DUFF COOPER

DUFF COOPER

The Authorized Biography

John Charmley

Weidenfeld and Nicolson · London

To Thea – without whom . . .

Copyright © John Charmley 1986

First published in Great Britain by
George Weidenfeld & Nicolson Limited
91 Clapham High Street, London SW4 7TA

ISBN 0 297 78857 4

Printed and bound in Great Britain by
Butler & Tanner Ltd, Frome and London

Contents

CONTENTS

Illustrations

Outdoing the French for style: Monsieur l'Ambassadeur and Lady Diana, 1945 (*Cecil Beaton photograph, courtesy of Sotheby's London*)

The statesman at work, Paris, November 1945 (*Cecil Beaton photograph, courtesy of Sotheby's London*)

Period piece at Chantilly, late 1940s (*Cecil Beaton photograph, courtesy of Sotheby's London*)

Duff and Louise de Vilmorin, late 1940s

Louise at the Embassy (*Cecil Beaton photograph, courtesy of Sotheby's London*)

In relaxed mood with Susan Mary Patten, late 1940s

Democratizing the Paris Embassy: Low's view in 1946 (*Evening Standard*)

With Bevin in Paris in 1947 at the Quai d'Orsay (*Illustrated London News*)

Caroline Paget's wedding, 1949

The Château de St Firmin at Chantilly

On the eve of retirement: at the presidential shoot at Rambouillet, December 1946 (*Popperfoto*)

Before the final cruise: Duff and Diana, 1953 (*Popperfoto*)

(*Unless otherwise indicated, all the photographs belong to Lady Diana Cooper's collection and are reprinted with her kind permission.*)

Acknowledgements

I am profoundly grateful to all those who have helped me in the research and writing of this book. That so many of Duff's friends should have been willing to see me and to talk to me about him seems to be the greatest proof one could wish of Duff's genius for friendship.

Chief amongst those to whom I am indebted is Lady Diana Cooper. She not only allowed me access to all her papers and bore with me through long interviews, but through her conversation made live again those days which are now forgotten by all but the oldest of men. To John Julius Norwich, who first placed faith in my ability to write this book, my debt is enormous. His help in contacting Duff's friends, in reading draft chapters and in offering encouragement, was invaluable; his insistence that I should write what I wanted regardless of the final portrait that emerged was characteristic of his generosity. Artemis Cooper placed at my disposal her notes for the edition of her grandparents' letters and her admirable *A Durable Fire* saved me many long hours at reference books – for which mercy I am grateful.

I owe a very special debt to Duff's nephew and literary executor, Sir Rupert Hart-Davis, and it is not easy to express my feelings without sounding effusive. That he and June should have given so generously of their hospitality would have been help enough. That Rupert should have found the time, amidst his other literary activities, to have read and commented in detail on successive drafts of the manuscript, was an overwhelming act of kindness. The debt I owe him is beyond computation.

The list of people without whom this book would have been far more difficult to write is a long one, but to all of them I am most grateful:

Miss Barley Alison; Mrs Susan Mary Alsop; Clarissa Avon; Lord Bessborough; Lord Blake; Lord Boothby; Sir John Coulson; Mrs

Daphne Fielding; Mr Alastair Forbes; Mr Frank Giles; Sir Robin Hooper; Lord Lansdowne; the late Sir Guy Salisbury-Jones and Lady Salisbury-Jones; Mr Peter Quennell; Sir Brooks Richards; Lord Rothschild; Mr Martin Russell; the Dowager Duchess of Rutland; and Mrs Daphne Wakefield.

I am most grateful to the staffs of the various archives where I have worked: the British Library; the British Library of Political and Economic Science; the House of Lords Record Office; the Liddell-Hart Centre for Military Archives, King's College, London; the Public Record Office at Kew; I would like to thank in particular Dr B. Benediktz of Birmingham University Library and Mrs J. Kavanagh of the BBC Written Archives Centre at Caversham.

For financial assistance in the early stages of my research I should like to thank the British Academy and the Twenty-Seven Foundation. The Supplementary Research Grants Fund of the School of English and American Studies at my own University has been most generous with my continuing requests for funds.

I should like to thank my agent, Felicity Bryan, for her cheerful good nature and her encouragement, and also my editors at Weidenfeld, John Curtis and Linda Osband: no one could have hoped for better assistance.

I would like to thank Mrs Hazel Bye and Mrs Vera Durell of my own University for coping so well with the mass of correspondence which the research for this book generated. I owe an especial debt to Mary Keavy for her comments on later drafts of the book. I am most grateful to my colleague, Professor J. R. Jones, for taking time off from his own labours to comment on the results of mine; his reading of the manuscript was much to its benefit. I would also like to thank him and my colleague Dr G. R. Searle for much stimulating conversation on Duff and on twentieth-century politics in general. I should also like to thank Albert and Vera Levine for the joy of their hospitality which made my London research such fun.

Only the wives of historians and writers can really appreciate what my wife Thea and my twin sons, Gervase and Gerard, had to put up with over the three years I was working on this book: of them it could be said that they had the dust and never sought the palm. Without them I could not have done it.

JOHN CHARMLEY
Norwich, 1985

Prologue

He still felt unwell as the liner sailed; unable to shake off the cough. He had brushed aside her suggestion to abandon the voyage. It was, after all, for the good of his health. It was not often that doctors prescribed something as agreeable as a holiday in the sun and it would be folly to reject it when they did. A winter in Jamaica would make spring back in Paris even more exhilarating than usual. It might even do something to lift her spirits.

His own rose at the thought of New Year's Eve parties: wine, good food and pretty women. The doctors had ruled out the first two pleasures – but not the last. Even at the age of sixty-three, life was very much worth living. A party to welcome it in, followed by a voyage and January in the West Indies, augured well for 1954.

Auguries can be misleading. There was to be no party for him. A few months before he had proclaimed that, much as he loved life, he could not 'fear the coming of the dark'. Nor was this bravado. Always a brave man, he had faced death in May; he had not been afraid, only regretful. The doctors had given him seven months since then; no doubt he would have welcomed another seven. But about noon the bleeding started. That interminable nose-bleed; bright scarlet blood. It had been a close thing before, but then there had been a hospital and blood transfusions; now there was only the tossing sea and the ship's doctor.

The *Colombie* turned back towards Vigo, but in vain. He died soon after midnight. It was 1 January 1954.

For her it was 'total loss'. The anguish of sitting by his side, as he tossed in agonies of thirst and pain would never wholly vanish. She had 'never dreamt of surviving – yet here I am'. She never again listened to a New Year's Eve party without memories welling up.

In London and Paris the newspapers gave his death banner-headlines. Readers of *The Times* even received a romantic touch with: 'Death at sea of Lord Norwich: body landed at Vigo.' The press reminded readers that Lord Norwich was 'better-known as Duff Cooper'; and so he was.

His death was reported in a dignified manner. One obituary struck a note which outraged his friends. With feline malice, *The Times* commented:

> The reason why Duff Cooper failed on the whole to realize the high hopes entertained for him can probably be found in a streak of dilettantism which made him good at many things but not in the first rank at anything.

The spectacle of a newspaper with a disgraceful record of pandering to Hitler's Germany commenting in this way on a man who had been right when it had been wrong, was too much for his friends to stomach; they hit back.

In the columns of newsprint thus spawned, the reader would have been able to discern the lineaments of Duff Cooper's character. Of his wit, courage, urbanity and intelligence, much that was eloquent was said; on these virtues there was unanimity. The *Daily Mail* spoke for many when commenting that he had been 'the epitome of the civilized man. He was a lover of wine and good company and talk. He was a scholar, a wit and a poet.' A statesman who composed sonnets over the gaming-tables; a wit whose patriotism impelled him to sacrifice all for honour; a *bon viveur* and London Club-man whose integrity and courage made him beloved by his many friends; this was an uncommon man who had died in his sixty-fourth year in such a dramatic fashion.

Time and again the principal episodes in his career were evoked in demonstration of his qualities. His wit and gaiety had won him the hand of the beauty of the age, Lady Diana Manners; his courage had brought him a DSO in the Great War; his oratorical prowess had carved out a political career; his scholarship was evident in half a dozen books. As for patriotism – well, his resignation over the Munich settlement in 1938 and his work as Ambassador to the French from 1944–7 both bore witness to that. But it was emphasized, for the sake of the many who had not known him, that what had really counted was the man himself. Quick-tempered and ardent in debate and conversation; witty and charming when at ease with those he loved, shy and uneasy with those he did not. Not 'a big public figure', but a friend whose passing took much of the savour out of life for those who had loved him. And the number of those who responded to the carping of *The Times* showed how many of these there were.

Although lapidary inscriptions bind no man to his oath, the portrait of a hard-drinking gambler, a scholar-diplomat and man of the world who loved life with a fierce passion, was not a bad likeness. Bob Boothby, writing in *Picture Post*, gave the perfect riposte to *The Times*: 'It has been said ... that he was a dilettante, that he belonged to the eighteenth century rather than the twentieth century. A truer description is that he was a civilized and integrated man in an uncivilized and disintegrated world.'

Duff had made a similar point in a tribute to his friend Hilaire Belloc:

> Success, as very well you knew,
>   Is not becoming rich and swell,
> But doing what you meant to do,
>   And doing it supremely well.

This would almost have served as his own epitaph, were it not for the fact that some lines of Belloc's do the job even better:

> From quiet homes and first beginning,
>   Out to the undiscovered ends,
> There's nothing worth the wear of winning,
>   But laughter and the love of friends.

1

First Beginning

The quiet home was 9 Henrietta Street, Cavendish Square, London; the first beginning was on 22 February 1890. Alfred Duff Cooper was the fourth surviving child and only son of Dr Alfred and Lady Agnes Cooper. His Christian names celebrated his parentage: Alfred after his father and Duff after his mother's maiden name. Despite the best efforts of later journalists, there was no hyphen in his name. No one ever called him 'Alfred', he was always 'Duff' or 'Duffie', and as his character showed more trace of maternal than paternal influence, this was as it should have been.

Although interested in history, Duff never cared for discussing that of his own family. In order that we should understand the nature of the quiet home which helped to form his character, it is necessary to disregard his example.

Family legend may trace the lineage of the Duffs of Fife back to that Macduff who slew Macbeth, but Debretts prefers to start with William Duff, MP for Banffshire in the early eighteenth century; we may begin with his grand-nephew, James, the fifth Earl Fife. It was he who added a dash of Hanoverian blood to the lineage. In 1846 he married Lady Agnes Hay whose mother, Lady Erroll, was one of the brood of nine Fitzclarences who were the offspring of the liaison between the future William IV and the actress Mrs Jordan. James and Lady Agnes were married in Paris, at the same Embassy over which their grandson was to preside a century later. Whenever one of the family behaved in an unconventional way, Duff's half-sister, Marie Hay, would attribute it to 'the Jordan blood'; the third child of the marriage of James and Agnes Fife, Lady Agnes Cecil Emmeline Duff, was evidently endowed with more than her fair share of it.

Born in 1852, she was brought up largely at Duff House, near Banff. The Prince of Wales, later Edward VII, was a frequent visitor, and his eldest daughter, Princess Louise, married the Fifes' only son in 1889. Lady Agnes was a pretty and lively young woman, slightly too lively perhaps, for in 1871 at the age of nineteen she eloped with the handsome and dashing Viscount Dupplin, heir to the Earldom of Kinnoul. It was a suitable match and received the family's blessing. At first all seemed well. In 1873 a daughter, christened Agnes Blanche Marie, was born; as Marie Hay she was to enjoy some reputation as an historical novelist; she married a relative of Field Marshal von Hindenburg and spent most of her life in Germany. Then, in 1875 came the rush of Jordan blood to the head. In April of that year Lady Agnes Dupplin eloped with a young man named Herbert Flower.

Herbert Flower had been a frequent visitor to the Dupplins' London residence, 13 Grosvenor Gardens, and evidently captured the heart of the unhappily married Lady Agnes. After her elopement they 'lived together as husband and wife from 20 May to 2 June' 1875 at the Castle Hotel, Dartmouth. They were living in a house in the same town when, in July 1876, Dupplin was granted a *decree nisi*. Little Marie went to live with her father's people, Lady Agnes married Herbert and they went on a world cruise.

'They are not long, the days of wine and roses'; and so it proved in this case. In 1880, at the age of twenty-seven, Herbert Flower, the great passion of Lady Agnes's life, died, leaving her grief-stricken and alone. Her family had ostracized her after her actions and the doors of Society remained firmly closed to the young widow. But the Jordan blood ran to resourcefulness as well as passion.

Agnes took herself off to London where, in the hope of learning to become a nurse, she took menial jobs at one of the big hospitals. While scrubbing the floor one day in 1882 she attracted the attention of one of the consulting surgeons; to appreciate what happened next we need to turn our attention to that surgeon – Alfred Cooper.

Born in Norwich in 1838, his was a classic Victorian success story. Although the Coopers had a tradition of following the law as a profession, he preferred medicine. After a spell at the Norfolk and Norwich Hospital, he completed his training at St Bartholomew's in London. It was there that he set up consulting rooms in Jermyn Street in the early 1860s; he must already have made some mark to have acquired a practice in such a fashionable area. His specialisms were the treatment of bronchial and venereal diseases and he became a consulting surgeon for several London hospitals. The former branch of medicine was to bring him the friendship of the Prince of Wales; the latter his most lasting claim to fame.

He was evidently a man of parts, for among his friends he counted noblemen such as the Duke of Hamilton, who presented him with a lodge on the Isle of Arran; he was a well-known figure in London Clubland and on the grouse-moors of Scotland. As a fashionable surgeon he accompanied the party which went to St Petersburg in 1874 for the wedding of the Duke of Edinburgh to the Tsar's daughter. The Prince of Wales, who suffered from bronchial trouble, fell ill during the visit and it fell to Alfred Cooper to treat him. Thus began a firm friendship which culminated in Edward VII giving his old friend a knighthood in his Coronation Honours list in 1902. The incident set the seal on Cooper's position in Society.

At some point during this successful career, Alfred Cooper had set eyes on Lady Agnes Duff – perhaps during one of the Prince of Wales's visits to Duff House. He fell in love with her, but it must have seemed that his passion was doomed to remain unfulfilled. She was fourteen years younger, highly born and romantic – and soon married to someone else. But the sight of the young woman scrubbing floors reminded him of his lost love.

He mentioned that she looked like someone he had once known, Lady Agnes Duff. She confessed to being Lady Agnes Duff. Whether it happened quite like that we do not know, but it happened quickly, for in 1882 Dr Cooper married the girl of his dreams, and Lady Agnes settled down to life as Lady Agnes Cooper. It remained to be seen whether the Jordan blood had spent itself, and how it would affect the next generation.

The Cooper marriage was a long and successful one, as it should have been; all fairy stories have happy endings. Safely ensconced at 9 Henrietta Street, Lady Agnes produced her second family: Stephanie (Steffie) was born in 1883, Hermione (Mione) in 1885, and twins in 1888. Of these only the female, Sybil (Sibbie) survived. It was some consolation for the little girl when little Duffie was born two years later; from the start she adored the fair-haired, blue-eyed infant. Lady Agnes, of course, equally worshipped her only son, and Alfred was delighted to have an heir.

Duff once remarked that 'in Heaven there is neither dining nor having to dine'; that was one of the respects in which home resembled Heaven. Lady Agnes's past was neither forgiven nor forgotten. Although it is said that the Prince of Wales told his son-in-law that he was not to cut his sister, contact between Lady Agnes and her family was strictly limited. As there were no Cooper relations, and as Lady Agnes's past was still remembered in Society, visitors at 9 Henrietta Street were not common. The Cooper children were thrown back on their own resources and lacked that extended family circle which so often acclimatizes children to the society of others.

Duff's childhood was made the more secluded by his delicate health and, despite pleasant visits to the Cooper–Angus lodge on Arran, it must have been excruciatingly boring had it not been for the attentions of Sibbie. It was she who introduced him to the delights of literature. Together they would act scenes from Shakespeare, memorize large chunks of Macaulay's *Lays of Ancient Rome*, and construct, from the contents of their parents' library, a world of make-believe.

This sheltered childhood made up in love and affection for what it lacked in social life. If we may trace the origin of his later shyness and his preference for small select groups to his early isolation, there are other respects in which the child seems the father of the man. Duff enjoyed to the full that feeling of being a conqueror which Freud attributes to the male child who knows he is the undisputed favourite of his mother. Lady Agnes adored her little boy, and his earliest years were spent with a mother and sister who gave him no reason to doubt that he was the centre of the universe. He retained always that unselfish egotism characteristic of the young child. His was, he once wrote, '*au fond* a happy nature', and he accepted the world with the assurance of one who knows that it is a place which values him.

It was a childhood which laid the foundations of his political success in the training which it gave to his remarkable memory and to the development of his oratorical skills; and it is not, perhaps, too fanciful to see in it some of the reasons why politics failed totally to absorb him. The world of literature beckoned. The ability to adapt to the company of strangers was never inculcated.

But amateur psychology is a dangerous speculation and had best not be pursued too far. Kindergarten at the age of six, followed by two prep schools left, however, little trace compared with 9 Henrietta Street. The shy and bookish little boy is only a stage or two removed from the man, but those stages were important ones. Eton, to which he went when he was thirteen, was to begin the process of forming the carapace behind which the youth would, as he approached adolescence, be able to cope in that wider world which lay outside the quiet home and first beginning.

2

The Shadow of Fox

In later life Duff was often compared to Charles James Fox, the rakish, charming, eighteenth-century Whig politician; Duff accepted the comparison with pleasure as an unconscious tribute to the artistry with which he had modelled himself on Fox, who became his great hero.

In his early years at Eton, Duff remained a rather shy youth, spending more time in the library than with his fellows or on the famous playing-fields. His academic performance was all that the fondest father could have asked for: he showed a considerable aptitude for the classics and for literature and history, reading widely and retaining what he read. His reports said that he was 'working splendidly in *every* way', which gave his father 'very great pleasure as I have ever hoped you would take such a position at Eton'. He became captain of his house, and his poetry was published not only in a college magazine but also in the *Saturday Review*, although this last feat may well have owed something to the fact that Sibbie was a friend of the proprietor.

In fact, poetry became Duff's great passion, and his earliest ambition was to become Poet Laureate, which amused his father who commented that it did not pay very well. Duff developed a particular fascination for Verlaine, Rimbaud and other poets of the Bohemian-romantic school, having a particular fondness for Ernest Dowson's 'Cynara'; he too longed to call for 'madder music and for stronger wine', at least in his imagination. In real life the adolescent Duff was more likely to ask for the latter; he remained deaf to the charms of music and could rarely sit through a concert, even if he could be lured into a concert hall. For wine, however, he was developing a taste.

During his many hours in the library, Duff read George Otto Trevelyan's *Life of Charles James Fox* and thus fell under the powerful, and

9

usually fatal, spell of that Whig hero. Fox's roistering, full-blooded life offered much to captivate the romantic adolescent. With no apparent effort he was the greatest orator of his age, a charming, worldly man, he spent his talents in friendship, his money (and his friends' money) on gaming and women, and his health on drink. Duff admired his 'brilliant success without undue application' and sought to emulate him, having a strong fellow-feeling for Fox; if success could be 'combined with dissipation', all the better.

In his final years at Eton, and during his time at Oxford, he moved in a set of like-minded young men. They wrote verses, gambled and cultivated the habit of drinking more than most people would have thought was good for them. The carapace behind which Duff would face the world was thus formed: the cultured libertine for whom the only business was pleasure, and pleasure the main aim of living.

As he was destined for diplomacy, it was necessary for him to perfect his foreign languages. This he did in two spells: before going up to Oxford he went to Tours to improve his French; and after coming down he went to Hanover to do the same for his German. He enjoyed Tours more than Hanover; he certainly learned more there.

It was hardly likely that a handsome, romantic youth, with an admiration for Gallic culture and poetry, would confine his activities in Tours to book-learning; Duff certainly did not. It seems entirely fitting that his first love affair should have taken place in France, and quite in keeping with his desire to emulate Dowson that it should have happened when he was seventeen and his lover an older, more experienced, French Comtesse. The affair can now be reconstructed only from some half-dozen letters, written in a sprawling, passionate, female hand. The Comtesse d'Aulby found the 'sweet, fresh lips' of the handsome young Englishman a temptation beyond her powers of resistance. Evidently Duff did nothing to help her poor powers of self-restraint. She told him that he made her wish that 'I were twenty years younger and that all sorts of impossible things were possible!!':

> A charming and attractive boy like you will always have many friends. Some may have a good influence over his life, others an evil one. I should not dare to say I could have a good one, but I hope at least it might not be the evil one. . . . You are so young, so unspoiled, so charming, so clever, one hates to think of all the worldliness that must be gone through with sooner or later.

If Duff's later behaviour is anything to judge by, she must have provided an attractive introduction to at least one aspect of that worldliness; for the rest of his life he was an eager pursuer and passionate lover of women.

His visit to Hanover, after leaving Oxford, was notable only for Duff being so bored that he even went to hear Caruso sing. It is no wonder that he was always a Francophile and a Germanophobe.

If his visit to Tours was one milestone passed, it was soon followed by another. In the spring of 1908, Sir Alfred Cooper died. This caused no unbearable sorrow; his father had always been a kind and affectionate parent, but never a close one. Duff felt that they had little, if anything, in common. In this he was probably wrong. Although he naturally felt a strong affinity with his romantic Duff ancestors, he was also his father's son. He inherited Sir Alfred's taste for the good things of life, for well-cut clothes and London Clubland. He also shared his father's passion for shooting. No doubt the penchant for the youngest daughter of a peer was accidental. Nor did Duff entirely forget his paternal roots. When he became a peer he took the title of Norwich as an act of filial piety; not that the officials of that fine and historic city were impressed.

Another veneer was added to the portrait by his experience of Oxford. In 1908 he went up to New College and found, in Edwardian Oxford, ample scope to develop his cult of Charles James Fox. The aristocratic, Whiggish milieu of his final years at Eton was even more predominant in his Oxford career. His best friends were those who shared his full-blooded enjoyment of pleasure, and he moved in a rakish set of 'bloods'. His closest friends, Denis Anson and Billy Grenfell, were both aristocratic rakehells. His set was patrician, reckless, cultivated and witty. Through Anson, Grenfell, and his other great friend, John Manners, Duff came to know most of the *jeunesse dorée* of his generation and first entered the sort of society in which he was to pass most of his life.

Philip Ziegler, in his biography of Lady Diana, has said all that needs to be said about the 'Corrupt Coterie'. Like all such coteries, its members imagined that they were the centre of the world and that their doings were of enormous importance to everyone else; such verdicts are seldom endorsed by posterity. Through Billy Grenfell Duff came to Taplow Court, the country home of his parents, Lord and Lady Desborough. In her youth, Lady Desborough had been a member of that other self-absorbed coterie of the 1870s, the 'Souls', and the children of her soulful friends were often to be found at Taplow, including the daughters of the Duchess of Rutland – the beautiful

Manners sisters. Another favourite haunt of Duff's vacations at this time was Clovelly Court in Devon, the home of John Manners's aunt. The house had its own private beach and was a favourite place for youthful flirtation. It was here that Duff carried on his early romances.

In his memoirs Duff wrote that the friends he made at Oxford helped to 'rid me of that lackadaisical admiration for failure into which I had fallen'. Harold Nicolson was nearer the mark in his notice in the *Dictionary of National Biography* when he commented that 'this was not apparent during his first two years at Oxford'.

Duff's Oxford career had a splendidly eighteenth-century tone to it. His prodigious memory, and his ability to master the essentials of any book he read without apparent effort, allowed him to cope with his history degree while leaving him plenty of time for more entertaining pursuits: chief among these were the Oxford Union, the theatre and gambling.

There was nothing in Duff's background to suggest that he would become a politician. He certainly lacked any early dedication to that career; for him, politics was a sphere in which he could exercise a talent for oratory which had become apparent while he was at Eton. Despite his admiration for Fox and the patrician life-style of the Whigs, he was instinctively a Tory. His own instincts were thoroughly Conservative, and he admired the romantic, doomed high Toryism which had supported the Stuarts and opposed the utilitarian doctrines of the nineteenth century. He naturally saw the Oxford Union as an arena in which to emulate Fox's oratorical prowess, and so joined those fledgling politicians who cut their parliamentary milk-teeth in that famous theatre.

He made his first speech on Guy Fawkes' night 1908, speaking against the motion that 'Drastic reform of the relations between the two Houses of Parliament is imperative'. With startling alacrity for a newcomer, Duff managed to get himself put down on the order paper as one of the main speakers. He turned up after the debate had started, fresh from a riotous party and trailing clouds of dissipation. One of his opponents in the debate was a Kingsman from Cambridge, Hugh Dalton, with whom he was to have weightier tussles in the Second World War. On this occasion Duff was the clear winner; it would not always be so.

Duff's conspicuous combining of business with pleasure soon gained him a reputation for idleness and frivolity among the more sobersided. His speech at the New College debating society in support of the Liberal Government was thought particularly perverse; he defended the Liberal Party on the grounds that as a Tory he was in favour of preserving all ancient institutions, among which was the Liberal Party.

The set in which he moved was not content with mere high spirits, inclining towards a brutal heartiness which could spill over into downright vandalism. But even Duff and Denis Anson realized that they had gone too far when they raided the rooms of a young don looking for things to throw on a bonfire and carried away a desk which, it transpired, contained the manuscript of a book he had been writing. Duff apologized profusely when he realized what he had done, but he was asked to find lodgings outside College.

He found digs at 22 Beaumont Street, conveniently near the theatre. His playgoing was prompted not only by his genuine love of drama; the fact that actresses' morals were reputed to be somewhat elastic was another incentive. He certainly found many lovers in that profession. This led to a conflict of wills with the College authorities in 1912 after he had gone down. During the course of the summer term Duff went up to celebrate the end of Final examinations with John Manners and other drinking companions. This led to him receiving a stern note from the junior dean of his College informing him that he was banned from entering Balliol College because:

> In company with a member of Balliol and a member of Trinity, you motored over to Oxford with some actresses and after getting out at 22 Beaumont Street you all went into Balliol ... there the ladies of your party behaved in a scandalous fashion.

'Actress' was often used as a polite euphemism for whore. Neither Duff, nor his partner in crime, Denis Anson, was contrite. Anson told Duff that he had instructed his father to tell the dean that 'if he was finding fault with me for being seen in his college with two perfectly respectable young women, he was a narrow-minded prig'. It seems unlikely that Anson *père* complied with this request. Duff wrote to the dean asking for further details, and got them: 'The particular behaviour of your friends which was most complained of was that they pulled their skirts above their knees and danced in the quad asking the porter whether he had ever seen anything like this before.'

The anxieties of the authorities were somewhat misplaced. Duff was to continue his romantic career for the next forty years without ever coming to any harm. The same could not be said of his other great passion – gambling.

To those who do not possess it, the gambling urge is all but inexplicable; why an intelligent man should put more money than he can possibly afford on the fall of a piece of pasteboard is beyond explanation; no doubt, in Duff's case, it was part of the Fox-like pose. In his case, as in that of his hero, the results were disastrous. Between 1908 and 1917 he lost a considerable portion of his patrimony at the green-baize table. On one evening in 1914 playing *chemin de fer*, he lost the colossal amount of £1,645 to a Captain Taylor; this was almost four times his salary. In order to have continued gambling on this scale, he must also have won handsomely on occasions. His recklessness at the gaming-tables certainly rivalled Fox's; but Duff had no friends who were willing to get up a subscription to pay his debts. When he lost £1,156 in 1917 to the future England cricket captain, Lionel Tennyson, the winner feared that he might not get his cash; he did. Duff was punctilious over such matters, even if others did not return the compliment. Tennyson bought himself a new white Rolls-Royce, which he had to sell at a loss a week later to cover a loss of £2,000 after a night's *chemin de fer*. Duff also found 'playing at railways'* a dangerous and expensive occupation.

It must have come as a surprise to some that he also managed to read for a good degree. His tutor, the historian and future Liberal Cabinet Minister, H.A.L. Fisher, wrote to console him on obtaining only an 'excellent level Second' when he had been 'considered for a "First" ', having been 'among the few unfortunates who gave the examiners a good deal of trouble'. No harm was done – except to Duff's pride.

He had no intention of remaining in Oxford and becoming a don; he wanted to enter the world of diplomacy. It was, however, first necessary to pass a stiff examination, and it was in order to prepare for this that he went off to Hanover and acquired a lasting dislike of all things German, along with a smattering of the language. It took him two attempts before he was successful, but in August 1913 he passed the exam, third out of four successful candidates. He was bound for diplomacy.

---

* *Chemin de fer* = railway.

3

Hot for Certainties

The Foreign Office was tolerant of eccentricities among its diplomats, and Duff probably found a more sympathetic attitude to his way of life there than he would have elsewhere. Lord Vansittart, some years Duff's senior and a future head of the Foreign Office, describes him at this time as 'a clever young thing, eager as I had been, for all experience but office work'. He certainly spent as much time as possible at Clovelly Court, flirting with young ladies on moonlit Devon beaches to the sound of the breaking of the waves, but he was, as one of them called him, 'a Pierrot of the moment'.

Duff loved romance: the secret assignations; writing and receiving love-letters; the excitement of the chase and the extravagant declarations of passion. As well as loving women he liked them, and they liked him, appreciating his sonnets and his chivalrous attentions; like many men of his generation he drew a distinction between the type of woman you dined with and the type you did other things with. He carried on flirtations with two or three young ladies at once, as well as the occasional more serious affair with a married woman.

For Duff, that summer of 1913, the last before the close-knit world in which he lived was plunged into the Armageddon of the Great War, was the essence of the *douceur de vivre*.

In the spring he had started a splendid new flirtation with the amusing, unpredictable and utterly ravishing Lady Diana Manners, who not only lapped up his passionate, witty and absurd letters, but responded with ones of her own. He had met her in March at a small party at the London home of her parents and, like almost every other young man who saw her, he fell in love with her. As she was in love with at least one other man, and he with two or three other women, neither of them took their epistolary love too seriously; but they did find great delight in writing each other elegant and lively love-letters.

15

Duff saw much of Diana that summer when they were both in Venice. Diana was with Lady Emerald Cunard, the wife of the shipping magnate, and Mr and Mrs Asquith. Duff's villa was distinctly more lively, containing his sister Sibbie, Denis Anson and Raymond and Katharine Asquith. Fancy-dress balls, parties and the heady atmosphere of Venice, which Duff discovered and fell in love with, all combined to make it a memorable summer. The fact that when they returned there in 1919 so many of their former companions were dead, gilded that summer and that city for Duff and Diana.

The first shadows began to fall even before the Great War. In early 1914, Gustav Hamel, a young Swedish aviator whom Duff and Diana knew well, failed to return from a flight. A poem mourning his loss was printed in *The Times*, written by 'A.D.C.'. Worse was to come.

A few weeks after Hamel's death, Anson was drowned after diving into the Thames, fully clothed, as a 'dare'. Duff was shocked. For the first time he realized that he and his set were mortal. At the age of twenty-four life seemed so 'various and so new'. It was to prove, for so many of his generation, quite otherwise.

The Great War had a crucial effect on Duff's life, as on the lives of so many others. In 1914 there seemed no reason why he should not continue to go his gay way, dissipating his talents and his money, acquiring a little fame and much love among his intimates, perhaps rising, one day, to the eminence of an Ambassadorship in some middle-ranking Embassy. There was certainly little sign that he would do anything notable. The problem with all this dilettantism was that it often led nowhere. The *beau-idéal* of their generation, Raymond Asquith, who became the symbol for the talent that was squandered on the fields of Flanders, was almost forty by the time he died and, with all his qualities, had not done anything to suggest that he was going to be an irreparable loss to the Nation. There was no reason to suppose that Duff would do any better. The war changed all this.

Because he was a diplomat, Duff was exempt from being called up to go to war; indeed, working sixteen hours a day for most of August, he was contributing more to the war effort than by getting himself killed. There were those who thought that Duff should volunteer to join up, but he was not among them. He saw no reason to prove his patriotism by getting killed; time enough for that when he was sent to war.

So it was that he remained in London. Like most people, he expected the war to be over quickly. It was not, and slowly and remorselessly it swallowed up the lives of most of his friends. The first to go was his beloved John Manners in September 1914. Katharine Asquith wrote to say that:

> I can hardly believe it even now. I suppose that the war will last for ever and that we shall all have our lives smashed sooner or later. I live in a shiver of fear now – but I can't bear that John should have gone out so soon.

Within three years her own adored Raymond had gone, leaving her own life smashed.

The slaughter of their friends drew Duff and Diana closer together and the nature of their relationship slowly changed. Diana's emotional and melancholic spirit found in Duff's calm and steady nature the prop it needed. It was Duff who evolved a method for coping with tragedy while continuing to live. Writing in the pre-dawn hours of 26 September, he told her that their code must be to 'make the most of what is left us' and not to 'put our eggs into one basket or our hearts into two hands'. Those who survived plunged themselves into a frenzied gaiety which scarcely concealed the fact that, as Angie Manners put it, 'it seemed such a little time ago that we didn't know sorrow, and now we are old and know nothing else'.

Diana sought to dull her pain with morphia and the labours of working in Guy's Hospital; Duff, as ever, took a less penitential line. He stuck to his code, sorrowed when friends died and rejoiced when they lived. He was profoundly unaffected by the wave of anti-German hysteria which swept over England in the early months of the war. He had always thought that the Germans were a bad lot and was only surprised that others had not shared this view. He was too sophisticated and too well-versed in history to imagine that the war was a Manichean conflict between good and evil. He was perfectly prepared to believe that, on the whole, his side was right and the other wrong, but felt no impulse to immolate himself on the altars of jingoism merely to prove his patriotism. Observing Asquith and other leading politicians at close quarters, Duff emulated their detachment. The only thing which he disliked more than the 'silly reactionary jingoism' of some sections of the press, was the 'silly contemptible pacifism' of other sections. The only statesman with whom he found common ground was Lord Lansdowne, the great Whig magnate and former Foreign Secretary, who made an appeal in 1917 for a compromise peace and was reviled for his pains. Duff thought the idea eminently sensible. However much of an extremist Duff may have been when it came to pleasure, he was a sensible and civilized moderate on most public issues.

The main effect of the war on Duff was that he lost the vast majority of his intimate friends and, although he was to make new ones, none of them achieved much intimacy with him. This helped to intensify the shyness which always seized Duff on social occasions and added to the impression that he was aloof and arrogant. A second effect of the slaughter in France was to remove rivals for Diana's hand.

The last point has been expanded by some to imply that but for this circumstance Diana would never have condescended to marry Duff. Lady Diana's own recollections are somewhat different. The only man she loved more than Duff was Raymond Asquith, but he was, as she put it, 'married and a decade older'. There was never any question of Raymond leaving Katharine, however much he returned Diana's feelings. So Duff's only rival was out of the way before the war began. What the slaughter of their friends did was to draw Duff and Diana together in a common bond of mourning.

Duff's presence in London undoubtedly gave him a great advantage in pressing his suit to Diana. The value of this advantage was increased enormously by the general relaxation of the rules of chaperonage and social behaviour. Many of Diana's female friends took advantage of the more permissive moral climate to part with their virginity; she did not join them. This was because she felt no desire to follow their example. Her lack of sexual desire set the limit to her developing relationship with Duff, who had rather been hoping that she would succumb to the prevailing permissiveness. She did allow him 'greater intimacy', but the sight of her 'naked to the waist' merely inflamed his passion all the more and, when she fought him off, added fuel to his temper. This sort of teasing would have brought problems with most men; with one of Duff's strong sensual nature it almost brought disaster. The second year of the war was a time of strain for Duff in many ways: overwork at the office; over-indulgence in the wine-cellar and the sins of the flesh added to a run of atrocious luck at the tables, all made him short-tempered; Diana's restraint was the final straw. He began to wonder just how much she really meant to him.

By the end of 1915 their love affair had entered a new and more intense phase, but it was still essentially light-hearted and can be summed up in the epitaph which Duff coined for himself in 1914: ' "He loved his lunch and Diana" or if you *will*, "Diana and his lunch".' As is so often the case, when she was most reserved his desire burned brightest and he longed to push aside 'that damnable spirit of camaraderie and friendship that makes our afternoons, but ruins our romance'. But when she did lower the barriers a little, or when his attention wandered elsewhere, he could 'not decide whether I'm in love with her or not'. He was, on the whole, inclined to think that he was not, 'but I have more fun with her than anyone'. Perhaps the most accurate description of his feelings is that given in a letter to Diana in late 1915: 'My love for you resembles a red, red rose less closely than a nasty attack of delirium tremens.' It was only in 1917 that they were forced to think clearly about what they meant to each other.

Duff had long had little opinion of the Prime Minister, Asquith. His habit of 'pawing' Diana's knee was one of the reasons for this, but another, and still more important one, was Asquith's inefficiency. He wrote to his mother in June 1916 from The Wharf (Asquith's country home) to complain that there had been 'no motor to meet me at the station and no champagne. I think it's high time the P.M. resigned.' Within six months Duff's wish had been granted, although it was his deficiencies as war-lord rather than host which occasioned his resignation.

Asquith's successor, Lloyd George, was expected to prosecute the war more vigorously. One of his early measures was to extend conscription to those hitherto immune. When the Foreign Office staff were given medical examinations in May 1917, the thought that he was likely to be sent to the Front filled Duff 'with exhilaration', although he did not 'own it, as people would think it was bluff, and I daresay that I shall very soon heartily wish myself back'. There were no mock-heroics in his attitude. As he told Diana, 'I have [felt] for so long that I am missing something.' In his memoirs Duff put it even more simply, writing that he joined up because 'it is plainly the decent thing to do, like giving up one's seat to an old lady or taking off one's hat in a holy place'. His main worry was how Lady Agnes and Diana would take the news.

Lady Agnes was upset but proud, Diana's reaction was equally uncomplicated – she feared that she would lose Duff for ever.

Duff's conscription came in time to clear away the misunderstandings which had dogged their relationship since late 1916. The death of Raymond Asquith in September 1916 came as a great blow to Diana. In a depressed and nervous state she found Duff's 'conspicuous sensuality' and his 'raging at the little I sometimes must deny you' too much to cope with. For his part, Duff found the burden of restraint increasingly intolerable. The result was inevitable. In November they quarrelled bitterly and Diana wrote sadly to suggest that 'We will rest from each other for a little.' Duff did not take this seriously, but he was careful, all the same, to deluge her with apologetic letters. They did patch things up, but the end of the year and early 1917 saw them on nothing like their former intimate terms. It was only when she realized that Duff was going to France that Diana appreciated how much she loved him: henceforth her letters match his in volume; and surpass them in emotion.

On 23 June Duff left the Foreign Office without 'a single regret', eager for new experience and hoping never to see the place again.

There were many people who shared the view of the Duchess of Rutland that it would do Duff good to 'rough it for a bit'; Duff disagreed. He told Diana that it would only be 'good' if it taught him to appreciate luxury even more:

> But that is impossible for me. .... I have drunk champagne every day for the last four years, but every evening I have looked forward to it with keener anticipation. .... I have worn a lot of clean linen and slept in the same, but my taste for it has only increased with the years.

He did promise to stay in bed until noon and drink even more champagne when he returned, just to show how much 'good' 'roughing it' had been for him.

All this was the fine flowering of his carefully cultivated image as the hedonistic epicurean, but it must not be accepted as the whole picture. Although he could tell Diana that he was 'mentally your only peer', he was painfully conscious that he was 'physically unworthy'. He wished that he could be 'tall and thin with a body like a Greek God and a face like Leonardo', like Raymond Asquith or some of her other admirers. But he was left with the fact that he was short and plumpish with a smooth, round, well-fed face. His most noteworthy features were an extremely large head and tiny feet, usually clad in elegant shoes. 'Can you imagine', he once asked Diana, 'anything more top-heavy than the fourth generation descended from me?' Underneath the carapace he remained a 'rather sentimental shy young man, with ambitions beyond my energy and dreams beyond my income'.

He looked forward to the new experiences the army would bring. His friend Eric Ednam (later Lord Dudley), who was already a veteran of the trenches, told Duff that as he was going to a training-camp first, he would probably arrive 'in time for the last charge of the war'. Less comfortingly, he added that a friend who had been through 'a cadet-corps says it's harder than anything, though he was in the ranks before'; which proved to be quite true. Equally accurate was Eddie Grant's description of the lot of the average officer: 'stuck in a six-foot bog, trained like an Olympian athlete and buggered about like a mulatto telegraph-boy'.

The hardest part of military existence for Duff was the squalor, discomfort and lack of privacy. It was the first time in his life that Duff had moved outside his own class – and he did not like the experience. The only advantage which his training-camp possessed was that it was at Bushey in Hertfordshire, which was conveniently near London. It was thence he fled in late July, suffering, for once, from depression. But not even the familiar sights of home could cheer him up, and all his friends were out of town. So he sought solace elsewhere:

> I went to the Junior Carlton and had a good dinner with a pint of champagne reading *Through the Looking-Glass* the while. Then, as by magic my untroubled mind came back to me, and not alone, but bringing courage, joy and hope.

Once again wine had proved itself 'a firm friend and a wise counsellor'. Thus did Duff pass the nadir of his army career. Henceforward his 'curiosity and avidity for novelty' would carry him through.

Despite the misgivings (and hopes) of the gossips Duff completed his course successfully and 'passed off the square' in November. Although he had not enjoyed Bushey, he was able to chalk up two good things from his time there: an improved handicap at golf, and the assurance that Diana really loved him.

Throughout his time in camp Diana had been a constant visitor, going on picnics with him, writing letters to him and generally cosseting him. After his departure for France in April 1918 she wrote to glory in the fact that all their friends asked *her* for news of him: 'I glow ... they cannot disassociate us. ... I have never loved you as I have in these last days.' She also wrote to Lady Agnes to say 'how much I love your Duff' and to hope that a 'small wound' would soon allow him to return to England: 'Beloved Duff. We both love him more than anything.'

All this at least gave Duff a good reason for surviving the war, even if there were other obstacles to be overcome later on.

4

A Different War

The lasting image of the Great War as it has come down to posterity is that created by the war poems of Owen, Sassoon and Rosenberg; one of muddy trenches, squalor and futile death. This was not Duff's experience. Writing to Diana from France in July 1918, he commented apropos of this view of the war:

> They can't see anything in it but lice and dirty feet and syphilis. God knows that nobody living loathes the war more than I do.... But there is romance in it. Nothing so big can be without it.

Duff thought that the war poets should try to express something of this, and he found their 'whining and jibing' as tiresome as the effusions of those 'who say it is all so glorious that we're fighting for liberty and to set the world free'.

His first experience of the war certainly confirmed his initial impressions. He wrote to Diana from a 'comfortable dug-out' that 'the horrors of war have been much exaggerated'. He did not imagine that he would 'like it in winter', but before then he would 'make a separate peace'. Duff had, in fact, had his usual luck where such things were concerned. He had been sent out to France in the late spring, after the failure of the last great German offensive of the war, when peace could not be far away. But he had enough experience of the sharp end of conflict to be able to escape any charge that he had had a cushy war.

Duff found himself with the third battalion of the Grenadiers, which was a piece of bad fortune, as it had 'a reputation as being the only one in which they set you down to three parades a day as though you were still on the square at Chelsea'. He did not find that the beauties of France made square-bashing any more pleasant than it had been in London. His chief amusements came from censoring the men's letters and following the notorious Pemberton Billing trial at home.

22

The men's letters yielded up pearls of folk-wisdom with which Duff found himself in full agreement. The man who wrote to his aunt 'Dear Aunt. This war's a bugger' had, Duff thought, hit the nail on the head. He also appreciated the macabre humour in the suggestion of one soldier that 'a lot of ships were needed to bring the British army to France – only two will be wanted to take it back again – one for the men and the other for the identity discs'. Like most of the British troops in France, Duff found the trial of the eccentric MP, Pemberton Billing, with its heady mix of sex and scandal, a source of never-flagging amusement; in his case the fun was enhanced because Billing's 'black book', which contained the names of forty-seven thousand persons who were being blackmailed by the Germans on account of their sexual perversions, included many of Duff's friends. He told Diana that 'no one here speaks or thinks of anything but the Billing trial' and that he was disappointed not to figure in the list. Some cheer was, however, provided by Duff's Commanding Officer, who called Margot Asquith a 'female bugger', only to correct himself a moment later by substituting the word 'lesbite'.

But such diversions were few, and life was, for the most part, a curious mixture of discomfort and luxury. When at the Front, it was impossible to wash, shave, or even take your boots off; but back at base it was a different story. There was, Duff wrote, 'capital food and plenty of it ... beefsteaks, butter, sugar without the restrictions, and ten sturdy waiters groaning under the weight of bottles of port and boxes of cigars'. So comfortably fed was he that he offered to send Diana a food-parcel. His only worry was that he would put on all the weight which he had lost at Bushey.

Duff's spirits remained high even when the fighting started – although his meals did become more infrequent and austere.

At five o'clock on the morning of 21 August, in what became known as 'the Battle of the Mist', Duff and his company went over the top as part of the Allied advance on the Albert Canal. In the thick mist and the confusion, Duff's platoon became separated from the rest of the Company. Pressing on alone, they 'picked up a fairly large part of the Shropshires' who had also gone astray. After some skirmishing with the enemy, Duff found that they had reached the Arras–Albert railway-line, which was the main objective of the attack; they were the only part of the Company to do so. But they soon found themselves pinned down by flanking-fire from a German machine-gun nest; Duff's Commanding Officer asked him to deal with it. He advanced with his platoon. Unknown to Duff, the men who were supposed to be following him were not doing so, having been hit by enemy-fire. Finding himself alone, he acted with the cool nerve of the gambler. Shooting one German he called upon the others – summoning up his scarcely remembered German – to surrender. The occupants of the machine-gun nest, supposing themselves to be outnumbered, came out with their hands up – only to find themselves confronted by one rather undersized Second Lieutenant. Before they could recover from their surprise, the rest of Duff's men had joined him. Thus it was that he captured, single-handedly, eighteen Germans. After that Duff needed a swig of the brandy, sent by Steffie, which he carried in his water-bottle. To his considerable embarrassment, he found himself singled out by his Commanding Officer as the hero of the hour.

After a few hours' sleep he was back on duty at two o'clock the next morning to face an enemy-attack which, fortunately for an exhausted Duff, failed to materialize. He did, however, receive a nasty gash on the cheek from a piece of shrapnel. He stayed at the Front to join in the attack on the morning of 23 August. It was 'one of the most memorable moments of my life': 'It was really a thrilling and beautiful attack, bright, bright moonlight and we guided ourselves by a star.' He was 'wild with excitement and glory and knew no fear'; it was 'what the old poets said it was and what the new poets say it isn't'.

Once again the attack was successful, and Duff felt that he had done even better this time when, after all, he was already tired, hungry and battle-weary. He even managed to repeat his exploit of capturing a German machine-gun nest. That evening his Company was relieved and they went back down the line to 'comparative comfort and safety', where Duff had sufficient time to write to Diana and Lady Agnes.

Lady Agnes had not, in fact, realized that Duff's battalion was fighting until she received a telegram from him, sent from the Front, telling her to 'sit tight'; thereafter she was a prey to all sorts of fears. Diana, who had realized that Duff was fighting, inundated the War Office with enquiries and set about planning a mission of mercy to the Front to look after Duff if he was injured. They were both relieved when Duff's letters arrived. He told Diana that the Germans were 'charming and always surrender'. He told his mother on 25 August that

the C.O. and the Brigadier rode past last night as we were coming out and the former pointed me out to the Brigadier who rode up to me and

> congratulated me. He said that the whole Brigade had done damned well but that I and my platoon had simply shone. You may imagine my delight and pride.

Swearing Diana to secrecy, he told her that there was a good chance that he would get a medal and asked how that 'would weigh in Her Grace's scales'? But he feared that it would not match the 'strawberry leaf' which denoted a ducal coronet.

Duff's bravery was indeed rewarded. The Colonel in charge of the regiment, Sir Henry Streatfeild, wrote to tell Lady Agnes on 4 September that 'your son has very greatly distinguished himself in the recent severe fighting ... for his gallantry and his leadership. You'll be very proud of him, as we all are here.' Duff had seen too many brave men die undecorated to put much store by his own medal. Writing to Diana he joked that the Goddess of Chance, who had so often deserted him at the gaming-table, had turned up trumps for once. He was awarded the DSO, which, as many of his obituarists noted, was not a decoration normally given to subalterns – especially in the Brigade of Guards; and when it was, it was generally recognized as a 'near-miss' for the Victoria Cross.

Before receiving these letters, Diana, worried by the long gap in their correspondence, wrote to accuse him of neglecting her because he was 'puffed up with military pride'. Nothing could have been further from the truth. When his adoring mother wrote to say that his old nurse had said that he was a 'born soldier', his comment had been that he was nothing of the sort and that he hated 'the bloody army and shall bless the day when I take off uniform never to put it on again'.

But that day seemed to belong to a distant future. At one point he had hoped that his shrapnel-wound would be serious enough to get him invalided back to London, but it healed with distressing speed. It was thus with a great sense of frustration that he reported to Diana that Foch 'says the war will be over in October. ... They always say October and they always lie.' This time 'they' were not far wrong.

Duff, however, still had one major battle left: the advance on the Canal du Nord. Fearing that he could not expect the Goddess of Chance to stay with him a second time, he was, for once, nervous. This came through in a letter written to Diana on the eve of battle: 'Tomorrow before dawn I fight a battle. I only fear death when I think of you because you are all that I cannot bear to leave in life.' Her anxiety for his safety and her fears that he did not love her 'paramountly', had convinced him that his love was reciprocated; it would, he thought, be a shame to die now.

The valedictory tone of this letter naturally aroused all Diana's worst fears, but by the time she received it there was no need to worry; Duff had emerged from the battle unharmed. Writing from the battlefield, he told her what had happened:

> I have fought another battle and am none the worse. I haven't done anything to be puffed up about this time you will be glad to hear, but we did what we had to do promptly, and effectively laid one of the foundation stones of a great battle. It was rather fun. We started in darkness after a wet night and there was a good deal of death about at first. Then the sun rose beautifully and the enemy fled in all directions including ours with their hands up, and one had a glorious Ironside feeling of Let God Arise and let his enemies be scattered. And then they came back again over the hill and one was terrified and had a ghastly feeling of God is sunk and His Enemies doing nicely. But we shot at them and back they went. This happened three times. And now the battle has rolled away and I am tired, tired and wondering where I shall lie tonight.

He spent the following afternoon sitting in the warm sunshine watching hordes of German prisoners being taken away. It was the end of his war.

On 27 September Bulgaria became the first of Germany's allies to sue for peace, and thenceforth it resembled, Duff thought, a scene from Shakespeare:

> *Scene:* A tent in Picardy. Soldiers playing cards.
> *Enter a Messenger:* 'Bulgaria asks for peace.'
> *Enter Second Messenger:* 'Bulgaria surrenders unconditionally.'
> *Enter Third Messenger:* 'We have taken 10,000 prisoners.'
> *Enter Fourth Messenger:* 'The French have taken 20,000 prisoners.'
> *Enter Fifth Messenger:* 'An American Army is surrounded.'
> *Enter Sixth Messenger:* 'Turkey has made peace.'

His guess that 'more spacious days' were in prospect was correct.

After this spell at the Front Duff was due for a spot of Paris leave. Before going he asked Diana, 'Should I tell you all that I did if I went to Paris?' Her replies set the tone for their marriage. Warning him to 'be careful baby – don't let's have conspicuous debauchery – or love made to my friends'; she would countenance 'anything else'. Writing on 14 September she added:

> Tell me every word of Paris, I'm bound to take it right and it's so perfect to feel lies unnecessary. On the other hand, except for gambling or con-

spicuousness, I wouldn't like the thought of me telling you to curb your enjoyment . . . have all the fun you can, but let me in on it.

He would, he replied, 'feel shy' of recounting all the details of his activities, which would be, to him, merely the necessary release after such a long period of sexual restraint. Diana's response was, again, characteristic of their relationship: 'Tell me as much or as little as you enjoy to confess. You know that I want your happiness above my own.'

Duff's leave was, in fact, not quite as licentious as the gossips would have liked to believe. Apart from the odd 'poll' or three, what he really enjoyed was the freedom of being in Paris in the autumn away from the shambles of the Front. Clean linen, hearty meals and good restaurants were what he really enjoyed.

He spent much of his leave in the company of an American, Carroll Carstairs, who had joined the British Army. Together they put up at the Ritz and set off to enjoy Paris. On one occasion he was stopped in the Crillon by a group of Canadian soldiers who told him that 'they knew what my decoration meant on the breast of a second lieutenant – and they would be honoured if I would drink with them', an offer he gladly took up. He was also invited to dine at the British Embassy with the Ambassador, Lord Derby, which was a curious foretaste of the future. He saw, for the first time, the interior of the place where he was to be at the end of the next great war, and did so at the request of the man who was to help him get the start in politics which set him on that road.

The saddest moment of his leave came when he popped in to see a play in which his old lover, Polaire, was starring; he was moved almost to tears by how old she now looked. But laughter kept breaking in. A few nights later he found himself hiding in his bedroom, his bed across the door, in order to escape the ravening clutches of a female admirer. To the accompaniment of bangs on his door he wrote to Diana, telling her how much he loved her and assuring her that 'black vice' was 'no competition'.

He was lying comfortably in his bath on the morning of 13 October when Carstairs rushed in to tell him: 'It's all over.'*

* A cease-fire had been announced.

~~~~~ 5 ~~~~~

Winning Diana

The Great War may have been over, but the battle to win the consent of Diana's parents to their marriage was just beginning.

There was never any question of Diana imitating Duff's mother and eloping. She did not want to lose her place in Society or to create any scandal. Moreover, without her allowance they would be poorer than those church mice everyone feels so sorry for. Duff had an income of about £700 a year, but that would scarcely suffice for an evening's *chemin de fer*, let alone keep them both in the style to which they were accustomed and would continue to demand.

Throughout the period that Duff had been at the Front, Diana had been thinking of ways of raising money, feeling that her mother might regard him more kindly if he arrived to press his suit laden down with doubloons. She toyed in a not altogether frivolous manner with the idea that they should live *en prince* on one of her many rich admirers. One of the most ardent of these, Lord Wimborne, did suggest to her in August 1918 that he would put up the money; but he did not press the offer, and she did not relish having to pay the price he would demand.

A less exacting source might be the Canadian millionaire, Max Beaverbrook, who had recently bought the *Daily Express*. Diana thought that 'Max' might give Duff a job on his paper, or, at the very least, give her advice on how to make a fortune quickly. In view of the later relationship between Duff and Beaverbrook, this first suggestion is not without its irony. Although grateful for her ingenuity, Duff was altogether more sanguine, telling her in September that 'I am sure we should arrange something suitable', adding later that, 'by gutter journalism, shady politics and crooked finance, we might climb to pinnacles of power and prosperity'.

It was probably nightmares of this sort which made the Duchess of Rutland so vehement in her opposition to the idea of Diana marrying

Duff. His reputation was quite sufficient to warrant any mother wanting to protect her daughter from marrying him; his gambling, drinking and womanizing were widely known.

Not even the war had prevented Duff from regular attendance at
the gaming-tables. By 1916 he had reached a point at which he 'had
very little capital left' and we find him writing to Diana to tell her,
'My bank won't let me overdraw any more and I haven't literally got
sixpence to get shaved with.... Oh for wealth and for you and the
war to be over – could I then want anything more?' His gambling
was a constant source of worry to Diana, who asked with some asperity what was the point of her trying to make money for them if he
was going to gamble it all away. When he lost £1,156 to Lionel
Tennyson at *chemin de fer* in December 1917, he concealed the fact
from Diana by telling her that he had 'lost a hundred' but that 'I
shall win next time'. She became somewhat suspicious when he
seemed to win every hand over the next two months. But even on his
own calculations, he only regained £560. He realized that it 'would
be a good thing if I promised you not to play at railways' but such a
promise would be worthless and would entail the danger 'of broken
faith followed by deceit'. It can hardly have reassured Diana to be
told by a friend that although Duff was one of the 'worst, the most
incorrigible' gamblers in the Grenadiers, 'he paid better, sooner than
anyone else'.

Duff was quite aware of his shortcomings. In October 1917 he
resolved 'to cultivate soberness, temperance and chastity' for two
weeks. But this laudable attempt had to be postponed because of 'an
argument after lunch as to whether one saved money by buying port
by the bottle rather than by the glass [which] ended up in my finish-
ing the better part of one of the former'. Not even his best friends
would have put 'soberness, temperance and chastity' amongst his
virtues.

But there was more to the Duchess's opposition than this. Diana
was quite incapable of telling her mother that she was in love with
Duff. Thus it was that when Duff approached the Duchess at the
fancy-dress victory ball at the Albert Hall in December 1918, and
asked if he could marry Diana, she did not believe that he was serious.
When Diana herself broached the subject the following morning, the
Duchess had a fit of hysterics. Diana's 'holiday task' of converting her
parents to the idea of her marrying Duff was going to be neither
pleasant nor easy.

She spent a 'grim' Christmas at Belvoir trying to drum up support for her endeavours, with mixed results. Her uncle Charlie, who was 'wonderfully sympathetic', spoiled the case he was making by warning her about Duff's excessive drinking, commenting that he had never heard of anyone who had seen him get up from the dinner-table sober. Her brother John suggested a compromise: she should wait for a year before announcing her engagement. She put this scheme to Duff on 31 December:

> I could hardly endure it, but if it is to be forced upon us by entreaty and the force of mother's health, I don't see how we are to stand out. Suppose we love each other less in a year? God what a conspiracy of cruelty it is.... Strengthen me Duffy – I feel in despair.

Part of her problem was of her own making: she still could never bring herself to tell her mother bluntly that she loved Duff.

There was nothing to be done save to carry this Victorian melodrama to its next act: suitor meets 'heavy father'. Early in the New Year, Duff called on the Duke formally to request his daughter's hand in marriage. The Duke wrote to him on 5 January 1919 to

> make the following offer; viz; that if you will undertake no further steps as regards your proposed engagement to Diana, and to completely hold your hand for one year from now, I will then, in conjunction with my family, provided you are both of the same mind as now, agree to place no further obstacles in your way and will let the engagement go on, at the same time rendering such assistance as may be possible.

If Duff refused to accept these terms, 'then I cannot take any further responsibility of any sort in the matter'.

Faced with this scene out of a nineteenth-century novel, Duff declined to behave like a Byronic hero, not least because Diana refused to imitate a Byronic heroine and one could hardly elope by oneself. Instead, he wrote to the Duke asking for some time to consider his position. On 19 January he finally accepted the ducal terms – with the caveat that he could always change his mind. The Duke's response was exquisitely polite. He accepted Duff's position, but made it clear that whatever happened to the mind of the young suitor, that of the 'heavy father' would remain unchanged. What made this whole drama so odd was the knowledge that the Duke was merely doing what the Duchess had told him to do.

Diana's mother was not convinced that her daughter was really in love. So muted was her behaviour that the Duchess had every reason for her suspicion; Diana found it impossible to say anything to her mother on the subject. However, a three-month-long sulk by Diana, in the best melodramatic tradition, broke down even her mother's resistance, and in April, she made it known that she would not frown on a renewed assault from the love-lorn swain.

Diana saw her father on the evening of 30 April and reported to Duff that he was 'perfect', not only giving his consent but also the game away by saying, ' "Don't go upstairs for a little. I don't want your mother to think I gave in at once." '

Like all good Victorian melodramas, this one ended happily at the church.

The wedding took place with due splendour at St Margaret's, Westminster. As the bride and groom emerged there was a huge crowd to greet them. The match between the beautiful and famous Duke's daughter and an impecunious Foreign Office clerk with a gallant war-record had caught the popular imagination. The wedding-presents displayed afterwards were suitably copious and exquisite. It really was 'the wedding of the year'.

After the reception Duff and Diana went down to Kent, where they spent the night at Philip Sassoon's beautiful house at Lympne; it was 'everything a wedding night should be'. The next day they left for the Continent. From Italy, Duff wrote to his mother: 'We have been perfectly, bliss-fully, incredibly happy.' So they were to remain.

~~~⁀ 6 ⁀~~~

Love and Ambition

It would have taken a brave soul to have prophesied that the young couple were going to remain 'blissfully happy'. Trouble could be expected from two directions: financial and sexual.

Duff, whatever his ambitions, was only a Foreign Office clerk on a salary which hardly provided him with money for an evening's journey on the 'railways'. With diligence and good fortune he might one day become an ambassador; but marriage to Diana seemed unlikely to stimulate either of these things. Although very beautiful, she was not very rich. She was not likely, either, to curb his own extravagances. They lived in an expensive set and, however adept Diana was in making sure that their rich friends paid for luxuries like Paris gowns and holidays on the Riviera, it cost them more than they could afford to keep their end up.

Their joint income came to £1,300 a year. It was enough to live a comfortable life, but that was not what they wanted. The one outward sign of their comparative lack of affluence was the fact that they lived in Bloomsbury. But, viewed from the inside, 90 Gower Street hardly seemed like the residence of a junior diplomat. It was true that there were those such as Chips Channon who described it as a 'tiny house', but they tended to be, like Channon, very rich and to own houses in Mayfair. With advice (and cheques) from her mother, Diana set her own mark on the house and, over the decade after 1920, the establishment expanded to include the first-floor flats of numbers 92 and 94 Gower Street. With *trompe l'œil* pictures by Rex Whistler on the walls of the drawing room, and a fine library designed by the Duchess for Duff, Gower Street brought an air of Belgravia to Bloomsbury.

The kind of life which Duff and Diana led did not endear him to his new chief at the Foreign Office, Lord Curzon. It seemed, to Curzon, that young Cooper was not behaving in a manner fitting to his

station in life and in October 1922 his lordship found occasion to
make his views known. When Duff asked for a period of leave, Curzon
told the Permanent Under-Secretary that he was 'having too much
leave'. After it was proved that this was not so, Curzon minuted that
'it is not so much his ordinary leave to which I object as his ability
while performing his duties to enjoy an amount of social relaxation
unclaimed by his fellow-workers'. This was, as Duff wrote in his diary,
'utterly meaningless drivel', but it reflected a not uncommon view
that young Cooper was not 'up to much except fun'.[1]

Duff was, even as Curzon was penning his orotund periods, thinking of ways out of the diplomatic service. His main problem, here as
elsewhere, was money.

It would have been easy to prophesy that the Coopers would have
financial problems; it would have been more difficult to have predicted the sexual difficulties encountered. Diana summed up the situation in her usual brisk fashion: 'Like most well-brought up girls of my
generation I was not much interested in it – sex I mean. But like most
men, Duff couldn't have enough of it.'[2] Duff was a sensualist. He
enjoyed making love, finding in it perfect relaxation and enormous
pleasure. Like most men of his class and generation he tended to draw
a distinction between women whom one married and women with
whom one went to bed. Given this, he would no doubt have encountered problems whoever he married. Diana presented special com-
plexities. For one thing she was a virgin when they married and it
soon became clear to Duff that her refusal to join most of her friends
in the flight towards permissiveness during the war reflected not just
maidenly modesty, but also a fundamental disinterest in sex. She was
utterly devoted to Duff, putting his comfort always before her own;
she loved him deeply, but she did not care for sex.

Duff was, in any event, unlikely to have proved a faithful husband.
His first extra-marital affair seems to have taken place in Venice while
they were on honeymoon, and it was quickly followed by many others;
he was incapable of restraining his carnal appetites.

No doubt these circumstances should have led to unhappiness and
a swift divorce; instead they produced a marriage which lasted until
Duff's death and which was the source of the greatest happiness to
both partners; for both Duff and Diana it was the rock upon which
all else was built. There were always those who thought that such talk
was merely a blind for Diana's great unhappiness, but her comment
on such nonsense was: 'I didn't mind adultery; I'm not a jealous

nature.' There were times, in the early years of their marriage, when Diana did complain to Duff about his affairs, but that was before she was sure that his love would not follow his lust. In one way, the very number of Duff's mistresses reassured Diana; other women were welcome to Duff's attentions provided she had his love. What Diana wanted was a father-figure to take care of her, and a romantic adoration; Duff provided both of these for his 'darling baby'. Thus it was that when, in 1921 when they were on holiday in Deauville and Duff went missing for several hours, Diana was far more upset by the idea that he might be dead than by the fact that he had been with his current mistress. No doubt it was an odd marriage, but it worked; Duff could not have endured a wife who insisted on fidelity and Diana, with her need to be admired, could not have lived with a jealous husband. They had, moreover, one overwhelmingly important concern in common – Duff's career.

Although he had been glad to leave the Foreign Office for the Front, Duff had failed to find any alternative source of income, and had been forced to return to his desk in 1919. He did well, despite the doubts of sober-sides like Curzon, and in 1922 he became Private Secretary to the Parliamentary Under-Secretary at the Foreign Office. This was a post usually held by one of the rising young men in the service and boded well for the future; yet it made Duff more dissatisfied than ever with his lot. The main reason for this was that it involved him in constant attendance on his chief in the House of Commons – which merely encouraged his ambition: 'When I sit in the House I do long to be in it – I feel that I must end there,' he told Diana in January 1924. These ambitions were stimulated by one of the most colourful figures in the diplomatic service, Sir Robert Vansittart.

He, like Duff, found the Foreign Office 'miserable'. The two men shared a common love of the theatre and literature and 'Van', admiring in the younger man those characteristics which he possessed and felt the service suppressed, urged Duff to 'leave it and go in for politics'. This was a line of thought Duff and Diana had been following ever since their marriage. At first it had seemed utterly impracticable for financial reasons. Gradually it dawned upon them that it might be possible, thanks to Diana's beauty, for them to make enough money to make the impracticable a reality. In 1922 Diana was asked to star in two films and made a substantial amount of money. Then, in the spring of 1923 she auditioned successfully for the part of the

Madonna in Max Reinhardt's play *The Miracle*. Although this would involve her in prolonged residence in America, it would also provide enough money to launch Duff on a political career. Thus, by the time Van made his comment, there was at least an even chance that Duff would take him at his word. But there were doubts.

In the first place it would mean giving up a regular salary of £900 a year with no guarantee of replacing it. In the second place, as Duff wrote to Diana on 14 January 1924 when she was about to make her Broadway debut, 'how could I make a practical success of politics with my reactionary views which become more confirmed and more reactionary daily?' The dilemma posed itself thus:

> Is it worth leaving a decent gentlemanlike job which may lead to an ambassadorship which I should like, in order to plunge into the cesspool of politics which can only lead to a few years of precarious power during which one is the Aunt Sally of the guttersnipes of the earth?

But the mere fact that he was posing the question, when common sense suggested the obvious answer was 'no', was evidence enough of the way his mind was moving.

His letters to Diana in the early months of 1924 show him fighting against common sense. When his income tax demand in early February suggested that Diana might have to pay £1,600 to the Inland Revenue, he thought that it seemed 'folly' to think of standing for Parliament – 'but think of it I do'. The advent of a Labour Government in January provided another good reason for leaving the Foreign Office. There were strong rumours that Oswald Mosley (who was at the 'radical chic' stage of his career before the term had been coined) would become Parliamentary Under-Secretary at the Foreign Office; Duff did not believe these, but determined that he would 'refuse to serve under him even for a day'. The prospect of that 'adulterous, canting, slimy, slobbering Bolshie' being able to order him about was a powerful inducement to Duff to quit diplomacy. The fact that Mosley could 'shine' seemed to suggest that the 'standard' required for success in politics was 'so low' that the odds in favour of Duff's gamble were not so bad. By March the die was cast – although Diana was adjured to say nothing until Duff had found a constituency.

This last hurdle almost proved a decisive barrier to his ambitions. His best hope of getting a seat lay in the Rutland connection. Belvoir Castle stood in the constituency of Melton. The MP for Melton, Sir Charles Yate, had announced that he would not stand at the next

35

election and Duff hoped that he might secure the nomination. On the surface his chances were good: the Duke of Rutland was a past President of the local Conservative association and Lord Granby (Diana's brother John) was the current President. Despite these advantages, Duff was not chosen. This was partly because John Granby was not on the best of terms with his colleagues, and partly because many Conservative associations wanted rich candidates who would pay for the local party organization. But Duff's continued difficulties in finding a seat suggest that the problem was more deep-rooted.

Had Duff wished to join the Liberal Party – an idea which never occurred to him – he would have been able to call on the assistance of a wide range of political contacts: Asquith, Edwin Montagu, Winston Churchill and even his old friend Hilaire Belloc; but on the Conservative side of the House of Commons he had few contacts. These few – his former boss at the Foreign Office, Ronald MacNeill, and his Oxford friend, Sidney Herbert – did what they could, and finally helped deliver the goods, but the fact that he knew so few Conservatives is significant.

Those Liberal politicians whom he knew tended to be those with at least a footing in the literary world, like Asquith and Churchill. The Conservative Party, Disraeli notwithstanding, did not run to literary men; and it was in the company of such men that Duff felt most at home.

It was this lack of Conservative contacts, as much as any defects of his own, which hindered his finding a constituency. There was also the fact of his unease in the company of strangers, which hardly suggested that he would make an ideal politician. This had gained him a reputation in some circles for arrogance; his friends called it shyness. Duff was well aware of this defect. Writing to Diana in March 1924, he commented that:

> I'm afraid I must confess, although I'm ashamed to confess it, that the only milieu I really like is the 'smart set'. I hate the provincialism of the respectable as much as I hate the bohemianism of the unrespectable.

It was, then, a nice irony and a pretty chance that brought this most metropolitan of figures to the industrial north, and which was to take him into Parliament.

Conservative Central Office was not blind to the problems caused by the tendency of local associations to choose rich, middle-aged businessmen as their MPs. In April 1923 the Conservative Principal

Agent, William Hall, wrote to that most important of Lancashire Tories, Lord Derby, expressing the hope that they would be able to 'get a small band of young men who talk well and offer them to constituencies. It is quite true we should have to finance most of them, but that is a matter for further discussion.'[3] The Conservatives had fared badly in Lancashire in 1923, mainly because of Stanley Baldwin's decision to fight the election on a platform of tariff reform. As the centre of the cotton industry, which depended on free trade, Lancashire had rejected protection – and its advocates. A much chastened Baldwin would not make the same mistake again, and all Conservatives hoped that the experiment of a minority Labour Government under Ramsay MacDonald would not be one which the country would want to repeat. But if the Conservatives were to win the next election then they needed to win marginal seats in industrial areas. This, in turn, required candidates of a high calibre. But as Hall explained to Lord Derby in May 1923: 'The trouble is that whilst one can find a young man quite able to win the seat when arrangements have been made regarding the expenses, so few of them have anything to live on when elected.' Duff was certainly a bright young prospect, as MacNeill told Central Office; and what was more, thanks to Diana, he would have something to live on once elected. Thus it was that his name was suggested to Albert Howcroft, Chairman of the Oldham Conservative Association. Howcroft wrote to Duff in early June 1924 urging him to consider standing for Oldham: 'I think someone like yourself has a good chance: Oldham was Mr Winston Churchill's first seat in Parliament.'

Duff was interested – especially as nothing better seemed in prospect. But before committing himself, he preferred to test the temperature of the political water in Oldham. On 20 June he wrote to the sitting Liberal MP, Sir Edward Grigg, to seek his advice. Oldham was one of the few remaining borough seats which returned two MPs. The Liberal decision to run two candidates in 1923 had split the anti-socialist vote and allowed Labour to take one seat; Duff asked Grigg if this was likely to happen again.[4] Grigg's reply on 8 July was courteous, but he made it plain that, given the divided nature of the Liberal Party, he could scarcely be sure of standing at the next election himself. Howcroft thought things would probably work out, but warned Duff against any formal pact with the Liberals: 'as a party the Liberals are not to be trusted'.

This seemed to Duff to be as much as he could hope for. On the

financial side things looked equally satisfactory. Central Office promised a proportion of the election expenses, and Howcroft assured Duff
that he would only have to pay £100 or £200 a year to the local
association: marginal seats may have been risky prospects, but they
were to be had on the cheap. Howcroft's main concern was that Duff
should have a 'good lady campaigner' to offset the influence exercised
by Lady Grigg. That would depend on whether the election fell
during the Broadway season of *The Miracle*.

Duff went to Oldham for the first time on 31 July. He made a great
and favourable impression on the selection committee and was
adopted as the Conservative candidate. Shortly afterwards he resigned
from the Foreign Office and set off for New York to join Diana.

From the very start of their enforced separation Diana had struck
a plaintive note in her letters. She had urged him to join her, but the
prospect of leaving the Foreign Office before he had found a seat,
merely to drink bad cocktails and 'hang around stage doors', did not
appeal to him.

During the dark and foggy London winter he did not, as he confessed, miss Diana 'intolerably'. But

> with the coming of the spring, reminder of all the possibilities and the
> importance of life, all the little pleasures which kept me going – bridge
> and Bucks, wine and friends, lose any keen-edged flavour which they ever
> possessed and which never begat distinction – and I feel acutely that days
> are limited and that every one passed without you is wasted.

Constantly he reassured her of the depth of his love: 'Whenever anyone
talks to me about marriage I feel as ill-fitted to give an opinion as the
winner of the Calcutta Sweep when asked for his views on gambling.'

But she was not altogether satisfied, and passages such as the following exchange of views with Lady Rosemary Ednam could hardly
have helped matters: 'I told her, which is true, that I only feel guilty
when I feel sentimental, never when I felt lascivious.' Nor was it long
before Diana accused him of lechery.

For once, her suspicions were misplaced and Duff really had been
only dining with the young lady Diana had accused him of dallying
with – Poppy Baring. His response speaks volumes for his understanding of Diana's nature. He denied her charges with mock indignation
and scolded her with a mixture of playfulness and sternness, calling
her a 'naughty, ugly, diseased, obstinate, perverse and disobedient
child'. He concluded the letter on the same paternal note:

I must now dine because I am hungry and they are waiting for me. But I do love my ugly little girl – not very much – but a good deal better than all the world beside.

And in his next letter he kept up the banter and the tone:

Well ugly – more letters from you this morning – nasty, plaintive, whining, suspicious but ever welcome, deeply cherished letters. You say it's dirty to be lecherous – but jealousy let me tell you is far dirtier – because the latter is of the mind.

He ticked her off soundly, but always adding the note of reassurance which she needed, including the first draft of a sonnet:

Doubt not, sweet love, oh never dare to doubt –
Lest doubting should conceive and bear distrust,
Lest the pure steel of our love show rust
And all our hosts of joy be put to rout.
Our citadel of love is girt about
By envious captains – Weariness, Disgust,
Estrangement, Disillusion, yea and Lust
But still the traitor at the gate is Doubt.

He improved upon the verses in his next letter, but the message remained the same.

In early April he told Diana that he would come over for a few weeks in New York and asked what boat he should take. With her innate parsimony she suggested a cheap liner – which prompted Duff to poke gentle fun at the contradiction between this advice and her repeated statements that she wanted him urgently:

Shall I sail by a leaky ship and slow,
One that the rats deserted long ago,
Or by the last, the largest and the best,
Whom no Atlantic tempest can molest?
I asked – your answer made the angels weep –
'Come darling by the one that is most cheap'.
You ungrammatical and graceless mite
You tiny Yid, you parsimonious fright.
When at the bottom of the deep blue sea
The hungry fishes make a feast of me
While the *Majestic* her untroubled way
Pursues in triumph, you perhaps will say –
While Nanny combs your hair and ties your sash
'I lost my Duffy but I saved my cash'.

It was all quite irresistible – and Diana did not want to resist.

Duff's long summer visit was cut short by politics. The MacDonald Labour Government fell from office in September and a general election was called for October. Duff left for England on the earliest liner, determined to put his all into what would be a crucial contest.

7

Oldham and Westminster

Then, as still to a large extent now, Oldham was a town of solid, grey terraced houses, dominated by the red-brick of the towering mill-chimneys, symbols of the source of the livelihood of most of the population. Like most mill-towns, Oldham was beginning to feel the effects of competition from Asia. My mother, who worked in one of those mills as a young girl, can remember her mother telling her that those 'little yellow men' who were being shown round the mills would soon put them all out of work; and so it proved. Yet the flame of the free-trade faith still burnt strong; strongly enough to fuel the Liberal Party and to make tariff reform a dirty word.

Oldham was not the sort of place that Duff would ever have visited for any reason other than getting into Parliament. Where it was not a working-class town, it was a stronghold of the sort of provincial, bourgeois respectability which was so alien to the metropolitan smart-set to which the Coopers belonged. Its Toryism was of the democratic variety: patriotic; anti-socialist; in favour of the drink trade and against the puritanism of the chapel. It opened Duff's eyes and emotions to a whole new world, although he was surely exaggerating when he wrote to Diana of finding 'seven or eight families' sharing two 'rooms' in a tenement. In such an atmosphere, the romantic high Toryism which no doubt sounded so well over the port in the precincts of White's began to falter.

One of Duff's reasons for hesitating to embark upon a political career was his fear that his 'reactionary' views were not fitted to modern politics. In fact his 'reactionary' views tended to be those cultivated in his own library or in St James's. He admired the doomed Toryism of the Jacobites, of the opponents of Peel; he saw himself voting with Disraeli, or advising the Young Pretender. Exposure to the realities of politics in his own time soon revealed the Liberal

41

lurking under the mask of the die-hard. On none of the great issues of the day was Duff to reveal anything save the most proper liberal-Tory sentiments.

Like almost every politician, Duff confessed to a loathing of electioneering; an odd characteristic of the genus *homo politicus*. But like all politicians, it was a tariff he was more than willing to pay for the attendant rewards. The year of 1924 was a good one to be fighting a marginal seat as a Tory. The election had been called because the minority Labour Government had lost a vote of confidence over its handling of the proposed prosecution of the editor of a Communist newspaper on charges of inciting troops to disaffection. Hardly had the campaign begun than the press came up with the famous 'Zinoviev letter', which seemed to show that the Labour Party was tarred with the brush of Bolshevism. The Labour Party was forced on the defensive, but at least it could rely on the bed-rock of class-based support. The Liberal Party, which had been responsible for letting Labour form a government in 1923, had no such refuge. Duff, like most Conservative candidates, drove home the message that the only sure way of keeping the socialists out was to vote Tory. With the 'Bolshevik bogey' working in his favour, and Baldwin's pledge that a Conservative Government would not introduce tariffs, Duff could not have asked for more favourable conditions. But he made the most of them; after all, hundreds of Conservatives enjoying similar advantages failed to get elected.

Duff arrived in the North on 5 October. There being no hotel in Oldham, he made his base at the Midland Hotel in Manchester. Sharing the curious belief, common among those from the metropolis, that civilization ended once Oxford was passed, Duff was delighted to find that he could procure good food and wine at the Midland – even after late-night election meetings. This, he thought, was a promising start.

The campaign was a gruelling one. The day after his arrival he went to Oldham, where he addressed three meetings at Conservative Working Men's clubs. As he told Diana:

> I addressed an audience of from fifty to eighty men and women. All the meetings went well. My speeches were not good, but they were good enough and as good as they had means of understanding. It was a dull performance, as all the audience are convinced Conservatives and would swallow anything. I only had one or two hecklers, to both of whom I was grateful as I dealt with them perfectly.

Assistance in the fight came from Diana's sisters, Letty and Marjorie, as well as from more weighty political figures such as Lord Derby; but one person was missing – Diana.

She was not able to turn up until the closing stages of the campaign, but from the moment of her arrival she stole the show. Lady Grigg may have been an experienced electioneer and Diana a tyro, but she had charisma. Diana had been terrified at the prospect of taking part in an election – not least because she was convinced that she would do something to damage Duff's chances of winning. She need not have worried. The mill-girls loved her, flocking to see her famed beauty and her fashionable clothes. Her way of recommending Duff to their good graces had the twin merits of novelty and brevity: 'I hope you'll vote for him. He's a very good husband.' Promising to perform a clog-dance if Duff won was final evidence that she was a 'good sport'. With Diana's arrival the election became 'news'; the danger was that the candidate himself might get overlooked.

Duff and Diana made a formidable electioneering team. She was able to provide the jollity and the 'gladhanding' that he shrank from, while he provided impressive oratory and a political platform. He addressed dozens of meetings during the campaign and demonstrated considerable power as an orator. His voice was a powerful weapon, strong and firm; given his size, he bore a marked resemblance to a bantam cock as he stood upon the platform excoriating the record of the 'Socialist Government'.

His main theme was spelt out in his election address – 'Socialism is the enemy'. Against the folly and the dogmatism of this foreign ideology, Duff set the solid Englishness of the Conservative Party which stood for 'union – union of all classes in one Nation, a union of all races in one Empire'. It was a strong and simple message, and he put it across excellently. Long before polling-day, Howcroft was confident that Duff would be elected; but the magnitude of his success caught them all by surprise.

Duff finished top of the poll with 37,419 votes, beating Grigg into second place with 36,761. The Conservatives of Oldham were jubilant, their paper, the *Oldham Evening Standard*, proudly declaring that 'never in the political history of Oldham has a Unionist gained such a sweeping and crushing victory as this'. At the age of thirty-four Duff found himself an MP and the senior burgess for Oldham; it remained to be seen whether he would be able to capitalize on this initial success.

At every point in Duff's public career there were not lacking those who claimed that he owed everything to Diana. He would have been the last to deny that, without Diana's earnings, his political career would have been impossible. But that was the extent of the help; and even that was two-edged. Diana was not a political animal and had no interest in founding a political salon to further her husband's career; moreover, the glamour and publicity which constantly surrounded her helped to reinforce the image of Duff as a political lightweight. This was to prove a considerable albatross around his neck.

Diana had been of considerable help in his struggle to clear the first hurdle on the political course, but he was on his own after that. The next major ordeal, the maiden speech in the Commons, he would have to undergo unaided. Given the press coverage of the election and Duff's career, there was considerable interest in how he would acquit himself.

Duff was due to make his maiden speech on 10 December 1924. He awoke at the unheard-of hour of six o'clock and spent the morning thinking out the lineaments of what he intended to say. He telephoned Winston Churchill to try to ensure that he would be called that afternoon, before making his way through a 'London as black as night' to the House. But despite 'hanging about' all afternoon, he failed to catch the Speaker's eye and had to postpone 'losing my maidenhead'.

This did nothing to help his nerves. In the 1920s newspapers were the only mass medium and speeches were reported at length. A man's whole reputation could rest upon his oratorical talents. There was, always glittering before the eyes of the tyro, the example in the previous generation of F. E. Smith's famous maiden speech in 1906, which had made his name and reputation in a night; and the names of Lloyd George, Winston Churchill and Ramsay MacDonald stood as testimony to the importance of rhetoric. There were, naturally, many men who came into Parliament as a natural part of their *curriculum vitae*, businessmen or local squires for whom the Commons was one of many interests. But for those who, like Duff, were professional politicians and who wished to rise to the top, success on the floor of the House was vital.

After his abortive attempt on 10 December, Duff retired to Hatfield House, at which shrine of high Toryism he polished up his speech. At seven o'clock on the evening of 15 December, having finally caught the Speaker's eye, Duff rose to give his maiden speech, and as he did so 'a thing happened to me which has never happened before – my mouth became perfectly dry'. However, he managed to get out a few words and, encouraged by the sound of his own voice, 'I gathered confidence'.

He was fortunate in his timing. He was speaking immediately after the Labour leader and former Prime Minister, Ramsay MacDonald, which meant that the House was fairly full. Moreover, he was speaking during a debate on the future of Egypt, a subject on which his recent experience in the Foreign Office gave him a particular right to be listened to with attention. Having overcome his initial nervousness, Duff was even more encouraged by the fact that 'people kept dribbling in instead of dribbling out as usually happens'. He heard the Foreign Secretary, Austen Chamberlain, tell Baldwin, ' "I hear he's very good." ' According to one newspaper Baldwin turned round to watch Duff and remained in that uncomfortable position for twenty minutes, while Austen Chamberlain was even seen to laugh; but as the same paper reported that Churchill, who was not even in the Chamber, joined in the laughter, this may be taken with a pinch of salt.

Read in the dusty columns of *Hansard* it is difficult to understand why Duff's speech was quite so successful; much must have rested upon the manner of delivery. The speech began with a reference to the famous Zinoviev letter, but dwelt, in the main, on the Egyptian question. Here his sentiments were impeccably liberal. As it was no longer possible to govern the country by force, he said, Britain should follow a policy of 'conciliation and concession'. Referring to the suggestion from the Labour benches that the whole problem should be laid at the door of the League of Nations, Duff poured scorn on the idea of 'high-brow Scandinavian professors' trying to acquaint themselves with the lineaments of the problem before delivering their long-delayed conclusion, and he warned that the League was 'in more danger from its friends than from its enemies ... from those who would lay on it burdens with which it is unequal to cope'. Having said that he was in favour of a settlement of the Egyptian problem on 'the most liberal and progressive lines' he sat down – with his name already made.

Maiden speeches are traditionally the subject of a great deal of polite congratulation, but the tributes in Duff's case were so numerous, so warm and so overwhelming, that there can be no doubt that it was 'a really brilliant and successful maiden speech'. The honour of delivering the first of the many encomia fell, by a happy chance, to Duff's old Oxford tutor, H. A. L. Fisher, who said that it was a 'brilliant' speech, 'perfect alike in form and distinguished by a liberality and generosity of spirit, and by a width of outlook which the whole House has appreciated'. The next speaker, Duff's old boss at the Foreign Office, Arthur Ponsonby, called the speech 'one of the most brilliant maiden speeches I have heard in this House'. Duff's colleague for Oldham, Sir Edward Grigg, was even more direct, calling it 'a brilliant maiden speech'.

The congratulations came, too, in less ephemeral forms. Sir George Lloyd, MP for Eastbourne and an acknowledged expert on the Middle East, pencilled a note on the back of a House of Commons menu saying that he 'agreed with every word' and passed it along the back-benches. Although Winston Churchill had missed the speech, he passed a note to Duff saying that Chamberlain had told him what a triumph it had been. Even more unusual than this homage from the Front Bench was a pencilled note of congratulation from the Speaker. All that evening, as he sat in the smoking-room, strangers came up to him and offered their felicitations. In short 'it was a triumph' – and his only regret was that Diana could not be there to share it. But then she was in America earning the money to make it all possible.

If a night's sleep had made Duff doubt the truth of what had happened the previous evening, a quick look at the morning papers was enough to convince him that, like Byron, he had woken to find himself famous. The press was loud, warm and almost unanimous in its praise of him. The *Daily Express*, trumpeting its own prophecy, called it 'undoubtedly the most successful maiden speech which the House of Commons has heard for many years', while the *Daily News* reported that Duff's 'singularly effective maiden speech' had been 'the brightest moment of the evening'. The *Evening Standard* noted that his speech was 'the subject of widespread comment in political circles today' and went on to add that 'by general consent no new member has commanded the ear of the House with such immediate and political success'; its leader-writer went so far as to say that 'a new personality had appeared on the political scene'. The comment of the *Evening News*, that he had at last escaped from his wife's shadow, seemed quite niggardly after these hymns of praise.

Duff's post for the next few mornings brought fresh causes for blushing. Letters of congratulation came from Lord Derby, who had been of great help, and from Lord Curzon, who had declined to speak for

Duff; his old chiefs, Cecil Harmsworth and Ronald MacNeill, offered their encomia; but the most satisfying letter came from Belvoir Castle. The Duke of Rutland wrote to congratulate him and to offer advice for the future; the scapegrace who had not been good enough to marry his daughter five years before had now been transformed into the most promising back-bencher on the Government side of the House. It was a sweet moment of triumph and Duff savoured it to the full. The gamble had paid off handsomely.

The question now was how to follow up this success. Soon after being elected Duff had written to the Conservative Minister whom he knew best, Winston Churchill, suggesting that he might become his parliamentary private secretary. But Churchill had written back urging him to keep his parliamentary freedom. Duff agreed with his advice that it was best for him to be able to speak freely upon whatever topic he chose. Churchill wrote back on 24 November saying that he was

> sure you have decided rightly not to sell your parliamentary birthright for a mess of quasi-official pottage. You can certainly count on any help that I can give you. The most practical form this help will take will be in talking over with you your interventions in debate and showing you how to secure the best chance of being called ... a Minister can also sometimes give an official hint to the Speaker quite informally that he happens to know that so-and-so is going to make a good speech and is particularly well-informed on the topic.

This advice turned out to be just right. But Duff drew the line when Diana tried to intercede with Churchill to get him promotion.

Had Duff become a PPS his room for intervention in debate would have been restricted and he would have had to stick closely to the Government line on most issues; as an independent back-bencher he was free to establish his reputation as an effective and brilliant speaker at his own pace.

Duff was well aware that the years before the next general election were 'the most important for me' and that he could afford to miss no opportunity during them. Unless he established his reputation quickly he would, he feared, 'slip back and relapse into a lazy idler supported by a rich, hard-working wife'.

As might have been expected, Duff paid least attention to the constituency side of his job; he was a Westminster politician, aiming for a position on the national stage. He would put in the necessary appearances in the provinces, but seldom spent the night in Man-

47

chester if he could catch the milk-train to London. Howcroft did find it necessary, in the early stages of Duff's career, to remind him, 'You are now a Member of Parliament with its obligations', which included opening church fêtes and attending Primrose League bazaars. But this reminder was not repeated. Duff was aware of the necessity of keeping his name before the Oldham public and he and Diana built up a great fund of goodwill during the next five years – as the efforts of their supporters in 1929 was to show. Although Duff may not have spent long in Oldham, when he was there there was scarcely a Chamber of Commerce dinner or a mothers' meeting which was not graced by a speech from the senior burgess.

The road to national fame was not an easy one. The Baldwin Government had a large majority and asked of its younger helots little more than their votes. Duff had no intention of remaining mere lobby-fodder, and his initial success had marked him out as a man with a future. He was careful to do nothing which might spoil this image. In the House he declined to become a bore, speaking on selected occasions upon topics where he could claim some special knowledge, establishing for himself a niche in foreign affairs, the League of Nations and kindred matters. His main efforts in the Conservative cause between 1925 and 1928 were on political platforms up and down the country. In a party which was not renowned for its platform orators, this was a certain avenue to success; provided, of course, Duff's oratory proved suitably compelling.

One of the most difficult things for a later generation to appreciate is the platform-style of a bygone political era. In the House of Commons the speaking style, influenced heavily by Baldwin, was becoming more conversational, and the rolling periods and majestic phrasing of Churchill's oratory was becoming outdated. But on the public platform there was, in this pre-microphone age, no substitute for a naturally powerful voice. Beaverbrook, who was no admirer, wrote to Duff in 1928 to say how impressed he had been by hearing him speak. As the comments of 'an onlooker who is incapable of doing the trick himself but knows enough to have some idea how the trick is done', Beaverbrook's words are worth some consideration.

His first comment was that Duff had shown 'great capacity and ability on the platform' and could, in time, 'become one of our leading orators and rank with the really big names in that art'. Beaverbrook's chief criticism was that 'you go to your main contention in too direct and deadly a manner'; he advised Duff to employ more humour and imagery in his speeches. The other criticisms were of technique: 'you ought to vary your tone more from time to time'; and 'when you want to rub in a point your voice goes harsh'. Duff was well aware of these various defects and his reply to 'dear Max' illustrates why he never became (in the words of one of his obituarists) 'a really big popular figure'. He accepted Beaverbrook's points, but on the subject of humour:

> I always feel that the difficulty ... lies in the fact that what amuses us would probably not amuse the audience, while what would amuse the audience is the kind of joke that we should be – but Lloyd George is not – ashamed to make.[1]

He never felt that rapport with the audience that truly great orators like Lloyd George or F. E. Smith felt, and he lacked that touch of the vulgarian which most successful democratic politicians cultivate. It was not just the manner of his speaking, nor the enormous number of his speaking engagements (as many as twenty-six during a parliamentary session) which established Duff as one of the coming young men.

If a model of a modern young Conservative had been required for show, Duff would have served for the purpose. He was anti-socialist, but mainly on the ground that socialism was a nasty foreign doctrine which perverted the thoughts of free-born Englishmen and wanted to 'transfer from the individual to the state certain functions, certain privileges, certain rights'. His Conservatism had a distinctly Whiggish, if not downright Liberal, tinge. His pamphlet, *The Conservative Point of View*, published by Conservative Central Office in 1925, was a work with which few Liberals would have had profound misgivings. Even that bastion of Lancashire Liberalism, the *Oldham Chronicle*, which took up eight columns of print in commenting upon Duff's 'errors', conceded that: 'If Oldham is to be represented by a Conservative, there is no private member for whom we would be disposed to change him.'

On domestic affairs his comments were few and simple: 'order and liberty' (in that order) were what was required. But, no die-hard, he wanted better housing, more jobs and a moderate attitude towards trades unions. Even during the General Strike he advocated conciliation. But his main specialization, on the platform and in the House, was foreign policy, where, once again, he was the paradigm of liberal Toryism. Was the great shibboleth of liberalism belief in the efficacy of the League of Nations at Geneva? – why then, Duff was for it.

Indeed, he made it his particular pet subject and became a vice-president of the League of Nations Union and did much speaking on its behalf. This phase of his career culminated in 1928 when he actually delivered an address on the 'Barbarians' at a meeting of the League in Geneva. What, one is tempted to ask, reviewing Duff's speeches between 1924 and 1928, had become of the young diplomat whose views had been too reactionary for success in modern politics?

Part of the answer to this question lies in noting that Duff was by no means alone in his views. He was one of a number of young Tories, including Harold Macmillan, Anthony Eden and Bob Boothby, whose attitudes earned for them the nickname of the 'Y.M.C.A.' and who, in turn, christened the harder-faced men who had done well out of the war and who thronged the Conservative back-benches, 'the forty thieves'. These young men looked to the party leader, Baldwin, for inspiration – and promotion.

Given the denigration to which Stanley Baldwin has been subjected since 1940, it now takes some effort to appreciate the tremendous impact which he had on British politics. After the untrustworthy brilliance of the self-styled 'first-class brains', Lloyd George, Churchill and Birkenhead, Baldwin shrewdly projected an image of himself as the quintessential Englishman: a 'second-class brain' with 'a first-class character'. This was, at least in part, a clever appeal to the deep-seated English preference for 'character' over 'intellect' which has been such a factor in the national decline, but it also reflected Baldwin's own instinctive belief in the virtues of bringing decency and honesty into public life. Taking up the Disraelian theme of 'One Nation', Baldwin strove to create an image of Conservatism that was as far removed from the crude materialism of the 'Boozer Swank', Birkenhead, as it was from the aristocratic remoteness of the Cecils of Hatfield House. This patriotic and romantic Conservatism, taking its sustenance from that vein of rural nostalgia which lies so near the surface of the English character, had a great appeal for Duff. He responded easily to Baldwin's sentimentality, which was similar to his own, and he had a great respect and affection for his leader. It is no accident that his career flourished while Baldwin reigned and then went into eclipse under his successors.

What Baldwin succeeded in representing was one version of Duff's rather literary, eighteenth-century vision of politics. Duff was not interested, as his pamphlet showed, in economics or social policy. He wanted to be at the centre of great and noble events – especially in diplomacy. But the age of the gentleman-amateur, to which Duff's spirit belonged, was passing. In an age of mass-electorates and economic decline, social and financial policy bulked increasingly large in the eyes of most politicians. He was fortunate in that he began his career in the twilight of the last age of British power and was thus able, to an extent, to have the sort of political career he wanted.

From almost the earliest days of his parliamentary life he was spoken of as a future Minister. In late 1925 he lost his habitual calm when the press tipped him for the job of Under-Secretary at the Foreign Office in succession to his old chief, Ronald MacNeill. It would have been astonishingly quick promotion, but it was the one job he really coveted, and he was disappointed when it went elsewhere – and furious with Diana when he discovered that she had asked Churchill to give what assistance he could: 'It is much better not to indulge in intrigue if one can get by without it.' In early 1928 promotion finally came when Baldwin asked him to go to the War Office as Financial Secretary. Henceforth, for the rest of his political career, with the exception of a self-imposed exile of eighteen months, Duff was to sit on the ministerial benches whenever the Conservatives were in power. He had arrived.

~~~~ 8 ~~~~

Finance and Friendships

The attainment of junior office is a landmark in the career of any politician; for Duff it was particularly important. He was in the Commons for fame and had, at the most, a guaranteed period of five years in which to make his claim. Oldham was a marginal seat which would be difficult to hold at the next election; as an ex-minister he would stand a better chance of finding a new (and safer) seat. As a junior minister Duff had placed his foot on the lowest rung of the ladder of preferment – and improved his chances of surviving long enough to climb a few more rungs.

Then there was the little matter of pay. In his memoirs Duff points out that although he received £1,400 a year, once the loss of the money which he had been receiving for journalism was taken into account, this amounted to a small increase in salary; that was true, but it was a safer source of income. In so far as Duff's finances did not depend on his political position they depended upon Diana.

One of the great unexplored areas of twentieth-century politics is how politicians financed their careers. It is, however, abundantly clear from what evidence there is that a political career could be ruinously expensive and that many politicians left office a good deal poorer for the experience: Asquith, Baldwin and Lord Birkenhead spring readily to mind. Duff's method of financing his political career was highly unusual, but had the merit of being successful. The bulk of the money which Diana earned from *The Miracle* was invested to provide for his needs, thus taking him outside the category of those bright young men who, once elected, struggled to support themselves. But, being Duff, this did not mean that money troubles ceased. Indeed, it was not until 1935 that he could really feel comfortably off.

This may sound ridiculous. Although in an unfashionable district of London, Gower Street was an imposing residence and both Duff and Diana lived in style. While she was in America Diana scrimped every penny she could to go towards Duff's career; it could hardly be said that Duff imitated her. Where she was eating macaroni cheese and persuading hoteliers to let her have her room for free, Duff was dining off oysters and champagne at Buck's, or flitting over to Paris for a weekend at the gaming tables and the whores; the contrast between her behaviour and his was one of the few things which drove Diana to complain to him. The simple fact was that Duff was incapable of thrift and as unrestrained in his financial behaviour as he was in his sexual appetites.

The roots of his extravagance no doubt lay in the extent to which his adoring mother had been willing, and able, to bail him out financially from his Oxford days onwards. His attitude to money was as 'Whiggish' as his political and sexual *mores*: money was not something which a gentleman worried about. The fact that he moved in a social circle which contained some extremely rich men who could afford to gamble for the sort of stakes which Duff felt obliged to match, merely exacerbated his financial troubles. But, as at Oxford, he had a woman to provide the wherewithal to meet his debts.

In November 1925 he confessed to Diana that he was in 'acute financial difficulty' – £423 overdrawn, with no means of meeting his debts. Characteristically, he had, upon receipt of this statement, sent a letter to his bank asking them to lend him another £600: this was 'Whig' finance with a vengeance. Diana, and capital from his mother's will, came to the rescue. He was able to report proudly to Diana that £700 from his mother's lawyers had seen him out of the woods. But in his next letter he waxed indignant, for having paid off his overdraft and asked his bank 'cheerfully' how his account now stood, he had been told that he was £2 overdrawn. This, he protested, was 'very discouraging'; but not so discouraging that it kept him in the black.

Diana forwarded him £470 at the end of 1925 to pay off various bills. This kept him afloat for a few months. Duff had a gambler's view of money; when he had it he spent it, and when he did not have it, he borrowed it. His long-suffering bankers finally protested to him in December 1926. He told Diana that he had just had 'the first unpleasant letter which I've ever had from my bank. They say they can't understand me. If they really can't they're not fit to be bankers.' He had a point. This time it took a cheque from Diana for £450 to clear the decks. But by February 1927 Duff was back in the red: 'It

53

is disheartening – but there it is – and I indulge in no extravagances.'
This last remark might well have raised eyebrows at his bank, but it
contains an important element of truth: trips to Paris or Cannes,
games of *chemin de fer*, champagne and pretty women were essentials
to Duff.

If Sidney Herbert or Eric Dudley went to Paris, so too must Duff.
If Duff could not run to a country house, he had at least to be able
to maintain a round of country-house visiting. Like many other young
Tories – for example, Harold Macmillan and Bob Boothby – Duff
had married his way into the British aristocracy; but unlike these
two, or that renegade Tory, Oswald Mosley, Duff scarcely had the
resources to sustain the social round. However, he would not have
been the man he was, in more than one way, if he had let that stop
him.

Duff's general attitude towards life is aptly summed up in a poem
which he wrote during the early 1920s:

> Young man sans melancholy
> To whom this world seems jolly
> Guard well your precious folly
> There wisdom lies.
>
> Love wine and song and beauty
> Nor give a hang for duty.
> Kiss girls when they are pretty
> With shining eyes.
>
> When things are going badly
> Don't frown upon them sadly
> But welcome winter gladly
> For spring is near.
>
> Play while it still is playtime
> To have made love in May-time....

Although it is unfinished, it is a succinct statement of Duff's hedonism.
He loved life and savoured it, as he did fine old wines and books.

Duff was, and remained, what he had always been, a metropolitan
boulevardier – and without Diana and his political career he might
have remained just that: an amusing man about town; a cultivated,
if rather raffish figure: a Birkenhead without the intellect, or a Randolph Churchill with literary talent.

There were, throughout his career, those who took him at face value, who saw him as an essentially lightweight figure; but they were fewer at this stage of his career than they were to become. His hard work for the party and the golden opinions he had won in liberal–Conservative quarters assured that the new junior minister had a warm welcome once the news of his promotion was announced.

Duff enjoyed his period as Financial Secretary at the War Office. His duties were not too demanding, and his chief, Sir Laming Worthington-Evans, was an amiable man who did not mind giving his junior a chance to shine; his habit, when perplexed, of suggesting that 'we should lubricate our intelligences with a cocktail', served to confirm him in Duff's favour.

The main job of the Financial Secretary was to help prepare the Army Estimates and, if necessary, to read them in the Commons. Duff made his Front Bench debut on 8 March and was pronounced a great success, with 'Worthy' congratulating him on a remarkable 'dayboo'. He turned the usually dreary business of reading a list of facts and figures into a dramatic performance, dispensing with notes and reciting from memory; a foretaste of his future success in this line in the 1930s.

During his eighteen months at the War Office Duff consolidated the reputation he had gained as a rising young man. The only ones who were in any way disappointed in him were some of his former supporters from the League of Nations Union who seemed disposed to censure him for 'failing to disband the Army forthwith'. The only cloud on the horizon was the fact that there was an election due in 1929. But it seemed certain that if he held his seat and if a Conservative Government was returned, Duff would attain ministerial office in the near future.

The nearer the election approached, the more unlikely did it become that there would be a Conservative Government and that Duff Cooper would be the MP for Oldham. This was through no fault of Duff's.

In 1924 the Conservatives had been in the happy position of being able to attack the record of their opponents; this time the position was reversed. Moreover, they could hardly hope for a new 'Zinoviev letter'. Nor was Baldwin's slogan of 'safety first' likely to enthuse the electorate. In Oldham Duff possessed some considerable advantages which he had not enjoyed five years before; as a junior minister and a respected local figure, he could count on considerable local support. But there was one major disadvantage: the Liberals had decided to run two candidates, which meant that the anti-Labour vote would be split three ways. Both Howcroft and Duff were well aware that this made defeat a probability.

But Duff was a fighter and threw himself into the campaign in May with great energy. Howcroft organized an effective series of meetings at which Duff spoke to large and enthusiastic audiences. Local helpers included a bevy of Lancashire beauties whose blue cloche-hats earned them the sobriquet of the 'blue belles'; their job was to marshal the 'flapper' vote. Alas for Duff's cause, that great lady electioneer, Diana, was unable to participate fully in the election because she was heavily pregnant.

Diana tried to make up for this by exercising influence in other quarters, most notably by badgering Max Beaverbrook to ensure that the northern editions of the *Express* featured Duff's speeches prominently. When she discovered that he was not doing as she asked, Diana berated him for his churlishness and he hid behind the excuse that he had no influence on the editor.[1] Needless to say, the *Express* was not loud in its praise of Duff Cooper.

But not even the much-vaunted power of the press, nor yet the toil and sweat of Duff's supporters, could prevail against the anti-Conservative tide in northern industrial towns. It is some testimony to Duff's talents that despite the fact that two Liberals were standing he managed to increase the Conservative vote by eleven thousand; but he still finished only a close third behind the second of the two Labour men to get elected. It was some small satisfaction to beat both Liberals, but it did not alter the fact that he was out.

Howcroft wrote to Duff to express the general feeling on the morrow of their defeat: 'Our people are dreadfully upset, as must be the case. You have grown into our affections, and to the Conservative men in the workshops you were a hero such as Oldham has never had before.' It was a generous tribute, and to judge from other letters which Duff received, a well-deserved one.

The fact that he also received messages of commiseration from grandees within the part such as Lords Salisbury and Birkenhead, as well as from Churchill and Baldwin, was a sign of his reputation within the Conservative Party. Neville Chamberlain, who was soon to become Chairman of the Party, wrote on 4 June to say that he was:

Confident that you will not be long out of the House, where you have already made such a mark in so short a time. We are looking to you as one of the men who, in the future, will carry the party to new achievements.

It was a nice letter – and one fully in tune with Duff's own thoughts. But until the next election, and until he could find himself a seat, he would have to find other things to occupy himself with.

Here he was fortunate. Duff was not one of those politicians whose minds dwelt exclusively upon his profession. Indeed, it was, perhaps, this fact that prevented his career going further than it did. Cut off from Parliament he could turn to literature – and to keeping his friendships in good repair. Given the nature of his acquaintanceship there was a close connection between the two things.

Duff's range of political friends was remarkably small for a politician. His closest friend was Baldwin's parliamentary private secretary, Sidney Herbert – but that was a friendship which dated back to Eton. He was on good terms with Lord Cranborne and Bob Boothby, but most of his closest friends were literary men – which reflects the fact that of all his interests, literature was the one closest to his heart.

The writer Hilaire Belloc was his dearest literary friend and they were bound together by a common Francophilia and love of wine. Belloc dedicated his *Heroic Poem in Praise of Wine* to Duff, a compliment which was returned when Duff dedicated his first book to Belloc. They shared a love of argument and poetry, and for more than two decades Belloc was a constant and welcome visitor at West House, the Coopers' small home near Bognor, where he would sit in the garden after lunch and declaim his verse. Duff fully agreed with him that:

> The world is full of double beds
> And sweet young things with maidenheads.
> This being so there's no excuse
> For sodomy or self-abuse.

Belloc would pepper his letters with amusing scraps of poetry:

> When little Charlie had the croup
> His mother gave him beastly soup
> Which made him sick, and when he cried
> She thrashed him till he nearly died.
> His sisters clouted him as well
> And made his life a perfect Hell
> With bellowing at him all the while,
> 'Smile! Damn your little gizzard! Smile!'
> And both his brothers kicked him too
> And punched his body black and blue,
> Until his father heard the row
> And shouting 'What's the matter now?'

Caught him a crack across the nut
And chucked him in the water-butt,
Wherein he drowned. And all they said
Was 'Little bastard! Better dead!'

Moral
Carissima Carol! Carol amandus!
Our near relations rarely understand us.

Duff, in return, plied the poet with 'princely gifts' of cases of port and boxes of oysters and kept in touch with him until the end. Although he was a selfish man in many ways, and his selfishness was encouraged by his mother and by Diana, he would always put himself out for friends he was fond of.

He numbered many of the literary elite of London among his acquaintanceship, although one will look in vain for the *avant-garde*. Duff's literary tastes were reflected in his friendships: Arnold Bennett, J. M. Barrie, Maurice Baring, A. E. W. Mason, Somerset Maugham, E. V. Lucas and H. G. Wells all appeared with varying degrees of frequency for dinner at Gower Street.

After the excitement of *The Miracle*, Diana found it difficult to settle down. With Duff busy in Parliament and no children, there was nothing to prevent her indulging her love of travel. She took the opportunity afforded by Sidney Herbert's ill-health to accompany him and Betty Cranborne to Nassau for Christmas 1928.

It was with some concern that she reported back to Duff that she was feeling sick, and it was only after days of worry that the doctors confirmed her suspicion that she was pregnant. For almost a decade she had wanted a child. She had tried everything, including a visit to Lourdes, and had given up hope. They were both delighted when their only child proved to be a son. From the very start John Julius was a great blessing, enriching both their lives and strengthening the emotional bonds which made their marriage so stable. Duff's way with the ailments of childhood was robust: 'Stuff the little bugger full of nourishing vitamins'; and, as the boy grew older, his quick intelligence and charm made Duff wonder what they had done to 'deserve such luck'.

John Julius also provided a much-needed expansion of the Cooper family circle. Duff's sister Steffie had died in 1918 and was followed by Mione in 1923 and Sibbie in 1927. Although their childhood friendship had not lasted, Sibbie had remained devoted to Duff. He had found her increasingly eccentric behaviour tiresome and 'could not pretend to be unhappy' at her death. He was, however, deeply moved by the devotion of her son, Rupert Hart-Davis. Indeed, he was seriously worried that Rupert's great grief would derange him, and did all that he could to help him and his sister Deirdre. Writing almost fifty years later, Sir Rupert Hart-Davis recalled that: 'He was always exceptionally good and generous to me. He gave me innumerable books and made a point of asking me to lunch or dinner at Gower Street when literary men were to be there.'[2]

His mother, Lady Agnes, had died in the South of France in January 1925. Duff, accompanied by Sibbie, reached her hotel only to find that she was already dead. At first Duff thought that he felt little, but when gathering up her things he was overwhelmed by sadness and, for one of the few times in his life, allowed Diana to glimpse his feelings:

> The futility of the possessions of the dead is so terribly pathetic – and Mother's poor little things were all so carefully and neatly arranged – chiefly my letters and things about me. It is terrible too to have it all happen in a hotel.

He took 'this thing far worse than I expected': 'We used to laugh at the "I saw him only last week" exclamation but it is based on a reality which is that the suddenness of death adds to the shock.' He was full of remorse when he remembered how he had left her just after Christmas – 'I might so easily have stayed another week':

> I oughtn't to harrow you my darling with all that is harrowing me and yet I must empty out my heart to you because I cannot bear that anybody else should see a corner of it – and I am even ashamed of my eyes. Only you could console, only you could companion me these days – but even the thought of you and the hope of you makes me happy, even now.

This was one of the few times he allowed the mask to slip. He did not like revealing tender emotions in public, although the theatre, where he was easily moved to tears, was an exception to this. This stoicism, which was part of the complete lack of fear which he had shown at the Front, lent itself to charges that he was a heartless man – particularly where Diana was concerned. As one of his White's club cronies, Raymond de Trafford, put it in 1921:

> Diana I suppose you have left in America to barter her youth and beauty in a vain effort to gather sufficient money to satisfy your tastes in old wine

and books and enable you to cut a fine enough figure to seduce her friends.

It was no doubt the same strand of thought which made at least one reviewer of Duff and Diana's letters doubt the sincerity of his protestations of sadness at their being apart while she was in America. Diana's friend Rudolf Kommer expressed surprise when he discovered that she and Duff wrote to each other every day they were separated. Duff sardonically commented that 'no doubt the lecherous wish was father to the silly thought'. He 'had rather that all my feelings and emotions should not be apparent'; but he knew, and so did Diana, that the most important of his friendships, and by far the deepest, was the one they shared together. That, indeed, was the secret of their long happiness. Diana enjoyed her theatrical career for its own sake, but the fact that it made her beloved Duffy's political career possible enabled her to rejoice in it.

Her love for him was deep and lasting, suffused with a spirit of self-sacrifice and devotion to his interests. Whether this was altogether a good thing for Duff is another question, and one which no outsider can be equipped to answer. Her initial unhappiness at his love affairs faded as she realized that he saw in them merely a means of physical release, and as she gained opportunities to tease him with references to her legions of devoted American admirers. These attempts were not very successful, as Duff was the least jealous of men. However, when one of the stars of *The Miracle*, Werner Krauss, bit her neck, Duff told her:

> Wicked Mr Krauss mustn't bite my baby. Will you tell him so and add that he's a bloody Hun anyway – and that if he doesn't behave himself I'll fill him so full of lead that he'll think he's a pencil.

Duff occasionally wondered 'how much I should mind' if Diana really loved one of her admirers, but decided that he would rather not know if she did – 'I'm with Othello on pioneers and all'.*

The depth of his feeling of loss at their long separation is not open to doubt. He missed her companionship and her inspiration and detested having to entertain company to dinner while she was away, knowing that without her to loosen tongues (not least his own) such gatherings were doomed to failure. After a particularly bad evening

---

* 'I had been happy if the general camp,
Pioneers and all, had tasted her sweet body,
So I had nothing known.' (*Othello*, III, 3.)

at the Café de Paris with Lady Carlisle, he confessed to Diana that:

> As I expected, conversation was a labour. She doesn't try.... There were
> pauses, long ones – during which I thought of you and envied your lovers,
> for I am sure you always help them.... Lady Carlisle is a poor conver-
> sationalist – but so, I begin to be afraid, am I. The difficulty of small talk
> increases with the years.

It was always much less difficult when Diana was there.

For her part, she got what she needed from Duff:

> I was born to be held safely in Duffy's arms, and be soothed and com-
> forted and loved – and then to get up on sunny mornings and take the
> winding road with him and lie sleeping in tall grass under summer trees
> in old countries – with an occasional visit with him to California wilds. I
> was born to see Duffy become great, and to treasure and never lose his
> love.

She never did lose it, and she did see 'Duffy become great'.

9

Battling in Belgravia

Supremely fortunate in his personal life, Duff seemed less so in his public one. The Conservative defeat in 1929 had left many former MPs looking for constituencies, and it was not easy for Duff to find a new seat to contest. An additional problem was that Stanley Baldwin, the leader whom Duff so admired, was coming under increasing pressure to resign. On the very morrow of defeat, Beaverbrook's *Evening Standard* had suggested that the Conservatives should appoint a committee to inquire into deficiencies in party organization, 'with Captain Macmillan and Mr Duff Cooper to represent the rising hopes';[1] it was nice for Duff to be so mentioned, but the implied attack on Baldwin was only the first round in a contest which was to culminate in March 1931.

While Beaverbrook, Rothermere and their 'Empire Free Trade' candidates began to snipe at the electoral foundations of Baldwinism, Duff occupied himself with the search for a constituency. His old boss, Worthington-Evans, suggested in February 1930 that he might try Reigate,[2] but by that time Duff had already fixed himself up at Winchester. Ironically, it was 'Worthy's' death in February 1931 which ensured that Duff would never stand for Winchester.

Worthington-Evans occupied the safest Conservative seat in the country, St George's, Westminster, which covered the Mayfair and Belgravia districts of London. Yet, in spite of the number of former MPs who were looking for a seat, Conservative Central Office found it impossible to find anyone to accept the nomination for the constituency once it was announced that the 'Empire Free Trade' campaign would support an 'independent Conservative' candidate in the form of Sir Ernest Petter.* Beaverbrook and Rothermere wished to commit the Conservative Party to a programme of protectionist tariffs – and

* 1873-1954, engineer and industrialist.

to get rid of Baldwin. That gentleman was already under fire from the right wing of his own party, led by Churchill and Lord Lloyd, for his acquiescence in the Labour Government's declared aim of granting India dominion status, and the 'crusade' of the newspaper tycoons was the final straw for potential MPs for St George's such as Duff's old companion in Oldham, Sir Edward Grigg. It was clear that the by-election would be seen as a test of confidence in Baldwin – and there were few politicians who felt like risking their careers for a leader who seemed to be on the way out.

So serious did he consider the position that Baldwin thought of resigning his own seat and fighting St George's. He did not need to; at the last moment Duff offered to fight the seat. Quite how he came to put himself in this position is unclear. He was well thought of in circles close to Baldwin, and Geoffrey Dawson, the editor of *The Times*, had mentioned his name to the Conservative leader.[3] It seems most likely that Duff was attracted by the gamble, and the principle, involved.

In retrospect his decision to stand for the safest Conservative seat in the country seems hardly to warrant the description of 'gamble', but in the context of the attacks on Baldwin's leadership it was just that. The 'Empire Free Traders' had won a by-election in Fulham the previous year and they enjoyed the support of the Beaverbrook and Rothermere press. Given Baldwin's failure in 1929 and his espousal of 'left-wing' policies towards India, there seemed a fair chance that his candidate would lose the election; in that event, leader and champion would go down together.

Baldwin in a corner was a dangerous opponent. It was too easy for his enemies to underestimate him. Duff was a good, perhaps the ideal, candidate for the constituency. The by-election was bound to take place in the full glare of publicity, and Duff, with the assistance of Diana, was ideally placed to take full advantage of this. He was a first-rate platform speaker and a good electioneer. He would provide the spearhead for a campaign which Baldwin cleverly turned into a moral crusade.

Beaverbrook knew that the contest was crucial. If Petter won then 'Baldwin must go, and Empire Free Trade must become the accepted policy of the Conservative Party';[4] if Petter failed then so did his backers.

To Beaverbrook's bewilderment, Baldwin and Duff shifted the issue of the election away from economic policy, where the press lords might reasonably expect to attract support, to the issue of whether the Conservative Party was to choose its leaders at the behest of the 'gutter press'. The issue, as Baldwin put it, was 'whether press or party is to rule'. By taking his stand on this issue Duff 'cast Beaverbrook and Rothermere in the role of evil and insolent conspirators whose presence on the political stage was a threat to the integrity of public life'.[5] As the campaign was to show, this was an issue on which the barons of the press could do nothing but lose.

One of the things which this issue did was to tap a rich vein of prejudice in the 'Establishment', and elsewhere, against the demeaning activities of the 'yellow press'.

The editor of the *Daily Telegraph*, Fred Lawson, assured Duff in early March that 'You will find all our people, editorial, circulation and everybody doing their damnedest for you, but if there is anything in particular you want, or anything we might do, let me know.' Dawson of *The Times* was equally helpful, telling Duff not to 'fail to let me know if I can do anything – by way of a letter from a correspondent or otherwise – to correct misstatements which the "stunt" newspapers decline to admit'. He had, he wrote, had to read

> the Riot Act about a headline this morning which followed the enemy's lead in concealing your name in a headline as 'Mr Cooper'. It is now laid down that you are never to be described in future without the 'Duff' and the 'DSO'.

Such vigilance was indeed necessary, given the report of one canvasser that the butler in one of the great houses in Mayfair had announced his intention of voting for '*Sir* Ernest' who was 'a gentleman' whilst '*Mr* Cooper' had 'been a clerk, and in a foreign office too'.

St George's was used to quiet election campaigns, but this time the battle raged from the Thames to Rotten Row. It reminded Duff of the famous eighteenth-century election when the beautiful Duchess of Devonshire had traded kisses for votes with the electors; certainly his own campaign team was a glamorous one, led by Diana and her sister-in-law, 'Kakoo', the Duchess of Rutland. It is not recorded whether they traded for votes.

The campaign was a bitter one. Beaverbrook's pet gossip-columnist, Lord Castlerosse, threatened to evict his wife from their Cheyne Row home if she dared to display a 'Duff Cooper' poster in the window; so she retaliated by putting one on their car instead. The *Daily Mail* took to calling Duff 'Mickey Mouse' – which can only have helped his campaign by giving further evidence of the low tone of the 'stunt press'. Empire Free Trade vans, equipped with loudspeakers, toured the streets of Belgravia, calling the butlers and housemaids to vote for *Sir* Ernest. The *Mail* and the *Express* waxed loud in Petter's favour, while the ranks of Duff's opponents were momentarily increased by the addition of Churchill who, on the eve of the poll, spoke in Chelsea against Baldwin and his India policy.

Duff's supporters were equally vociferous. The widow of the former Liberal Prime Minister, Margot Asquith, wrote him long letters full of unhelpful advice and delicious malice, telling him that she had won him 'twenty Liberal votes – half from loathing of the press peers'. She reported that Harold Macmillan 'reproaches himself bitterly upon going on Winston's platform – and other foolish intrigues against Baldwin'. As for Churchill himself, her fury knew no bounds and, despite protestations that she could not trust herself to write about him, she did so at great length, castigating him for his 'fundamental disloyalty and lack of character (another word for lack of judgement). He is the falsest of political gods to worship and has done for himself now.'

Macmillan wrote to Duff on 12 March, offering to deny the 'fantastic and unscrupulous' charges made by the *Mail* that he had been a member of the 'Y.M.C.A.' group of 'semi-socialist' Tories. Rothermere had been making some play out of the 'fact' that Duff was not really a Conservative. These allegations seemed to be based on the fact that he had once lectured to a Labour Party summer school and had 'apologized' for the Empire when giving a talk in Sweden. The lecture had been entitled 'An apologia for the British Empire'; presumably the press lord thought that his readers were too ignorant to be able to distinguish 'apology' from 'apologia'.

The main problem about such lines of attack was that Duff was the official Conservative candidate, and so the charge that he was not a real Tory could only be sustained by alleging that the Conservative Party had been taken over by non-Conservative forces, which, given the activities of the press lords themselves, was rather an unconvincing line of approach.

Baldwin threw the full weight of the party machine behind Duff's campaign. A hundred and thirty-two messages of support from local Conservative and Unionist organizations revealed the hollowness of the claim that Baldwin enjoyed no real backing in the country.

Leading Liberals, including Lords Crewe, Grey and Reading, issued a manifesto declaring, *inter alia*, that:

> At a time when the bulk of our electorate is still in the elementary stages of its political education, the power which the multiple-newspaper gives to irresponsible amateur politicians to mislead their readers by the weapons of distortion and suppression constitutes a menace to our treasured political institutions, the gravity of which it would be impossible to overstate.

The Conservative leader drove this particular shaft home in a famous speech at the Queen's Hall in which he accused the press lords of wanting 'power without responsibility – the prerogative of the harlot throughout the ages'.

Support came for Duff even from quarters that were, by convention, non-political. The Duchess of York took a great interest in the campaign and 'despatched a busload of servants up to London in support of Duff's candidature. This initiative was successful. Longing to vote herself, but barred by custom from so doing, the Duchess gave vent to her feelings by taking her election communication from Petter and placing it in the waste-paper basket.

Fiercely fought though the contest was, it was not wholly without chivalry. At one point Duff cast some aspersion on Petter's war record which, if reported, might have damaged his cause slightly. Diana, already upset by this open breach with Max Beaverbrook, telephoned him, asking him to keep the thing out of the papers. This he did, saying to his editor, 'Do you love your wife? Well, I love Duff Cooper's wife, so lay off him.'

Duff won comfortably, taking 17,242 votes to Petter's 11,532; decency had prevailed and St George had slain his dragon.

The congratulations flooded in, not least from the reprieved Baldwin. Neville Chamberlain, the Party Chairman, wrote to say 'how much I have admired the manner in which you have conducted your campaign' and that although

> you had plenty of capable helpers, in my opinion your own personality was the winning factor. It was a courageous thing to undertake a contest which everyone knew was likely to be a dirty one, but the spirit and ability with which you not only repelled attacks but carried the war into the enemy's country has given you the reward you so richly deserved.

The errant Churchill wrote to Diana in apologetic vein on 20 March: 'On every personal and several public grounds I am very glad indeed that D is safe in Parliament, and with so many feathers in his cap or tail, and such good marks in Mr B's book.'

Duff had indeed done himself a power of good with the leaders of his party – Baldwin himself was one of his sponsors when he took his seat.

Among the hundreds of letters which poured into 90 Gower Street one in particular stood out, not least because it was written in green ink. Dated 29 March from the White Hart Hotel, it was from Ernest Petter. Referring to Baldwin's post-election appeal for party unity and Beaverbrook's announcement that he was going to 'make his peace' with the Conservatives, Petter asked, 'Don't you think I should be included?' He went on to say, rather truculently, that the 'enormous number of letters' which he had received had convinced him that his entry into Parliament 'would be extremely popular'. All this was the prologue to asking if Duff would kindly use his influence to get him the vacant candidature at Winchester. This breath-taking piece of effrontery seems to have gone unanswered.

Behold him then at the age of forty-one: MP for the safest Conservative seat in the country with a guaranteed place in the Commons as long as he cared to hold it; in high good favour with Mr Baldwin and Neville Chamberlain, the two most powerful men in the Conservative Party; his place in a future Baldwin administration seemingly assured. Behold his domestic felicity: happily married to the most celebrated beauty of the day, with a healthy and prepossessing young son; embarked upon his first major book which was nearing completion. He was indeed in favour with fortune and men's eyes.

10

Junior Minister

The election had exhausted Duff: two weeks after polling his health broke down and he needed several months to recover. He and Diana decided to spend the summer on the Continent. Early August found them at Lake Annecy where they met Mr and Mrs Baldwin. During their holiday, rumours of the imminent collapse of sterling and of the Labour Government had grown increasingly strident; Diana saw in their meeting with Baldwin an ideal opportunity to find out what was really happening. Duff, who had been anxious enough at her insistence on wearing red slacks and relieved when she had abandoned them for something more staid, was horrified to hear Diana say: 'Come on now, tell us every word that Ramsay said, for Duff tells me nothing.' Baldwin gave a 'smiling grunt as answer' and Duff's 'face blazed into a sunset of shame and embarrassment', made all the worse by Lucy Baldwin's reply: 'My husband tells me nothing either, but then I would *never* ask him'; he felt that his 'political future was at the bottom of the lake'.[1]

Recalled to London by a telegram from the Speaker of the House, Duff arrived to find the clubs full of gossip about the Coalition Government which was being formed to stave off what seemed an imminent economic collapse. It was to be led by the former Labour leader, Ramsay MacDonald and, as an all-party coalition, there would be fierce competition for ministerial posts.

Duff's mind was naturally on his prospects of office; but, after dinner on the train bound for Calais, his thoughts turned to Diana. It was not often, as she commented in her reply to his letter, that he said 'serious things to me'. But now he did in a 'tender and truly loving fashion' which 'dissolved' her.

I was never so miserable at leaving you tonight – not even that first time when I left you in New York. I had again that horrible home-sick, hope-

68

less feeling which makes everything seem vanity and vexation. I haven't had it for such a long time – not because I have ever ceased to love you as much but because we never had such an unexpected, perhaps unnecessary and anyhow beastly parting.

It was, therefore, with some asperity that he greeted rumours that he was not to be included in the Government. But, even as he packed for the return journey to Venice, Baldwin's secretary rang up to ask for his address. Duff said that he should send Baldwin's letter round at once. When it arrived it contained the news that 'your holiday is going west too'; he was to be Financial Secretary at the War Office under Lord Crewe. As he confessed to Diana, 'I received it with feelings as mixed as it is possible for feelings to be.' Crewe was an ageing Liberal peer whose appointment lost Brendan Bracken his bet that 'Crewe was dead'; however, he refused to pay up, 'saying it hasn't been proved'. So there would be scope for greater initiative for Duff; and, as Crewe was a peer, he would be the sole spokesman for the War Office in the Commons. But it was disappointing to be no further on than he had been in 1929. He cheered up slightly when Baldwin told him on 30 August that he was to have the better post of Under-Secretary at the War Office.

From Duff's point of view the National Government was a mixed blessing. The massive support for it meant that he did not even have to fight a contest in the election in October and this augured well for the future. But there was a price to be paid. Duff had reasonable hopes of junior ministerial office in a purely Conservative administration; in a coalition these hopes had to be deferred.

Neither Crewe, nor his successor, Lord Hailsham, proved a demanding master, and with the Government secure behind a huge majority in the Commons, there was enough leisure at the disposal of the Under-Secretary of State at the War Office to allow the completion of *Talleyrand*.

Much of the book was written at West House, Aldwick, a mile or two west of Bognor; this was Duff's 'terrestrial paradise'[2] – an eighteenth-century farmhouse which the Duke of Portland had given to Diana's mother who, in turn, had given it to Duff and Diana. It was a place for picnics on the Downs and sea-bathing; for Sunday luncheons with friends which lasted all afternoon; for fun and relaxation; and for literary inspiration.

Duff wrote in longhand, very slowly and carefully, with scarcely a correction. Diana imagined that he composed effortlessly, but it was quite otherwise. He would read, take notes, and then think for hours before putting pen to paper, forming the sentences in his mind, turning them over, and finally writing. His elegant, right-sloping script was as clear and beautiful as his prose; his manuscript, almost unblemished, free of any signs of hesitation, is enough to make those less fluent despair.

Talleyrand was finished early in 1932 and published by Jonathan Cape in October. Rupert Hart-Davis, Duff's nephew, was a director and had suggested that his firm should take the book. Its subsequent success was one of the earliest signs of his eye for quality.

It is an elegant book, wearing much learning lightly and striking a middle course between the moralizing of previous biographers and the slick, undergraduate cruelty of Lytton Strachey and his imitators. Some indication of its style can be gleaned from the deathbed scene:

> The old diplomatist had set forth upon his last mission. Some doubts he may have felt as to the country whither he was travelling, some uncertainty as to the form of government that there prevailed; but he had made enquiries of those best qualified to advise him; he had obtained the most reliable information available; he had taken, not a moment too soon, all possible precautions and he departed in order, his passport signed.

Contemporary reviewers were favourably impressed. That greatest of modern historians, Lewis Namier, writing in the *Manchester Guardian*, described it most accurately as

> what a book on Talleyrand should be – it is charming, leisurely in appearance, has a glittering surface, on which the glitter is so cleverly distributed as to be unobtrusive and seems almost natural; it is full of elaborate cleverness and upholstery, mental and stylistical, and is written with an easy humour such as comes to writers who themselves are genuinely amused.

Harold Nicolson, in the *New Statesman*, drew attention to the way in which Duff's own political career had enriched his writing, and called the book 'a deliberate work of art'. *Talleyrand* received over a hundred notices – and not one of them was bad.

Diana, who had not even dared to read the manuscript, so great was her dread of his failing, telegraphed to Duff with delight from Manchester, where she was playing in *The Miracle*'s British tour.

He was in Scotland, enjoying the tail-end of the parliamentary recess with his fellow MP, Captain Euan Wallace, on a shooting-trip at Innerleithen. Late on the evening of 9 October he penned a sleepy reply to Diana's felicitations:

> We had a long day's shooting in heavy rain. The sport was good and there was a pony to ride which I rode most of the day. Otherwise I don't believe I could have walked it. How the others managed was a marvel to me.

Much as he loved shooting, he liked it even better when it was not accompanied by too strenuous exercise. He told her that 'Euan's loader asked whether I was "*the* Mr Duff Cooper" which, coupled with your telegram, might have sent me to bed with a swelled head had it not been too tired and too muzzy with good wine'.

Duff travelled down to join Diana before Parliament reassembled. They spent three days together before he had to leave for London. From the Commons on 7 November he wrote longingly to her:

> I don't think I have ever minded leaving you so much.... I couldn't bear to think of that poor little creature going up alone to those big empty rooms where we had been so happy for three days. My only consolation was the thought that our unhappiness itself was such a tribute to our happiness and love and how much sadder it would have been had we parted with a sigh. I don't think I ever loved you more than those three days.

He had, he confessed, wondered whether it was really necessary for him to leave for London: 'On that score my mind was set at rest by having the busiest morning in the War Office that I have had for a long time.' Another thing had also been settled, he told her, by his early arrival in London; they would not be inviting Ramsay Mac-Donald to the party which they were planning for the following week. He had 'just made the worst speech that I should think any Prime Minister has ever made in the House of Commons. Everybody is saying "It can't go on".'

Whatever troubles poor MacDonald was having, Duff was still in fine good humour, not least because Baldwin had just told him that: 'My Missus is crazy about your book. She can talk of nothing else.'

But it was not all sweetness and light for a junior minister. Even as his leader's praises were ringing in his ears, Duff was setting off for Coventry to speak at a Conservative meeting, where he found himself sitting next to the local MP who could have bored for Britain at international level. He had, he wrote to Diana, 'a dull time': 'A good meeting but a bad hotel – the King's Head. If I had to run a hotel

71

in Coventry I'd call it something more traditional – Lady Godiva's bottom for instance.'

The success of *Talleyrand* apart, 1932 had been, Duff reflected at the year's turning, 'uneventful', at least in comparison with the heroics of 1931. Saluted on his birthday by Diana's friend Rudolf Kommer ('Kaetchen' was the 'only person' who ever remembered Duff's birthday) as the 'star of three stars: one wife, one son, one book', Duff mused that 'At forty-three Napoleon was starting the campaign to Moscow – more behind him than I have – but very little in front.' He was, however, in better condition than Talleyrand, who at forty-three had been a 'discredited and penniless exile'. He was, he told Diana, unable to give her any more famous 'forty-threes' as 'the Westminster Housing Association are waiting for an interview'.

The success of *Talleyrand* brought more than money and fame. In March he was asked by the executors of Lord Haig's estate to write the official biography of the Field Marshal. It was, perhaps, rather ominous that difficulties with Lady Haig had already caused John Buchan and G.M. Trevelyan to decline the honour; then there was the fact that Duff had never known Haig and 'was not interested really in military matters'. On the other hand, 'It is a great opportunity. The material is wonderful – many volumes of Haig's diary, most carefully kept, which have never seen the light. The book, whoever wrote it, would be of the greatest importance.' It was not, he concluded, a chance he should let pass. His main fear once he had accepted the commission was that he 'should probably be criticized for undertaking such heavy work while a Minister' – and that if he was promoted to the Cabinet, he might not be able to finish the book. Despite such misgivings he settled down to work, mainly at weekends and during parliamentary recesses.

The task turned out to be far more difficult than he had imagined. *Talleyrand* had been a labour of love, and one compiled mainly from secondary sources; it had been a biography of a man with whom he had felt a great empathy. Duff had no such feeling about Haig and faced novel difficulties in dealing with the great mass of primary material. Haig's diaries occupied forty stout volumes and were guarded by his widow.

Most biographers find widows tiresome, and Duff would have envied the co-operation and kindness which his own biographer has received; he certainly enjoyed no such favour from Lady Haig. When he took on the task he stipulated that he should have access to all available materials and the right to publish what he wanted. Haig had left a copy of his diary with General Edmonds, the director of the historical section of the Committee of Imperial Defence; given his official position, Duff was able to borrow these copies – which greatly speeded up the process of composition. However, in October 1934 Edmonds wrote to him to say that Lady Haig had told him that she would be 'forced to legally arrange for these diaries to be reclaimed' unless he returned them forthwith. This placed the whole project in peril.

Duff was fortunate in being at the War Office. The Permanent Under-Secretary, Sir Herbert Creedy, who admired Duff's work, was one of Haig's trustees and instructed Edmonds to allow Duff access to the diaries. When Edmonds replied that he would do so only if Duff would read them in his rooms at the Committee of Imperial Defence, Duff told Creedy that he was prepared to resign his task. Only after a prolonged exchange of lawyers' letters was Duff allowed to get on with his writing.

Haig did not go to Cape's. Somewhat to Rupert Hart-Davis's disapproval, his uncle utilized the services of a literary agent who sold the book to Faber's for a large advance. Faber's subsequently took fright and decided to bring the book out in two volumes in an attempt to recoup their money; this did not succeed.[3]

Despite the pressure of work, Duff managed to get the first volume out in 1935 and its successor in the following year. Where *Talleyrand* had been handed over to the literary editors and had received bouquets of praise, *Haig* was given to the military correspondents, who greeted it with a sustained barrage of criticism; such, at least, was Duff's explanation for the bad reviews which he received. In fact, his severest critic, Basil Liddell Hart of *The Times*, actually toned down his criticisms for publication. In public he concentrated on demonstrating that Duff's reading had been insufficiently thorough and that he had been too kind by half to an obtuse old fool of a general whose stubborn stupidity had wasted thousands of young lives. In private he thought that Duff had skimped the job disgracefully, serving neither his employers nor his subject particularly well.[4] No doubt Duff had worked quickly, but there was one fact of which Liddell Hart was not aware.

Duff had faced a difficult problem when coming to write *Haig*. It became clear from his diaries that the Field Marshal had disliked and mistrusted the French. Duff feared that the revelation of such feelings at such a time, and from the pen of one who was in the Government, would damage Anglo–French relations; so, as he told Robert Blake, who edited Haig's diaries almost twenty years later, he decided to omit these references.[5] Naturally this made some of Haig's actions a little difficult to explain.

Not everyone shared Liddell Hart's feelings. Buchan, Baldwin, Rupert Hart-Davis and the Duchess of York were among those who wrote admiringly. But the barbs of the reviewers stung. There was one consolation: with the publication of the second volume of *Haig* in 1936, Duff could feel free of money troubles for the first time in his adult life.

The reason for his caution in publishing Haig's views of the French stemmed not merely from Francophilia, but from a feeling that Anglo–French solidarity would soon be necessary again.

Duff and Diana decided to spend part of the summer recess on a motoring tour through Germany on their way to stay at Chips Channon's Schloss in Austria. They spent the first night on German soil in a small village called Montjoie. It seemed an ideal spot, rural and unspoilt, but during the course of the night they were woken 'by the sound of men marching and words of command given in a raucous voice. It was my first contact with the Nazis.' Subsequent contacts proved equally unpleasant.

Finding Bayreuth unbearable because of the presence of large numbers of uniformed men and no festival, they made their way to a small hotel at Berneck. There, to their surprise, they found that Hitler was in residence, preparing a speech for a rally at Nuremberg. One of his myrmidons, Alfred Rosenberg, knowing that Duff was an MP, asked him if he would like to meet the great man. They went upstairs, leaving Diana behind 'picturing Duff reforming anti-Christ'.[6] But he never did meet the man who was to have such an effect on his future career; the Führer was too tired, and Duff returned to Diana bearing tickets for the Nuremberg rally.

Diana, who liked to see her celebrities the hard way, rose early the following morning and, clad in dressing-gown and curlers, hid behind a curtain in the lounge in the hope of glimpsing the departing dictator. Unfortunately the lounge soon filled up with other people on the same mission and, to get to the window, Diana had to 'run the gauntlet of surprised pilgrims', which she did 'with my eyes closed like an ostrich's'. A helpful Nazi told her that Hitler was leaving the back way, but by the time she got there all there was to see was a cloud of dust – and 'the horrified gaze of an old Hun in bed' – for she had stumbled into someone's bedroom.

She finally got to see him at Nuremberg and was disappointed to see how common he looked. Duff managed to put up with part of the Führer's diatribe before scandalizing the audience by leaving before the end.

From the safety of Channon's Austrian residence, Duff gave his sister-in-law, 'Kakoo' Rutland, his reflections on Nazi Germany. He was in no doubt about the implications of what he had seen:

> The whole of that country is preparing for war on a scale and with an enthusiasm that are astounding and terrible. We heard Hitler speak at Nuremberg and were very disappointed. He read his speech, which he doesn't normally do and it aroused no enthusiasm.[7]

He preached the same message to Churchill, telling him that the Germans were 'preparing for war with more general enthusiasm than a whole Nation has ever before put into such preparation'.[8]

Not only did Duff enjoy the distinction of being one of the first (if not the first) to alert Churchill to the dangers of Nazi Germany, he was the first British politician to speak publicly of those dangers. On his return to England he gave a speech on the perils of Nazism to the St George's Junior Imperial League. For his pains he was denounced by the Beaverbrook and Rothermere press as a 'warmonger'. Writing to Kaetchen Kommer on 18 October Duff commented that 'Great events seem to be taking place. Max has been attacking me violently in the *Express* for having said that we should observe the Treaty of Locarno and that Germany is preparing for war.' Despite this storm, he and Diana had dined that day at the German Embassy, where the Ambassador, Hoesch, had tried, without success, to convince Duff that Hitler was 'a great man'.

This was the first of many occasions on which Duff was to sound the warning tocsin about the dangers of Nazism; for his efforts he was attacked in the press and from the pulpit. Nor was it much consolation to such a hard-headed realist to reflect that Cassandra had ended her days as a slave in the house of her enemies.

Beaverbrook hastened to assure Duff that there had been nothing 'personal' in the attacks made by the *Express*. Duff replied on 31 October, saying that he was glad to hear it: 'I like plain speaking and hard knocks both in political and private controversy and I know that you rejoice as much as I do in the exchange of blows. We hate the

mealy-mouthed and the thin-skinned.' He concluded with a revealing
Freudian slip: 'Although I fear we shall seldom agree, I hope that we
shall continue to slosh one another in public and like one another in
public as much as we do today. Yours ever, M. Mouse, Duff.'⁹ For
Diana's sake he was willing to put up with 'Max' in public, but there
was no love lost between the two men and, as Duff was to discover in
1940, Beaverbrook had a long memory where grudges were concerned.

Henceforth the 'shadow of the swastika' (as Duff called it in a letter
to Kommer in 1934) hung over his political career. In 1933 it was no
bigger than a man's hand, but it was to grow until it engulfed Duff
and the rest of the world. To Duff belongs the honour of having been
one of the first to point out the menace of Hitler; it was not his fault
if others refused to listen.

Duff had no particular ideological objection to dictators; what he
found repulsive and dangerous about the Hitler regime was the obvious fact that it was preparing for war. Mussolini, whom he met
during the Easter recess in 1934, he found a quite different proposi-
tion: 'He was nicer than I expected – simpler, more humorous and
completely lacking in pose. We talked chiefly about disarmament and
were quite in agreement.'¹⁰ Mussolini laughed when Duff said that
the idea that armaments produced wars was as ridiculous as saying
that umbrellas produced rain. He foresaw, at this point, no danger
from Italy; indeed he shared the view of many other British politicians
and diplomats that the Italians might be useful allies against Hitler,
particularly in defending Austria. He saw no reason to alter his view
until the spring of 1939.

A gulf was opening between Duff and his former supporters in the
League of Nations Union. They continued to believe that wars could
be averted by the League; Duff saw that Hitler could only be stopped
by the threat of force. He was moving away from the idealism of the
1920s towards a *realpolitik* that was appropriate for the 1930s.

Despite predictions from the *Express* that Duff Cooper would be
dropped from the Government, he received promotion in June 1934
when he went to the Treasury as Financial Secretary – a post usually
regarded as the antechamber to the Cabinet. Duff was delighted, but
feared that his mathematics might not be up to the job; but he found
Lord Derby's words to Disraeli apposite: 'You know as much about
finance as Mr Canning did – and anyway, they give you the figures.'

His new chief was the most powerful and dynamic man in the

Cabinet, Neville Chamberlain. Their previous relations had been confined to Chamberlain's kind letters in 1929 and 1931. The Chancellor was not a great one for frequenting the smoking-room of the Commons, and preferred bird-watching and life at home to the social round in which Duff was so conspicuous a figure. Duff did not find the first interview with his boss an auspicious occasion. Chamberlain referred to Duff's speech about Germany, commenting that he had gained thereby a 'reputation for indiscretion'. He 'warned me that while the unguarded words of most Junior Ministers mattered little, an indiscretion by the Financial Secretary to the Treasury might bring down the Government'.

Despite this start the two men worked well together, and Duff was pleased and relieved when Sidney Herbert reported in December that Chamberlain had spoken

> in glowing terms of your work as Financial Secretary. After paying a tribute to your answers to questions and speeches, he praised also your judgement and wise reticence. He added that he was very pleased at the assiduity you showed in your own work as Financial Secretary and at the fact that you were not continually asking to see the Chancellor or do his work for him instead of your own (a habit, apparently, of his former Financial Secretaries). He was full of optimism about your future.

He would hardly have spoken in such a way to one of Duff's closest friends unless he had wished to encourage him.

Ironically, in the light of future events, at this time when Duff's relations with Chamberlain were so good, those with Churchill were rather poor.

Churchill had been Duff's earliest political friend and their common interest in history provided an enduring bond between them; but the nature of their relations was now very different from what it had been a decade earlier. Then Duff had been a young MP seeking help from the Chancellor of the Exchequer; now Churchill was in a self-imposed political exile and Duff was a rising star in the political firmament. Duff commented at length on the draft of Churchill's first volume of *Marlborough* and, on a purely personal level, their relations had continued to be good. Diana recorded a pleasant visit to Chartwell in September 1934 when, despite the coldness of the afternoon, they all went swimming in Churchill's heated pool. He called for his servants to put more coal on the furnace and, learning that it was their afternoon off, 'The darling old schoolboy went surreptitiously and stoked it himself for half an hour, coming in on the verge of apoplexy.'[11]

Things were rather different in the political world. Churchill was one of the fiercest critics of the Government of which Duff hoped to become an ornament. The 'Other Club', the dining club formed by Churchill and F. E. Smith in 1911 to which Duff belonged, had as one of its rules that 'nothing in the rules or intercourse of the Club shall interfere with the rancour or asperity of party politics'; but the virulence of Churchill's attacks on the National Government seemed to go beyond the bounds of reasonableness – especially when he was still a Conservative MP. Duff wrote to Kommer in March 1934 that

> Winston grows more foolish and factious. Odd that he should not realize that the game is up. I suppose that he goes on intriguing and making speeches in the same spirit that my mother-in-law goes on painting her face and wearing a wig.

He clashed publicly with Winston over the intervention of the latter's son, Randolph, as an 'independent Conservative' in the Wavertree by-election in February 1935; and he won £5 from Winston and £5 from Randolph when the Labour candidate was elected.

Duff was quietly satisfied with life in early 1935; *Haig* was progressing well and he was being tipped for promotion in the event of a ministerial reshuffle. The only disappointment was that Diana was not there to enliven the 'pretty dull' round of dinner-parties and politics. He wrote to her in May, longing 'to hear some news of you': 'Wednesday is the ball at Guildhall, but I shan't go as you aren't here. One couldn't go alone. It might have amused us together.' He was particularly nervous at this time. He was sure that his successful speech on the Army Estimates in March 1933 had helped to win him promotion; delivered without notes, his recapitulation of a mass of facts and figures had been much admired. He hoped to repeat the trick on the second reading of the Finance Bill in late May, which might be the last chance to show his mettle before the General Election. Writing to Diana on the evening of 22 May he described what had happened:

> I sat on the bench from 3 till 11, speaking at 10.15. I did very well. Neville was delighted with me. I received many congratulations.... I think now that there is going to be some shuffling at Whitsun.

There had been one tantalizing moment when Baldwin

> asked me to join him at dinner in the House. He was just, I thought, going to tell me something when a third party sat down beside him which

reduced him to a toad-like silence. He is extremely affable to me these days. But is that a very good sign? And again Neville is so pleased that he might wish to keep me. However, in any case, I am quite happy and in no hurry for a change.

Parliament, clubland and the country houses of the political world hummed with gossip and rumour: who was going to be out? who was in?

A wet weekend in Norfolk, at Venetia Montagu's house in Breccles, was something of a break from such preoccupations. A non-political house party allowed Duff to occupy himself with 'bridge and backgammon, delicious food and drink' – and with gossip that was only tangentially political. 'We had', he told Diana, 'a great discussion on toadies.' It was generally agreed that Diana 'had the most', but that she 'waited until a toady had been properly trained by someone else' – the MP for Southend, 'Chips' Channon, being a recent example. But she was not the only one with 'toadies'.

Political preoccupations pressed hard. A week later, at the end of May, Channon dined with Duff, Diana and Baldwin at the Commons; he noted that 'Dormouse' Baldwin was 'the centre of all eyes since he must reconstruct the Cabinet next week. Duff hopes for preferment and all the young men were sucking up to him.'[12] Considering the part which Duff had played in saving the 'Dormouse's' career in 1931, promotion to Cabinet office was slow. Nor was this entirely due to the number of claimants for office in a coalition Government.

Baldwin's doubts about Duff manifested themselves in delay. There was no Whitsun promotion. The election came in November, when Duff held St George's with a massive majority over his Labour opponent, Mrs Fremantle. A week after the results were announced Duff was invited to join the Cabinet as Secretary of State for War. The sense of achievement might have been tempered had he heard Baldwin tell his friend, Tom Jones, 'I'm doubtful about Duff Cooper. Must try him out for a year, and Neville can decide whether to carry him on.'[13]

~~~ 11 ~~~

Politics and Pleasures

All politicians present to the public a face which is more or less different from their private one. In this there is an element, greater or lesser according to the example chosen, of hypocrisy. Baldwin was far from being the simple English countryman he liked to be portrayed as, but it was his public *persona* which created the characteristic political tone of the age: decency, sobriety and respectability. The Lloyd George coalition cast a long shadow; glittering brilliance was equated with untrustworthiness.

Not even the Conservative Party could get by without an admixture of brilliance, and both Lord Birkenhead and Winston Churchill were taken into Baldwin's Cabinet; but they were not trusted. 'Our two *banditti*', as Neville Chamberlain once called them, were never at home in the Baldwinian ethos. The Prime Minister, when refusing to take Birkenhead into the Shadow Cabinet, had said: 'We are a Cabinet of faithful husbands, and think we will remain so.'[1] 'F.E.' offended against the chief virtues of the political tone established by Baldwin. Churchill was also seen to lack balance, temperance and restraint. As Lord Robert Cecil once commented of him:

> I don't believe Winston takes any interest in public affairs unless they involve the possibility of bloodshed. Preferably he likes to kill foreigners, but if that cannot be done I believe he would be satisfied with a few native Communists.[2]

Baldwin's Governments rested, as Neville Chamberlain observed, 'largely on public confidence in our character'.[3] In this respect what is striking is not that Baldwin should have had doubts about Duff, but that he should have fostered his political career at all. His style of living, his well-known tastes for wine and other men's wives, all served to distance him from the provincial respectability personified by Baldwin and Chamberlain. In a political climate where private virtue was so clearly linked to public effectiveness, it was but a short step from condemning Duff's morals to writing him off as a political dilettante.

When he had first received office in 1928, Betty Cranborne had written: 'I suppose you will be known as "the Little Minister". It is the first sensible thing Baldwin has done. I am so glad. I suppose he felt a need of the Boy Orator.' He had, and continued to do so. The back-benches were not so thronged with Conservative talent that Duff's claims to Cabinet office could be ignored indefinitely; so to the War Office he went. It would be up to Chamberlain to judge if his public qualities outweighed any defects of character.

At the time, Neville Chamberlain welcomed the promotion. He wrote a letter of congratulation on 21 November which reveals so much about his conception of politics that it must detain us a while. He was, he said, 'very sorry to lose you at the Treasury, but I rejoice in the opportunity that has come to you now to show your quality as the head of a Department'. He proffered the advice that 'many people take a little time to find their feet in the Cabinet, I don't know that they lose much thereby', and hoped Duff would not 'feel obliged to express your opinions before you want to'. 'It is', he went on, 'by what a man is in Cabinet, rather than what he is as a departmental chief that ministers are ultimately weighed and assessed.' It was nice to be told, by the man who would be doing the assessing, that 'I have formed the opinion that you have the right qualities of mind to make a good Cabinet Minister and I am confidently looking forward to seeing that opinion confirmed.'

Chamberlain was to be disappointed. In private and in public, Duff did not live up to the image of the Baldwinian minister. Betty Cranborne's comment proved nearer the mark: 'I can't see you settling down as a sedate little Minister – you are always the centre of gaiety and amusement and there is always fun and enjoyment wherever you are.'

Even as a junior minister he had failed to fit the required mould. Off on a jaunt to the Riviera with Sidney and Michael Herbert in early 1932, Duff had written to Diana that 'I shall be back in a jiffy – and you will like me all the better – like one of those angel faces which you have loved long since and lost a while.' He said he would 'be good' and promised not to fall:

1) Out of the puffer
2) into bad habits

81

3) for the girls
4) by the way
5) at the tables
6) off the boat
7) from grace.

He was quite successful with numbers one and six.

There were two things wrong with the Herbert villa at Cap d'Ail: it was uncomfortable and it was too near to Max Beaverbrook. Still, by dint of spending a lot of time in the Casino or on the beach, Duff could mitigate both circumstances. He reported back with delight that in his first evening at the tables he had won £60, lamenting only that it had not been on his last night, when he might have kept some of it. Betty Cranborne was not amused; she thought 'it wicked to gamble in France in view of the state of the national finances' – this was not an opinion which recommended itself to Duff or the Herberts. Arriving home at 1.30 a.m. and bundling his towel under the bolster to get a comfortable pillow, he could feel some smugness when Michael Herbert arrived back four hours later and was then 'astonished to feel ill the next day'.

The Riviera, like his other favourite haunt, Venice, offered 'many women only too anxious to be made love to'. For Duff, making love was as essential a part of enjoying himself as wine and the gaming-tables; he was an unashamed sensualist and delighted in his own prowess. Cap d'Ail may have harboured Beaverbrook, but nearby at Cap Martin was the more welcome figure of an old flame, 'Daisy "Wanton" Fellowes'.

An heiress to the Singer sewing machine fortune, Mrs Reginald Fellowes was reputed to be one of the best-dressed women in the world; she was also a lady after Duff's own heart. Playing 'the copulation game' in 1926, he had placed her fourth on his own list of the women he would most like to sleep with, and she provided a long-standing diversion. Her forthright attitude mirrored his own: 'Duff, my darling, love me. I do adore being loved and cannot think of a safer sedentary occupation for anyone between the ages of 30 and 60.' Quite so, he thought. She could, however, be too much even for him, and he confessed to being 'shocked' by the revelation that she and a friend had followed her husband to a brothel and, with the aid of a two-way mirror, 'watched him performing with a poll'.

Her unconcealed delight in love-making, her enjoyment of the little deceits which add a *frisson* to illicit passion – secret letters in lovers' code and late-night assignations – all made her a most congenial companion. He liked the fact that she 'loved' his letters, but shared her view that 'when all is said and done I prefer the flesh to the spirit'. She appealed to the worldling in him; and there was certainly a good deal of that.

She also helped make political visits to Paris more interesting. When Duff went there in early 1935 she suggested they should meet and asked what he wanted her to arrange – perhaps 'a nice room with a sitting room in a quiet hotel?', followed by dinner *à deux* and 'a play or music-hall'. She told him that she felt 'like being very 1900. A veil, garters, a gift in morocco case tucked inside a napkin, caviar, violets and champagne. What say you?' She had little need to ask. When he went to the Admiralty in 1937 she lamented that as he 'became grander and grander' he would

> miss all the nice, pleasant gardens of Eden and warm sunshine and the scent of tuberoses in the evenings, and your eyes will become ringed not with the purple shadows of passion well-spent, but through the burning of midnight oil in palaces of state.

This sad state of affairs never quite came to pass.

Associations like that with Daisy Fellowes can only have confirmed the view that Duff was a lecherous drunkard which was held in some quarters. Yet this was wide of the mark. Had he been nothing more than a 'pouncer' (and he was certainly that), his former mistresses would hardly have remained in correspondence with him or have sought his help in their own matrimonial problems. The number of letters from female friends, lovers and otherwise, in his papers, bears witness to his role as (to use the words of a Scottish peeress) 'my good archiepiscopal adviser and comforter'.

His sympathetic ear, his ease in female company, his wit and his beautifully turned sonnets, all made his an obvious shoulder to cry on when the going got rough. But, as many of those who sought him in this capacity found out, what started as a friendly pat on the knee often ended in bed. Indeed, the peeress who coined the phrase quoted above, soon found herself falling for his charms and, feeling 'thoroughly unsettled', wrote somewhat crossly:

> Why the Hell can't you leave ruts alone, they're so easy. You had the satisfaction of sending me out of mine so high that the rut became a yawning and *magnetic* chasm – you're really responsible for both processes.

She wondered: 'Is that your fun – to place little dynamite fuses under dull people?' Suggesting that they might lunch together, she later regretted 'letting myself be bullied by you': 'Why I liked you before was 'cos you were softened enough to be sympathetic and understanding – now you have ceased to be softened and your cruel nature comes out.' It could not have been that 'cruel', for she was soon inviting him to supper at her London home, telling him that her husband would be out on business.

It was Duff's openness which irritated some people – the man did not even pretend (as others did) that he was a faithful husband. There were occasions when this had its disadvantages. One evening when he did want merely to dine with a pretty young lady he felt obliged to add a postscript to his invitation – 'no rape'.

It was clearly too much for some men to bear: not only was Duff married to the most beautiful woman of her generation, whose earnings had financed his political career, he was also free to love elsewhere. But outsiders were apt to confuse lust with love.

Throughout the 1920s, thanks to *The Miracle* and politics, Duff and Diana were often apart. This state of affairs led many to prophesy imminent divorce, and the list of co-respondents whom Diana could cite were legion. But this was to judge an unusual marriage by the standards applicable to 'normal' marriages. Few of the latter could have survived Duff's constant infidelities or Diana's need for constant reassurance; but then Duff and Diana were most uncommon people. The only opinions worth listening to as to the success or otherwise of a marriage are those of the participants. Judged by this standard it was enormously successful, bringing both partners much happiness; not once was the question of divorce or separation even raised.

That Diana was free from jealousy is not, as we have seen, altogether true. In the early years of their marriage she was anxious when friends reported Duff's infidelities. But, as she came to recognize that these really were 'only of the flesh' and not the spirit, so too did she come to accept them. She adored him:

My darling Duffy,
   I am missing you. I cannot tell you how much. It will get better. I have a lump in the throat. It is more than a year that I have been away for more than two days from you – and yet I used to go for six months and bear it alright. I have been a mess and a weight for six weeks – no-one

can continue to love nurotics [*sic*].... My darling love – I weary you with my love.

D.

Thus Diana wrote in June 1934. Where others saw the beauty and the vivacity, Diana saw only her own shortcomings and neuroses. She never truly believed in her beauty, or, rather, she never saw that any merit attached to her for something which she had been blessed with. She needed a protecting father-figure; this Duff gave her.

When they were apart she worried constantly, not about his infidelity but about his health and safety. When he went to Paris in the Easter of 1932, she wrote anxiously:

> Oh Mr Baby be carefull [*sic*]. I do love you so and I am in more distress than ever I can tell you – I am bound to be when you are out for a good time. I pray you'll have one and justify my desolation and fears.... I want you back Duffy, don't tarry too long. I love you better than all the world beside. You know it. I know that freedom is enviously binding in our case. I know that I am as glad to see you and hear that front door bang by your hand ... as it is possible to be ... every day you are away holds an unchanging degree of pain. Remember me my darling and come back soon.

B.

Little John Julius's assurances that ' "Papa *will* come back. I *know* he will, in a few days" ', made 'my blood run cold', and she was 'so frightened that some harm may befall you'. But such was her love that she could write, a few days later, 'you must not feel bound, if you want to have a few more days in the south'. Like Sibbie and Lady Agnes, Diana was prepared to make sacrifices so that Duffy could have a good time.

But what of his feelings for her? How did he react to the weight of this adoration and depth of love? The *persona* of the eighteenth-century man of the world was so firmly established that many came to accept it as the real face of the man, and not a mask. But behind it lay the reality of a deep love for Diana. He missed her when she was away. Such occasions had only one advantage: they gave him time to be with the growing John Julius, whose presence he came increasingly to appreciate, and who provided a new bond between himself and Diana. Whatever outsiders might think, the marriage worked, and it worked well.

Duff's all too evident pursuit of pleasure soon gave rise to other rumours. If private morality was thought to have some connection

85

with the public effectiveness of a politician then it was natural that
the belief should have spread that Duff was a lazy minister, too busy
with other things to attend to his work. His sister-in-law, 'Kakoo'
Rutland, passed on such gossip to him in July 1936. He replied that
it 'contained that germ of truth' without which no rumour could
spread, but went on to say that 'I know I am not lazy, but I may
devote too much energy to the kind of work that is congenial and
neglect unduly what I find dull. I shall try, and am trying now, to
correct this failing.'[4] There is no necessary connection between private
morality and public performance: a 'good' man may be a bad minister
and *vice versa*. If Duff got across Neville Chamberlain he did so for
quite different reasons than might be supposed; although differences
of temperament no doubt contributed to the process.

He made himself unpopular with Chamberlain in two ways: by his
fierce opposition to the Chancellor's own plans for the army; and by
his 'blazing indiscretions' on the subject of foreign policy.

Duff went to the War Office in the middle of a dispute with the
Treasury over the size of the Army Estimates; a dispute which scarcely
concealed two opposing views of what the army was for. The Defence
Requirements Committee (DRC) of the Cabinet had reported in 1934
that the army should be of a size, and sufficiently equipped, to participate in a Continental war; to defend the Low Countries in co-
operation with the French against a German attack. This was the
thinking of the Army Council and the official view of the Chiefs of
Staff; it was a view which Duff, as Haig's biographer, as a Francophile
and as a student of foreign policy, came to share. Unfortunately for
him it was not one which Chamberlain favoured.[5]

The Chancellor disliked the idea of spending £40 million on the
army and wanted the figure reduced to £19 million. He may well
have hoped that his former assistant at the Treasury would help in
this endeavour; the fact that Duff so swiftly took the War Office's
view – and then argued it persistently in the Cabinet – did nothing
to help his relationship with Chamberlain, or his political career.

The problem was not that there was any flaw in Duff's argument,
it was that Chamberlain fundamentally disagreed with it. His reasons
were not wholly, or even mainly, financial; he saw no need for a large
army. From one of his fishing companions, the GOC Southern Command, Sir John Burnett-Stuart, he had imbibed some of the ideas
associated with that *enfant terrible* of the military world, Basil Liddell
Hart; what Duff called 'the pernicious doctrine that if we contributed

Above left: Father and son:
Sir Alfred and Duff, *c.* 1893
Above right: Lady Agnes Cooper
Right: Young page-boy: Duff, *c.* 1895

Left: Regency Buck: Duff and Clare
Tennant, 1914
Below left: Young Diplomat, 1913
Below right: Second-Lieutenant Cooper,
1917

'Bliss-fully, incredibly happy' – leaving
the church with Diana, June 1919

In sombre vein: portrait of Duff
by Lavery

The young couple on holiday with Raimund von Hofmannsthal (centre)

‘MP in dreamland’, 1925

Mother and son: Diana and John
Julius, 1929

Battling in Belgravia: Diana and Duff, March 1931

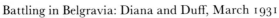

The Secretary of State for War leaving Gower Street, 1935

Post-prandial mood at Bognor, mid-1930s

The Czech crisis: arriving at 10 Downing Street to hear Chamberlain's report on his meeting with Hitler

Duff and a lady-friend at Randolph Churchill's wedding, 1939

Above and right: 'Perfect partners':
Duff and Diana in the late 1930s

At the Ministry of Information with
Lord Hood, 1940

Pensive, after-lunch mood at Bognor, early 1940s

to the cause the greatest Navy in the world and a first-rate Air Force our Allies could hardly expect more'.[6]

Chamberlain, like Liddell Hart, took the view that the Army Council was being short-sighted and 'blimpish' in its insistence upon a large army; he wanted a strategy of limited liability on both economic and strategic grounds. There was no point in preparing for a rerun of the shambles of 1914–18; this time the air force and the mechanized arm would dominate affairs, so it was futile to spend money on a large army. Moreover, Chamberlain's instincts as a politician told him that the public would not stand for a military posture which promised a repeat of the battle of the Somme.

Duff quickly took up the cudgels which his predecessor at the War Office, Lord Hailsham, had wielded. Hailsham had been forced to accept a budget of only £20 million along with a commitment to create a 'Field Force' (it was thought that 'Expeditionary Force' held too many overtones of 1914).

However, the moment was ripe for a fresh effort to get the War Office view accepted. In November 1935 another DRC report was submitted to the Cabinet, drawn up to take account of the need to take precautions against Italy in the light of her invasion of Abyssinia; like its two predecessors, it emphasized the need for an army capable of playing an active role in Continental warfare.[7]

Duff had his own views on British foreign policy. He was a firm believer in the French alliance and could not see how that would be strengthened by an announcement that the British were willing to fight to the last French *poilu* whilst providing aircraft and a navy to help against the Germans. When the DRC report came before the Cabinet in February 1936 Duff argued the case for a large army. He won the congratulations of the Cabinet Secretary, Sir Maurice Hankey, for 'the brilliance and lucidity of his remarks', but little else. The Chancellor's opposition was too strong and so Baldwin decided upon a compromise: the Field Force would be re-equipped in line with the DRC report, but the major recommendation, that the Territorial Army should be brought up to a high enough standard to become the cadre from which a Continental army could be created, was held over for five years.[8]

The Abyssinian crisis added another dark shade to Duff's already gloomy outlook on foreign affairs; but even high drama has its *longueurs* and, during a long debate in the Commons, he whiled away some time by writing a piece of doggerel:

The Duce gives the order
To march against the foe,
And off to Abyssinia
The organ-grinders go,
But now they're quite incapable
Of any sort of grind
And they're back to Mussolini
With their organs left behind.

The hosts of Ethiopia
March back to hearth and home
With knick-knacks for the mantelpiece
Imported straight from Rome.

The Pope is inundated
With pleas to join his choir
From wops whose tenor voices
Are now an octave higher.

The Duce calls a rally
Of veterans tried and true,
'Heroes' he cries, 'My heroes
What can we do for you?'

'What price is theirs who answer
Their country when she calls?
What shall your Duce give you?'
The soldiers answered '-----.'

Here at least was some relief from the unpleasant results of the crisis: Italian enmity; French confidence in Britain badly shaken; the resignation of Sir Samuel Hoare, the Foreign Secretary, in the wake of a public outburst against attempts to negotiate with Italy; and the feeling that public opinion was unduly pacifist.

Duff had acquired, as a junior minister, a reputation for indiscretion; he was to build upon this in 1936.

No one would have called Duff Cooper a man of equable temperament. Elizabethans would have labelled him as a man of 'choleric humour', for such he was, with strong likes and dislikes. Among the latter were, as he told Diana in August 1937, 'men who live, by choice, out of their own country. I don't like interior decorators, I don't like Germans, I don't like buggers and I don't like Christian Scientists.' To this list could be added; pacifists, socialists and Lord Beaverbrook. Randolph Churchill recalled that:

Anyone meeting Duff Cooper for the first time might have judged him markedly choleric. To praise Mr Lloyd George or the Germans was an infallible method of producing an outburst of passionate personal vituperation which, like a tropical storm, passed away as quickly as it had arrived.[9]

These outbursts of temper 'which suffused and distorted his face', were known, among his friends, as 'Duff's veiners', and Diana would sometimes refer to him as 'the dear old turkey-cock'. Intimates took these 'veiners' for granted, they were part of his charm, but strangers found them alarming. Duff's private and public outbursts during 1936 gained him few new friends and finally lost him some old supporters.

During the 1920s he had enjoyed the support of those liberal minds who were in favour of the League of Nations. His warnings about Germany in 1933 had done him no good in such quarters, nor anywhere else for that matter. It may take an effort of imagination, but it should be remembered that, at this time, the view was widely held that Germany had been badly treated in 1919 and that the French were the main villains of the piece; Germanophilia, if not outright approval of some aspects of Nazism, was widespread in Conservative circles; while Francophobia was equally common both there and in socialist quarters. Duff had little time and even less patience for such opinions.

Outraged by the pacifist views of some members of the bench of Bishops, Duff did not hesitate to make his feelings plain. When a Canon Davey of Liverpool refused to say prayers for the Government because it had suggested that the German reoccupation of the Rhineland was not wholly a good thing, Duff denounced him. He later urged the Bishops to say plainly 'whether it was right or wrong for a Christian to take up arms in defence of his country'. This gained him 'an undesired and undeserved reputation as a baiter of Bishops and an enemy of the Church'.[10] This sort of thing may have gone down well in some quarters, but it was not to everyone's taste.

During the summer, when he went on a tour to boost the recruiting drive which the army was mounting, Duff widened his attacks to include those outside the Churches who preached pacifism and he put the case for higher spending on defence. Liddell Hart did not approve of the way Duff went about things:

> If the cleavage is to be reduced rather than increased, it is essential to understand the intellectual position that underlies the pacifist case. It is only too clear that Duff Cooper fails to do so – and by the recent trend

of his speeches he is tending not only to stiffen the pacifists but to strengthen their forces by driving moderate opinion further that way.

He is apt to talk a Kiplingesque language which is out of date, and fails to realize that any savour of jingoism is repugnant to most thinking people today in this country.[11]

Those inclined to liberalism have always suffered from the illusion that they alone have minds in good working order, but even so, he was correct in thinking that Duff had lost the support of many of his old friends in the League of Nations. In the summer Duff gave a speech in Paris which argued the need for Britain and France to stand together and brought a storm of controversy blowing about his ears.

The Labour Party was not at all happy about press reports that Duff had advocated an Anglo-French alliance to guard against the dangers from Germany, and the Labour leader, Attlee, tried to get a debate on the subject of the speech at the end of the session in July. A debate was granted and Duff found himself accused of advocating a policy 'which conflicts with the declared foreign policy of His Majesty's Government'.

Attlee and other Labour MPs sought to foist that charge on the Secretary of State for War, and they were supported by Liberals, including Sir Archibald Sinclair and Lloyd George. Churchill found himself in the unusual position of defending the National Government, a fact which was commented upon by some Labour members. Duff's friend Sidney Herbert accused the Opposition of frivolity, and neither he, nor Sir John Simon, had any difficulty in disposing of the allegations made by Labour. At the end of the debate the House divided, with 136 in favour of Attlee's line and 284 against it.[12]

Duff's Francophilia and his fears about Germany had, in fact, caused him to utter words which were close to his heart; closer, one suspects, than they were to Neville Chamberlain's: 'Your frontier is our frontier,' he had said; and he believed it.

Although the Government had never been in any danger, the debate had been unwelcome and it helped to weaken Duff's political position. This was hardly strengthened when, upon bringing his recruiting plans to the Cabinet in the early autumn, he was forced to withdraw them again because he had forgotten that they should first have been cleared with the Treasury.

Duff's Francophile, Germanophobe views were not common in his Party, and their expression and the manner in which they were aired served only to distance him from other MPs. In private he expressed his opinions without any restraint. Chips Channon witnessed a scene at Philip Sassoon's beautiful house at Lympne where 'There was the usual German argument after dinner with Philip and Duff attacking the Nazis with the violence born of personal prejudice.' The impact of this 'veiner' on Channon's companion, a young RAF officer, is instructive: 'Is Duff Cooper off his rocker, or what?'[13] Channon, who defended the Nazis with all the personal prejudice of an American trying to forget his roots, was the disapproving witness of another occasion on which Duff aired his own views. He recorded how, at dinner at Venetia Montagu's London house in November 1936, he found the 'usual lot' present, the 'cleverest, wordiest, quickest people in London'. But for once he was not impressed; they were, he thought, 'boring, and worse, out of date'. Their sin was that 'they do not know what it is all about now. I fear that they are all too pro-Semite'; a dreadful social solecism, no doubt. 'Crinks' Harcourt-Johnstone, a former Liberal MP, began dinner by saying, 'Here's death to Ribbentrop'; when Diana 'turned on him', Duff 'laughingly said, "I only hope he dies in pain." Then the usual long, anti-German tirade began.'[14]

In Channon's mind, and possibly in other minds, Duff became identified with a strain of 'warmongering' that could only cause trouble. As the Baldwin era began to draw to its close, speculation arose about the future. Channon, who heard from Diana that Duff was growing tired of politics and of Chamberlain's obstruction of his wishes, hoped that he would retire and had heard that the Chancellor 'dislikes and disapproves' of him.[15] Beaverbrook predicted to Lloyd George in October: 'I think Baldwin will retire soon. And when Chamberlain comes to form his Government he will demote Duff Cooper who has been a dreadful failure at the War Office.'[16]

～9 12 c～

Distractions and Duties

His first year as a Cabinet Minister had been one of mixed fortunes. Duff felt that had it not been for the inflexible Chancellor he would have been more successful. Between the two men was fixed a gulf of temperament which could only have been widened by their differing visions of the role of the army. It was unlikely that the Minister of War would win a tussle with Baldwin's heir apparent. The 'cleverest, wordiest, quickest people in London'[1] whom Channon so admired, commanded few guns in the political world. Whatever else Duff was he was not a 'serious' politician; Chamberlain was that *par excellence* – if nothing else. Politics was a mistress whose jealousy surpassed that of any woman and Duff's infidelities were not pardoned; it was necessary for success that he should at least give the appearance of worshipping solely at her shrine. But there was too much fun in him for that.

To his friends (and he was always at his ease in small gatherings of intimates) he was 'the best of talkers', the 'most lovable of companions'.[2] To those in any kind of trouble or with problems he was the truest friend; he was in Lord Boothby's words, 'absolute for friendship'.[3]

At his clubs – the Beefsteak, the Carlton, Buck's, occasionally the Garrick and, most often of all, White's – and in Society, Duff seemed 'more a man of fashion or a man of letters than a man of affairs';[4] it was a description that would have pleased him. He aspired to a breadth of culture and a wealth of pleasure, rather than to the narrowness of the corridors of power. He was always something of a dandy. The Lavery portrait which hung in his study at Gower Street showed him in top hat, opera-cloak and evening dress; the very image of the man about town. He had a taste for well-cut suits, fine ties and, at dining clubs, embroidered waistcoats. Conscious of his tiny feet, he was always elegantly shod, his footwear sometimes tending to the

92

exoticism of yellow pumps. He was equally fond of hats, possessing at the time of his death twenty-seven of the things, including such items as a yachting cap and a grey bowler. Not for him the morning coat and pin-stripes of Neville Chamberlain, or the country-tweeds of Mr Baldwin; if he could not match the physical elegance of Anthony Eden, he could equal his sartorial excellence.

Wit, charm, genius for friendship, conversational brilliance, all these are transitory qualities not easily captured on paper and difficult to fix in pen and ink; but they were the qualities which Duff's friends remembered most. In the absence of a Boswell it is impossible to translate the excellence of his conversation into print. Bob Boothby recalled a lunch with Duff and Belloc when 'the food was excellent, the claret superb' and where he could never again 'hope to listen to talk of such incandescent brilliance'. Belloc started to recite some of his own poems, but laughed so much that Duff had to finish them. It was with reluctance that Boothby bade his hosts farewell and departed to keep an appointment for 3 o'clock, only to discover that it was already half-past four.[5]

Belloc was also one of the presiding spirits at West House, which was, for Duff, that 'small house in the country, not too far away from the capital' which the poet Horace thought so desirable. Chips Channon and his wife motored down to Bognor in mid-July 1936 to find Venetia Montagu, Conrad Russell and Belloc as their companions. Dinner was 'preceded by much drink' and then enlivened by the poet singing 'Provençal lyrics' and reciting French poetry and Jacobite ballads: 'it was quite a unique experience – but not to be repeated'.[6]

The company there was usually more literary than political: in addition to Belloc there would be Maurice Baring 'reading his new novels aloud' and reciting poems which he had written in honour of Diana; H. G. Wells, Arnold Bennett and lesser luminaries such as J. C. Squire were other visitors to West House. But for all its rural charm, Duff could not settle there for too long; with him it was a matter of (to quote from his own translation of Horace):

> In Rome you cry 'Give me my country house';
> But in the country 'There's no place like Rome.'[7]

Although politics was occupying more of his time than it once had, he was hardly on a political treadmill. Some idea of the pace of his social life in the mid 1930s can be gleaned from the letters which he wrote to Diana in early 1935 while she was off on a cruise with

Beaverbrook and his entourage. He was, he lamented, leading a 'pretty dull life'. This included, in the first week of Diana's absence: a trip to Brussels and Paris (where he lunched with Daisy Fellowes); dinner with Brendan Bracken (where, despite promises of Churchill's company, they dined *à deux* 'in his dark room on filthy food'); a more enjoyable dinner at Lord Derby's (to listen to his host's recollections of Haig); a party for forty at the French Embassy; and a night at the Other Club – 'which passed off without any insults'. The following week included not only lunch with the Queen of Spain and dining out every evening, but also 'a foretaste of heaven' at a 'men's dinner for eight': 'I don't think I have had better food anywhere, and wonderful drink. We played bridge afterwards and I won every rubber.' Not everyone's idea of the dull life.

And yet Duff meant what he wrote. As he commented to Diana on 12 February: 'I am just longing for you to come back, my beloved. Nothing seems much fun without you.' Life without her was like champagne without the bubbles: 'Oh won't it be fun when you come back.'

At Gower Street there was work – and John Julius – to keep him occupied. Duff kept Diana informed of all their son's latest exploits: 'He is very well and very charming. He sits in my big armchair quite quietly reading his book while I am working.' A telegram from Mummy would take him to Duff's bedroom in the morning to see if his father had been similarly honoured, after which they would pore over maps together, plotting her wanderings. When he accompanied Duff to a wedding in early February, John Julius

> behaved with such calm dignity. His *mot* of the day was when the organ pealed out one of the other little boys exclaimed, 'What a noise' to which J.J. replied indignantly, 'It isn't a noise, it's music.'

A remark which suggests that his ear for these things was rather better than his father's.

For Duff, the social and political worlds were intermingled; his problem was that his enemies were all too willing to believe that it was impossible to combine business with pleasure: hence the rumours about his future.

But the Baldwin era was not quite over. Duff and Diana were good friends with the new King, Edward VIII; they had been the first guests to stay with him at Fort Belvedere after his accession and had accompanied him and Mrs Simpson on a cruise of the Mediterranean in the summer of 1936. Diana found Wallis Simpson uncongenial, telling Conrad Russell: 'She is wearing badly; her commonness and Becky Sharpishness irritate.' They were thus aware of the rumours that Edward's intentions towards her were strictly honourable. But it had not occurred to Duff that a man might be willing to renounce his throne for love.

He first became aware of such a possibility when Baldwin stopped him in the lobby of the Commons on the afternoon of 16 November.[8] Duff was told that Edward was talking of abdication if he could not 'marry Wallis and remain King'. Baldwin, who already wondered whether 'the Yorks would not prove the best solution', said that the King wanted to see Duff. He went to see him the following afternoon.

He pointed out that if the King did abdicate 'the whole blame for the catastrophe ... would be placed upon Wallis, both now and in history'; this seemed to shake Edward who longed, above everything else, to protect Mrs Simpson's good name. Duff's second line of argument was to ask him to reflect upon the sort of life that would be his as an ex-monarch, but Edward merely gave the cheery reply: 'Oh you know me, Duff, I'm always busy. I shall find plenty to do'; this was to sound ironic to Duff a decade later. The sensible and worldly advice which he proceeded to give the King, that he should keep Mrs Simpson as his mistress, fell on deaf ears. Edward was too besotted, too naïve, too straight, to contemplate such a step.

Duff did not think that it need come to abdication. Why, he asked, did Edward not go ahead with his coronation and the planned Indian durbar while staying away from Wallis? After a year Edward's 'position would be immensely strengthened'. People, Duff said, 'would see that he had done his best to get on without her but had found it impossible'. In such an atmosphere he might be able to have Mrs Simpson and his Crown; but the King could not, he said, do such a thing.

Back at the Commons, Duff found that Churchill was most indignant with the King. The man who was to become the royal champion took the line that 'just as men had given arms and legs and indeed their lives, for the sake of the country, so the King must be prepared to give up a woman'.

Perhaps Duff's advice to the King percolated through, or perhaps Edward simply disliked being lectured by Baldwin, but by 22 November it was rumoured that he was showing signs of fight. A midnight call at Gower Street by Esmond Harmsworth, Rothermere's son, confirmed these rumours for Duff. The King now seemed to favour a morganatic marriage; Duff thought this was a good idea, provided Edward did not insist on marrying Mrs Simpson at once.

But Baldwin poured cold water on this idea at the following morning's Cabinet, and Duff left 'feeling for the first time that it really would come to abdication'. He did suggest that the King should speak to Churchill, whose robust language might change his mind.

Alas, by this point it was Churchill who had changed his mind. When Duff saw him in the House after the weekend, Churchill was arguing that the King must be defended. To his evident annoyance, Duff proceeded to attribute his change of mind to the influence of Lord Beaverbrook who had just returned from America to see the King.

By the time the matter became public the next day, 1 December, the battle-lines were already drawn up: Baldwin would not accept the King with Mrs Simpson at any price; the King would give up his throne but not his beloved; Churchill and Beaverbrook, for their several motives, intended to defend the King and attack Baldwin. Some of the more excitable members of the Cabinet, including Hore-Belisha and 'Shakes' Morrison,* feared that a *'coup d'état* was not impossible', with Churchill being called upon by the King to form a Government and then calling an election on the issue of the 'King's marriage' which might undermine democracy and lead to a Fascist Government. Baldwin took a more sober view.

The one moment when it appeared that the Prime Minister was losing his touch came on 4 December when, in addition to allowing the King to see Churchill, he suggested that they might 'pass special legislation in order to render absolute without further delay Mrs Simpson's decree nisi, so that he should be able to marry her as soon as he goes'. Duff pointed out that not only was this procedure somewhat amoral, it also laid the Government open to the charge of wanting to get rid of the King. It would be said that while they had been unwilling to pass special legislation for a morganatic marriage in order to keep him, they had been willing to 'introduce legislation which, according to existing law, would legalize adultery, to expedite his departure'. That was the end of that scheme.

The crisis rumbled on until 9 December with opinion, according to Duff, moving away from the King. At the Cabinet that morning Duff

---

* William Shepheard Morrison (1893–1961), at this time Minister of Agriculture. Later Speaker of the House (1951–9) and still later Viscount Dunrossil (1959).

learnt of the abdication and of Prince Albert's decision to take the title of George VI. Baldwin had told the new King that 'I never thought I should serve again under a Queen Elizabeth', drawing the acid comment from Sir John Simon that 'Now, with Lord Burghley's permission, we will get back to business.'

The same afternoon Baldwin enjoyed one of his greatest parliamentary triumphs with a moving speech announcing the abdication. Duff met him in the lobby afterwards, commenting: 'Looking back on it, how right you were to agree to the King seeing Winston.' Baldwin replied: 'I never doubted that I was right for a minute. I am only a simple lad you know, Duff, but there were reasons why I thought it best to put it to the Cabinet in the way I did.' He did not elaborate on what they were, but the fact that both Churchill and Beaverbrook were damaged by their involvement in the crisis can hardly have upset him.

Duff wrote to Beaverbrook on 16 December: 'In the recent catastrophe I think that you and I were in sympathy.... I'm afraid it was a lost cause from the start – but that was not your fault or mine.' He reassured Beaverbrook that he had not, as had been reported, criticized him violently.[9] By this time Duff needed whatever help he could get, for he was in the middle of what proved to be another battle which was lost from the start.

Although he seemed to have lost the battle with Chamberlain over the role of the British Army, he found an opportunity to raise the whole question again in December, just as the abdication crisis was reaching its peak. He circulated a paper to his colleagues on 3 December in which he put his case forcefully.

Duff pointed out that there was general agreement that the Territorial Army (TA) was 'an integral part of the British Army' and that when the Cabinet had postponed its rearmament earlier in the year this had been because of the limitations of industrial production. The Director-General of Munitions had, however, now decided that it would be possible to start rearming the TA, in which case, Duff argued, it was time to begin expanding Britain's 'production capacity'. He made it clear that he expected the Cabinet to approve the creation of a large army.[10]

Writing to Duff in 1938, Malcolm MacDonald recalled

the way in which, when you were at the War Office, you fought an almost ceaseless duel with the then Chancellor of the Exchequer, regardless of the facts that he was to become Prime Minister within a few months and that his displeasure might result in your exclusion from the new Government. Some people would have done anything rather than quarrel with Neville Chamberlain then.

He was quite right.

Chamberlain's response was swift and powerful. In a paper dated 11 December he sought to undermine the very foundations of Duff's policy. He argued that the country could not and need not afford such an expense. Although he denied that he was advocating a policy of 'limited liability', there can be no doubt that he was doing just that.

Chamberlain's memorandum is a breath-taking testimony to his own self-confidence. Despite the fact that three DRC reports had assumed that Britain would need a large army because the most likely war would be a Continental one against Germany, he called for a 'survey by the competent authorities of all possible alternatives'. Public opinion would not, he warned, tolerate 'large-scale military operations on the Continent'.[11] Chamberlain, wisely, did not deal with what would happen if Hitler ignored British public opinion.

Duff made a spirited response to all this on 14 December, making the point that the 'competent authorities' were all agreed that 'the simplest and gravest emergency which can be envisaged is an attack by Germany on France and Belgium'; that, after all, was why three DRC reports had recommended a large army. If Chamberlain was arguing that this was not a possibility, he should say so, for there would follow 'immediate and fundamental' adjustments to British foreign and defence policy.[12]

None of this deterred Chamberlain, who in his reply in Cabinet on 16 December made the astonishing statement that:

> The fact that successive Chiefs of Staff and Secretaries of State for War had taken the view that, in the event of an attack by Germany on France, we should be prepared to send a land force to Belgium and France did not weigh very much with him as the War Office was the interested department.[13]

According to this peculiar doctrine only a department with no 'interest' to declare could propound a policy; an odd conclusion, and one which would have ruled out the Treasury from taking an opinion.

The simple fact was that Chamberlain disagreed with the Army Staff and intended to get his own way. When Baldwin decided that the whole question should be referred back to the Chiefs of Staff,

Hankey commented that Chamberlain would have to do the job himself 'because I know of no one else who shares it with sufficient conviction to put it forward'.

The Chiefs of Staff report, which came before the Cabinet on 28 January 1937, broadly confirmed Duff's views and argued for an increase in production which would allow the Territorials to be re-equipped quickly. However, the final victory went to the big battalions commanded by the Chancellor; money was not forthcoming to create the large Continental army which Duff wanted:[14] the results were to be apparent in 1939 and 1940.

The defeat of his plans for the army left him rather uselessly occupying the War Office by late spring 1937. Baldwin's retirement was near and, given Duff's recent clashes with the heir apparent, the hot money was on the rumours that he would be replaced. He had, alas, acquired little credit from his tenure of office, but the verdict of the official historian should be borne in mind:

> While it is true that he had failed to persuade his colleagues of the correctness of his views, the official records suggest not that he put his case clumsily, but simply that his views were unpopular.

Professor Gibbs observed correctly that arrayed against Duff were 'the tides of finance and of strategic thinking'. Nevertheless 'whatever else he had failed to do' Duff had 'argued the case for a comprehensive plan for the Regular and Territorial Army in the kind of war which was becoming more and more likely'.[15]

Such reflections were not, alas, available to console Duff as the moment for Baldwin's resignation came close. It was widely expected that Duff would be left out of a Chamberlain Cabinet, indeed one newspaper editor offered him a contract to write articles, anticipating the evil day.

Chamberlain, as one historian has observed, 'preferred Cabinet Ministers whose detached, unemotional and empirical approach to problems made them resemble good civil servants rather than politicians in touch with the mood of the electorate'.[16] This description hardly applied to Duff, who thus had little hope that he would survive in office. He wrote to Liddell Hart on 4 May 1937 to say that he had not 'lost sight' of the question of a peerage for him and 'would try again in the next regime, if I am in it'.[17] He wrote to Chamberlain on the same day, assuring him that if he was kept at the War Office he was perfectly prepared to implement Chamberlain's army policy.[18]

Chamberlain became Prime Minister at the end of May. He wrote to his sisters saying that he was 'convinced that many and drastic changes' would have to be made at the War Office, which would require 'great application and much courage to carry out'. He would, he said, be removing Duff who 'has been lazy and until lately has shown no sign of getting down to work on any of the big problems'.[19] As the letter which he had sent to Duff in November 1935 had revealed, Chamberlain saw himself as a chief policy-maker, with his colleagues confining themselves to their departmental responsibilities; hence his penchant for appointing 'experts' to run departments rather than politicians.

Duff told Liddell Hart that he was 'very sorry to leave the War Office' and that he had

> argued with Neville. But Neville was influenced by mine and Jock Stuart's arguments about a British Expeditionary Force and felt somebody else better to implement the policy. Unfair to D.C., D.C. demurred, and said he wanted to carry on and could carry out, but Neville adamant.[20]

Nor was this surprising, Chamberlain wanted someone who would do what he wanted at the War Office and chose Hore-Belisha.

Duff, before the axe fell, was haunted by a recurring nightmare that he was to be dismissed.[21] For once, his habitual sang-froid deserted him. He did not, in any case, expect to like the new regime. Baldwin had been his leader and he regretted the passing of the great man. He wrote to Baldwin on 30 May, the day before his retirement, to send a 'last message of gratitude and good-bye'.[22]

Now that Baldwin was going Duff could, he said, 'speak frankly of the deep admiration and affection I have felt for you for so long'. Having, he said, 'a horror of those who curry favour I unfortunately find it difficult to be barely more than civil to an individual upon whom my fortunes may depend'. This, Duff thought, 'is one of the many reasons why I often doubt whether I am really suited to politics in spite of such success as I have had'. He told Baldwin that the fact that he owed 'that success' to him made it 'more precious to me', because 'to have won your approval is more important to me than to have got into the Cabinet'.

It was not often that Duff allowed himself to write freely about politics and what he wanted out of them, but in this valedictory mood he did so, telling Baldwin that he would 'miss you more than you would expect' because he had

100

brought to politics – and what is more, retained in politics – the tradition of a broader age in which politics left room for leisure and literature and philosophy – when there was time to read something besides F.O. telegrams and Cabinet papers.

This was why he liked Baldwin so much. He feared that

the whole atmosphere in which we politicians live will grow stuffier, foggier, thicker now you've left it. That is at any rate how it seems to me and that is why I am so unhappy to say good-bye to you.

There cannot be many Prime Ministers (if any) who have received a sonnet from one of their colleagues, but Baldwin did. Duff sent him a revised version of one he had written in 1926, after the General Strike; he told Baldwin to pay attention to the initial letter on each line:

> Steadfast of purpose have you proved – and true,
> Thrice-tried custodian of your country's fate,
> And neither sought the many to placate
> Nor feared the private malice of the few.
> Later when civil faction fiercer grew
> Engendered out of misery by hate
> You were the statesman who preserved the state
> By faith in those whose faith stood firm in you.
> And when your task is ended and the cheers
> Loud echoing round you shall have died away
> Down the long corridor of crowded years,
> Welcome awaits you where you longed to stay,
> In books and woods and fields and quiet spheres
> Not unremembered in your noisier day.

Indeed, Duff was tempted by 'quiet spheres'; he was certainly right in his foreboding that the Baldwinian protégés were about to fall on harder times. But he was not totally accurate.

He was indeed, as in his nightmare, asked to see the new Prime Minister, but instead of the sack he was offered the post of First Lord of the Admiralty, which was, technically, a promotion. Duff was surprised and delighted, but never did understand why Chamberlain had acted in the way he did. He reflected later that the future Prime Minister had paid particular attention to his speech introducing the Army Estimates in the spring, and wondered if this had influenced the final decision. Duff may have been right. One historian has written that Chamberlain considered 'seriously' the idea of 'dropping Duff

Cooper', but 'apparently decided that it would be better having him in the Cabinet than asking embarrassing questions about the rearmament programme from the Conservative back-benches'.[23] This is a highly plausible suggestion, but Dr Shay offers no hard evidence for it; maybe there is none.

There are some problems with it, however. Chamberlain had a majority in the Commons of nearly three hundred and had no need to fear an isolated dissident. It was true that Duff, as a recent Cabinet Minister with inside knowledge, would be a more dangerous rebel than Churchill, who was regarded by most people as an ageing and politically bankrupt has-been,[24] but Chamberlain was not the sort of man to let that worry him; he certainly did not do so in 1938.

But, whatever Duff's defects, there may have been two reasons why Chamberlain hesitated to sack him. For one thing he was one of the leading figures in the small group of pro-French Conservatives in the House of Commons. His dismissal would have been read as a clear signal in both Berlin and Paris, and Chamberlain had good reasons for not wanting to give any signals to either capital. In the second place Duff was, along with Eden, Oliver Stanley and Walter Elliot,* firmly identified as one of the inheritors of the Baldwinian tradition. Chamberlain needed to be more firmly in the saddle before he could be sure which parts of that inheritance he could discard. Moreover, if Duff fought as hard for the navy as he had for the army, he would make it even easier for Chamberlain to restrain spending on the army. If Duff showed that he could abide by Chamberlain's Cabinet rules then he could remain, provided he performed his departmental duties efficiently. If he was inefficient he would destroy a political career which was already waning; and if he did not abide by Chamberlain's rules, then he would be sacked. Unlike Baldwin, Chamberlain knew where he wanted to go.

* Ministers of Labour and Agriculture, respectively.

~~13~~

First Lord

Having confounded the sceptics, Duff's feelings about his survival were ambivalent. He was anxious to erase the impression that he had been a failure as a minister, and he wanted to make a success of his new post; but, at the same time, he was growing weary of politics. He had entered the Commons with the ambition of becoming Prime Minister, but, as he noted in his diary at the beginning of 1938, 'my political ambitions have dwindled'. He had been close enough to the centre of power to see the 'endless, thankless work' and the 'worry and responsibility and abuse'; he now looked towards literature for his future, rather than Downing Street.

His appetite was not, however, sated, and the mood of disenchantment passed – for the moment. The Admiralty was a fascinating and congenial job, and it provided Diana with a place in his political career. She had not cared over-much for the War Office; military manœuvres and elderly generals were not much fun. Now, however, she was mistress of the First Lord's yacht, *HMS Enchantress*, and of Admiralty House; both gave her much enjoyment.

Admiralty House was one of the grander government residences. With the help of her old friend Philip Sassoon, who was Minister of Works, Diana did away with Lady Hoare's 'Brunhilde's pyre' colour scheme, and imprinted her own unique touch on the building. It took months before Duff and Diana could move into the house, but it was, from her point of view, well worth it.

Sassoon provided her with a bust of Nelson and other 'Trafalgar trophies' to surround a Danish mermaid figure in the hall. All this fitted in well with the existing furniture. Some of this had come from a Mr Fish and had, appropriately enough, arms and legs in the fashion of dolphins or other aquatic creatures. Large portraits of

Cook's voyages to the South Seas were placed on the walls, and the whole decor had a pronounced maritime flavour.

Wherever she lived, Diana's bedroom was the centre of her universe; like Louis XIV she held court from her bedchamber. For Admiralty House she had the most amazing bed constructed *in situ*:

> The room was at least twenty feet high, and from close to the ceiling hung a wreath of gilded dolphins and crowns. Blue curtains, lined with white satin and falling to the ground spread open to reveal a headpiece of more dolphins, tridents and shells. At the bottom corners of the bed two life-sized dolphins, arch-backed and curved, menaced intruders.[1]

They evidently expected a longish stay at the Admiralty, for in addition to these extensive refurbishments, Duff moved most of his books from Gower Street (with the exception of 'twelve shelves full of dull books' which were sold). This presaged the final abandonment of Gower Street, with its splendid library and *trompe l'œil* decorations. When Diana's mother died early in 1938 she left them her magnificent house at 34 Chapel Street, which precipitated the decision to sell the house in which they had lived so happily since their marriage. It was a decision which they were both to regret.

Even better than Admiralty House was the *Enchantress*, a thousand-ton sloop. It was the first (and last) time that they had had a yacht, and they both delighted in it. There were unkind souls, mostly socialists, who looked askance at what they termed 'pleasure trips' taken by the First Lord and his Lady, but these were, in the main, visits to the Fleet or on government business.

The first cruise came in the summer of 1937 and was hardly a 'pleasure'. Duff went to visit the Fleet at Invergordon, taking Diana, John Julius and other friends with him. It was exceedingly pleasant to be able to stop for a few days with Diana's sister Marjorie at Plas Newydd. However, the next stage of the voyage was ghastly. As the yacht reached the Minches it was hit by a violent gale. Diana described the scene in a letter to her friend Conrad Russell: 'My God, it was *three* hours of hell! My poor child was sick four times. Captain Wallace was taken very ill too. I'm thankful to say that Duff and I both felt rotten but were not sick.' Cape Wrath, living up to its name, was even worse:

> By 3.30 the tide was rolling hysterically and I was bathed in sweat.... Suddenly there was a super-roll followed by a series of crashes, and I leapt up and ran to Duff's cabin.... What should I find but a scene of chaos!

The bed had 'got away' from its mooring, the whole of the bedding, mattress, blankets, pillows on the floor in a tangle and poor Duff picking himself up, bruised and bewildered.[2]

Fortunately, the next cruise, in October, was in the eastern Mediterranean, where Neptune is in gentler mood.

Thus it was that Duff continued to make hay while the sun shone; he was aware, more so than most, of the dangers from Berlin, but he did not let them overshadow his existence – that would not have been his way.

Duff's mood at this time can be gauged from a letter written to Diana in August, just before their voyage to Invergordon: 'I have been thinking during my dinner – which was better than average – how very fortunate I am at the moment. I have been tapping wood and crossing fingers to try to avert the wrath of the Gods.' He had, he wrote, 'no money troubles' and 'all three of us' were in good health. The blessings multiplied with thought: 'No love troubles, no political troubles – and a perfect job. Can it last?' He could even, he thought, see some good in the fact that they had been apart for three weeks: 'It makes me realize how much I love you, how much I miss you – how you are the backbone and the bottom, the beginning and the end of me.' It was a nice mood but, like all such, was not fated to last; the Gods were not propitiated by crossed fingers.

The New Year of 1938 began the rot. It opened with demands from the income-tax people for £1,600 in back taxes. The bad luck continued in even worse vein, marked by a series of political storms of increasing severity, and culminating in one of such strength that Duff's 'political bunk' came away from its moorings.

Income-tax demands were the least of his troubles, even though he had only £900 in the bank. Far greater were those stemming from the planning of British defence policy. But it may be worth noting that Duff's defence policy, like his personal economic policy, was one untrammelled by considerations of the amount of money actually reposing in a bank-vault.

The central point at issue between Duff and Chamberlain hinged on this, for while the former wanted a policy which would meet Britain's strategic needs, the latter insisted on tailoring a defence programme which kept to a reasonable level of expenditure. The argument between the two men touched the very fundamentals of policy: what was a 'reasonable' level when Britain was, according to Duff, faced with possible extinction?

There was then a fundamental divide between Chamberlain and Duff. The former Chancellor saw it as one of his main objectives to reduce defence expenditure. He realized that this could be achieved most easily if international tensions were reduced – hence his active appeasement of Hitler. He was supported in his policy by the most powerful figures in the Cabinet: Sir John Simon, the Chancellor of the Exchequer; Sir Samuel Hoare, at the Home Office, and Sir Thomas Inskip, the Minister for the Co-ordination of Defence. They all took the view that finance was the 'fourth arm' of defence. If, so they reasoned, Britain's enemies saw that her rearmament programme was destroying her economic stability, they would be further strengthened in their nefarious designs. Moreover it was essential, if war did come, that Britain had the financial strength to fight a long war, for her defence plans were based upon that assumption.[3]

Although historians have long abandoned the idea that there was any coherent group of anti-appeasers, there persists a popular belief in such a thing, mainly because of the image of Churchill battling 'in the wilderness'. Historians have also, for the most part, abandoned the idea that appeasement was something motivated by a mixture of cowardice, naïveté and short-sightedness; but again, thanks to the powerful portrait given by Churchill in his memoirs, popular perceptions have not been much influenced by the historians. And yet, if Duff's actions are to be understood, two things must be appreciated: that there was no widespread opposition to appeasement; and that this was mainly because the policy was firmly rooted in fertile political soil. Those who opposed war – and what politician has ever declared himself to be in favour of killing people? – whether on the Left or Right of the political spectrum, could find a hero in Chamberlain; and those who feared Bolshevism more than Fascism could also approve of appeasement. Arguments of financial prudence told heavily in its favour too. Those Conservatives with their eyes on the 1940 election could see massive party political gains in Chamberlain 'solving' the external problems which seemed to threaten the peace of the world: 'vote for Chamberlain the dove of peace' would be an election-winner.[4] And what, indeed, was the alternative? To argue that the vital interests of the British Empire demanded the defence of Czech frontiers was to meet with the inevitable response: but how can naval power do that? As one critic of Chamberlain's diplomacy, Liddell Hart, was to write in September 1938:

On each successive international issue the Government has had persuasive arguments for dishonouring our obligations – but the fact remains that each surrender has led to a worse one, and to a worsening of our situation as well as that of civilization.[5]

This was the view which subsequent history seemed to vindicate, but its proponents were not popular at the time.

Nor were they united. When Chamberlain manœuvred Eden out of the Foreign Office in February 1938 over the issue of appeasing Italy, Duff had no idea of how bad the differences were between the two men until they surfaced in the Cabinet meetings which immediately preceded Eden's resignation. Even had he known, he would have been unlikely to have helped Eden. For one thing, as we have seen, Duff deprecated the policy of driving Mussolini into Hitler's arms by snubbing him. For another thing he did not much care for Eden. As he told Diana in August 1937: 'People tell me that Anthony says the vilest things about me. I cannot imagine any reason why he should and yet I believe what people tell me.' Philip Sassoon assured him that he had been 'misinformed there', but there was not a great deal of love lost between Duff and Eden.

Oliver Lyttelton wrote of Duff that: 'As a politician he would have gone even further if he could have been cast more readily for other roles than Foreign Secretary.'[6] One reason he did not achieve that position was Eden's having established a prior claim to it during the period 1929–31 when Duff had been out of the Commons. He bore no grudge, but he was unlikely to feel much sorrow at Eden's departure.

The First Lord was having his own problems with the Prime Minister and was too busy with those and with naval planning to see what was happening at the Foreign Office.

The good relations which Duff had enjoyed with Chamberlain in the early 1930s had been seriously soured by their quarrels over the role of the army, and the Prime Minister had little faith in his First Lord. In December 1937 Duff managed to commit two gaffes which brought down upon him the weight of Chamberlain's displeasure.

In a speech at Pimlico, Duff attacked Attlee and the Labour Party for their policy on the Spanish Civil War, this despite a warning from Chamberlain that no minister should comment on the matter; he was then reported by the press as having said that Britain should accept a Japanese apology over a diplomatic incident in the Far East, when no such apology had been tendered. Chamberlain seized his opportunity. As he wrote to his sister Hilda on 17 December:

I have twice verbally warned Duff Cooper about his habit of committing blazing indiscretions. This time he hasn't got Stanley Baldwin to deal with and I have written him such a letter as I expect he has never received in his life before. It will be interesting to see whether it penetrates. In his place I should bring my resignation to the Prime Minister at once and hope that he wouldn't accept it.[7]

Chamberlain's letter was certainly a stiff document,[8] but it failed to bring Duff running with his resignation; he had, perhaps, too good an idea of how that would be received. He expressed his 'sorrow' and 'deepest distress' at having 'incurred your displeasure', and tried to excuse himself. He concluded by saying that he had taken 'your letter very much to heart' and assuring him that 'you'll never have cause to complain of me in this way again'.[9]

This was hardly the political posture from which to conduct a successful campaign against Chamberlain's attempts to cut spending on the Fleet.

Duff's predecessor, Sir Samuel Hoare, had presided over the introduction of a plan for a 'New Standard Fleet' (NSF). This was meant to update the plan laid down in the 1934 DRC paper to take into account changes for the worse in the international situation. Chamberlain, his Chancellor, Sir John Simon, and the Minister for the Coordination of Defence, Sir Thomas Inskip, wanted to cut back the construction programme to the levels set out in the DRC paper.[10]

Just before Christmas 1937, Duff sent Simon a detailed account of why the navy needed an extra £55½ million in the coming year, only to receive a 'discouraging response'.[11] Duff then tried to lift the matter onto the political plane in a forceful Cabinet paper written on 11 February in which he stigmatized the DRC Fleet as a 'purely paper conception' bearing no relation to 'the present international situation'; the NSF programme 'represented the minimum consistent with national security'. He warned his colleagues that the position of any minister who could not say that he was doing everything to 'hasten the completion of his preparations for the worst eventuality' would be 'unenviable'.[12]

However, when the Cabinet met on 16 February, a ceiling of £1,650 million was set on defence spending for the next quinquennium. This was a decision which opened the way for a free-for-all among the Service departments – and also put the NSF in danger. Duff said that his naval advisers reckoned that that would leave the Admiralty with only £12 million for the following year, which would not even keep up with the outmoded DRC requirements. He also put forward the line which he was to stick to throughout the dispute: that if a war had actually started 'we should not dream of accepting an arbitrary figure given us by the Treasury'. But he received little support.[13]

The international situation continued to deteriorate. In March Hitler's troops entered Vienna and announced the incorporation of Austria into the Reich. It seemed to many that Czechoslovakia, with its German Sudetens, would be next on the Führer's agenda. The fact that France was Czechoslovakia's ally gave the British Government an interest in the matter: how should Britain respond in the event of the French being asked to shoulder their obligations to Czechoslovakia?

Duff had other, and more personal, worries; in the last week of March he was struck down with 'the worst attack of influenza' from which he had 'ever suffered'. He was confined to bed under doctor's orders for nearly three weeks. From there he wrote to Chamberlain on 12 March, sufficiently well to see a connection between his own naval programme and events on the Continent. He urged the Prime Minister to take some striking action which would show the Germans how much their moves had been deplored. The quickest thing he could do would be to announce an increase in the Naval Estimates. Chamberlain responded by proposing to increase the Air Estimates, to which Duff replied that 'nothing we can do in the air is going to alarm Germany who is steadily increasing her lead in that element ... the war won't be won in the air'. He reminded Chamberlain that the blockade, which had been so effective in the Great War, would again be 'our principal weapon'. Moreover, the plans for an expansion of the navy already existed.[14] But only Sam Hoare backed this line in Cabinet.

What Diana thought of all this activity from his sick-bed may be imagined. She lived in constant fear that Duff was about to be taken away from her by illness or accident and was alarmed when he tried to get up after a fortnight in order to deliver his speech on the Estimates to the House. The result of this was that his temperature went up and that his Under-Secretary had to deliver the speech. It was, Duff complained to Hoare, 'rather hard to be done out of one's annual appearance'.[15] He never was to deliver the Naval Estimates. He was, however, quite determined to get up when he saw the agenda for the Cabinet meeting on 23 March.

The agenda contained the texts of statements which Chamberlain proposed to make about Britain's likely reaction to problems over Czechoslovakia: one was a 'cold refusal' to the French Government to offer any assistance if they went to war; the other was the text of a parliamentary declaration which amounted to a statement of British isolationism. Duff's temperature soared when he read these documents, but he made it plain that he was going to Downing Street the following morning. Diana persuaded him to wear a scarf – and asked Hore-Belisha to make sure that Duff stayed out of draughts.

The Cabinet of 23 March was almost a dress rehearsal for the greater drama that was to be played out later in the year. Duff wanted Britain to make it clear that 'when France fought Germany we should have to fight Germany too, whether we liked it or not'. Oliver Stanley and Lord De La Warr supported this line, but the rest of the Cabinet followed their leader; a depressing foretaste of the lines of cleavage which opened wider in September.

Duff retired to convalesce with Euan and Barbie Wallace at Lavington in Sussex. Belloc, who came to lunch one day, gave poetic expression to Chamberlain's policy:

> Dear Czecho-Slovakia,
> I don't think they'll attack yer
> But I'm not going to back yer.[16]

However, Chamberlain's statement in the Commons on 24 March adopted a very different tone, implying that Britain would support France and the Czechs; it remained to be seen whether there was anything more to this than a rhetorical gesture.

Duff spent most of Easter in Paris, talking to French politicians, including the Prime Minister, Daladier, his own opposite number, Campinchi, and Georges Mandel, Minister for the Colonies. He gave his opinions of the visit to the British Ambassador, Sir Eric Phipps, in a letter on 20 April: 'On one subject I found them all inclined to take the same view, namely the unimportance of friendship with Italy. They argue that when the time comes she will pursue her own interests.' Duff was rather worried to hear Daladier say that the recent Anglo–Italian agreement over Spain had saved Mussolini from disaster; as he told Phipps, 'I do hope he won't say that to our P.M. Neither the P.M. nor Edward Halifax know much about the French ... Daladier might do infinite harm.'[17]

The omens for any Anglo–French staff talks were hardly good.

When the Committee of Imperial Defence (CID) had met just before Easter to discuss the question of giving some concrete effect to Chamberlain's statement in the Commons, there had been an obvious reluctance to commit British troops to the Continent. Chamberlain had the nerve to argue that the army was too small to play any significant role there anyway; Duff managed to restrain himself from telling the Prime Minister who was responsible for this state of affairs, but did point out that the French would hardly be reassured if they knew that they could expect no Continental commitment from the British. Chamberlain's reply, that he had never been 'dogmatic' about whether to send a force to the Continent or not, has been well described by the official historian as 'disingenuous'.[18] But there had been no commitment to staff talks on this basis. Duff hardly felt that Anglo–French relations were in any fit state to admit of firm action being taken against Hitler.

Duff and his First Sea Lord, Chatfield,* made a fresh attempt after Easter to provoke the Cabinet into taking a firm decision on the future of the NSF. Duff made a devastating attack on the whole principle of 'rationing' in a paper which he sent to Chamberlain, Inskip and Simon on 28 April. It was, he pointed out, their first duty to 'ensure the adequate defence of the country'. It was much easier to ascertain what these defences were than to discover what the country's financial resources were, and he thought that 'the danger of underrating the former seems to me greater than the danger of overrating the latter'. After all, he went on, if they made mistakes about what an adequate defence policy was, it could lead to 'defeat in war and complete destruction' whereas a mistake which led to overspending can only lead to 'severe embarrassment, heavy taxation, lowering of the standard of living and reduction of the social services'.[19] A Prime Minister with an election to fight by 1940, and who did not believe that the choice confronting him was this stark, could hardly be won over by such arguments.

Duff had picked out the key point at issue between himself and the Prime Minister. He stated that they faced a choice between altering the 'whole of our social system or the whole of our foreign and imperial policy'. Chamberlain regarded the former as too high a price to pay and hoped to avoid having to pay it by a successful diplomatic policy.

Simon refused to allow Duff's paper to go before the Cabinet. The

* Alfred Ernle Montacute Chatfield (1873–1967).

Treasury were worried about the accuracy of the figures which the navy had presented, and about the way the other Service departments would react if the Admiralty were allowed to 'proceed with their programme without any financial limitation'. When Duff sent a further long memorandum to Simon on 28 May, Chamberlain minuted his copy: 'The same old Admiralty and, I expect, the same old reply from the Treasury.'[20] By this time Duff was inclined to shy away from trying to get a definite decision and to 'rely upon the Treasury being obliged to agree to what we want from time to time as we want it'. The decision of Chamberlain to allow Anglo–French naval talks at staff level seemed the thin end of the wedge for this 'wait and see' policy.

Inskip was alive to this danger and in July he pressed for a definite decision on the NSF, pointing out that financial constraints made it impossible to build.[21] Duff wrote to Hoare on 19 July to seek his support when the matter reached the Cabinet. He gave vent to his feelings about Inskip's role: 'I am sure it was never intended when a Minister for the Co-ordination of Defence was created that our future naval policy should be based upon the opinion of a well-meaning and terribly overworked barrister.' He thought that Inskip's 'lamentable' conclusions had been arrived at 'simply on his study of previous documents' and without any consultation. The problem with Chamberlain's style of government was that ministers were so overworked in their own fields that they did not have 'the time to consider great questions which do not concern their own departments'. Instead they were 'inclined to think that Tom is a very good chap and a very fair-minded man, his opinion must be the last word and that they had better let it go at that'.[22]

Duff and Hoare did manage to increase Inskip's figure of £355 million to £410 million, which was within striking distance of the £433 million the Admiralty had asked for; for this Duff earned praise from his officials. He could feel quietly satisfied as he and Diana set out on the *Enchantress* for a cruise in the Baltic. But if he was expecting it to be better than Cape Wrath had been, then he was wrong.

14

Munich

The name of Duff Cooper will always be associated with Munich. When the name of that treaty and the word 'appeasement' were excoriated then Duff's reputation stood high; a reading of his obituary notices is enough to make that point. But as appeasement has come to enjoy a better press, then so too has Duff's reputation declined. Even so, there can be no doubt that it was the major political event in his career and that it must occupy a prominent place in his biography.

There was little thought of such portentous matters on the *Enchantress* as she sailed the Baltic in August 1938. The most vexing matter for Duff was having to propose a toast to Hitler at Kiel, something which almost induced apoplexy. Dinner with Colonel Beck, the Polish Foreign Minister, at Gdynia, on 8 August was a less trying occasion, at least for Duff; Diana found his drunken boasting rather a bore.[1] But when she, Beck, Brendan Bracken and Liz Paget* all went off to a night-club where there was much pinching of thighs, Duff retired to his cabin, 'the Duff cot', to write home his impressions to the Foreign Secretary, Edward Halifax.

Duff did not think that what Beck had had to say was 'of great importance', but he had been impressed with the man's insistence that it should all be repeated to Whitehall. He had been most emphatic that Poland, like other Baltic powers, wanted to preserve the status quo. Duff pointed out that Britain and France were its main supporters and 'therefore the natural friends of all Powers whose existence depended upon its maintenance'. Duff thought that the main danger to the peace of Europe lay in Hitler, encouraged by his previous successes, taking a 'step, which once taken, he could not withdraw'. It should, therefore, 'in fairness to him and to Germany' be

* The daughter of Diana's sister, Marjorie.

113

'made plain now what forces he would find himself up against'. Duff felt that if it was clear that Germany would have to face the coalition of 1914-18, with America entering the lists at an early stage, there would be no war.[2]

Gdynia was followed by Danzig, a free city by the terms of the Versailles settlement, its administration run by an uneasy combination of a League of Nations Commissioner, Carl Burckhardt, and a Nazi official, Greiser. Burckhardt was one of Diana's great passions, 'a Swiss, a philosopher and an historian', in Duff's words. His mood, according to Duff, was more optimistic than might have been expected, and he even thought 'that the Nazi regime may yet come to a good end'. Forster, the Nazi *gauleiter*, had, according to Burckhardt, been 'very much altered' by his recent visit to England and had begun, like other Nazis, to realize that there were other 'forces in the world besides Nazism and other countries besides Germany'. Duff tended to agree with the British naval attaché, Tom Troubridge, that 'If somebody were to ask Göring over to England and give him a few days' good shooting, you could have him feeding out of your hand for the rest of his life.' He told Halifax that 'Some of these people belong to a world so different from that to which we are accustomed that a real effort of imagination is required if we are to make a successful appeal to them.' There were, however, 'plenty of ominous signs in Germany': the calling up of the reserve and the retention of conscripts for an extra month's training; but these might be 'purely precautionary'. It seemed to Duff unlikely that 'if the Germans had really decided to have a war in the autumn' they would 'give us warning of this intention'.[3]

However, towards the end of August reports were received in London that German troops were massing on the Czech frontier; Chamberlain summoned an emergency Cabinet for 30 August. Duff's cruise was brought to an abrupt end; the crisis which led to Munich had started.

In Chamberlain's eyes the crisis was one about the fate of Czechoslovakia; what had to be found was a solution which would allow Hitler to have the Sudeten Germans and allow the Czechs to keep as much of their self-respect as was compatible with giving in to the Germans. Duff took a wider view. What was at stake was the balance of power in Europe, the Anglo-French entente and British honour. Chamberlain 'was depressed by a total want of confidence in France',[4] and not without reason. Daladier, the French Prime Minister, and his

Foreign Minister, Georges Bonnet, looked, in A. J. P. Taylor's words, 'plaintively to London for some twist which would enable them to escape from their impossible situation'.[5] They had an obligation to defend the Czechs, but saw that they could not fulfil it; to have admitted as much would have been to say that France was no longer a Great Power. The blame would have to rest, or be made to rest, on *La Perfide Albion*. Chamberlain, seeing the problem in these terms, argued that Britain could not help the Czechs. Duff saw things differently. He thought that the French needed their spines stiffening and suspected that Hitler was bluffing; even if he was not, then war now, with morale intact, was better than war later when morale had plummeted. It took time for this gulf to become clear, but there were traces of it at that first Cabinet meeting on 30 August.[6]

Duff wanted the Government to make it clear to Hitler that there would be a general European war if he attacked Czechoslovakia. Halifax and Chamberlain wanted to keep him 'guessing'. Duff's argument that 'we should do everything in our power to make sure that he guessed right' was not accepted. Halifax feared that any warnings from Britain might exacerbate Hitler's anger, while Chamberlain refused to countenance any threats which it might prove difficult to put into action. This remained the only ground of dispute between Duff and the Prime Minister, at least until 25 September.

After the meeting, the Lord Privy Seal, Lord De La Warr, complained to Duff that there seemed to be only 'five bright boys' in the Cabinet. The four who spoke against Chamberlain's intentions at that meeting were the ones who backed Duff throughout the crisis – at least until the final stage; they were: De La Warr, Oliver Stanley (the President of the Board of Trade), Walter Elliot (the Minister of Health), and Lord Winterton (Chancellor of the Duchy of Lancaster). Stanley was Duff's closest friend, but their reasons for not wanting to 'form any sort of group of those who share our opinion' throws a light on the reasons for the ineffectiveness of Chamberlain's opponents: 'those who do are three of the lightest weights in the Cabinet'. Elliot, Winterton and De La Warr were, he told Diana on 13 September, 'more liabilities than assets'.

This was one of the main problems facing Duff during the Munich crisis. De La Warr was a young National Labour peer who carried few votes and even less influence. Winterton, despite having been in the Commons for almost forty years, was still only a junior minister; and few took him as seriously as he took himself. A pompous man, he did not seek to cabal with those who felt uneasy about Chamberlain's policy, and they did not seek to cabal with him. He had hoped to get the War Office in 1935 and felt a certain coolness towards the man who had got the post. Nor were Walter Elliot and Oliver Stanley of much heavier calibre. Both were hampered by their reputation of being rising young men who had not lived up to expectations. Duff was the only one of the doubters with a large government department behind him, but he was not regarded as a political heavyweight. Even had they caballed together it is doubtful whether the dissentients would have achieved much; but they never even managed to do that. They were never anything more than individuals with doubts about Chamberlain's policy; to call them a 'group' within the Cabinet would be a misleading description.

Like most political problems, the Munich crisis appears simpler to historians in retrospect than it did to the participants at the time. With the knowledge that the war was to come in 1939, it is easy to say that the dissenters should have banded together and opposed Chamberlain at all costs; but the temptation to do so should be resisted. It was not easy to oppose a leader as autocratic as Neville Chamberlain. He had not only the advantages of being leader of the Conservative Party and Prime Minister, but also of having popular opinion on his side. No one wanted war, and he offered an honourable way of preserving the peace. It is sometimes, regrettably, necessary to sacrifice people in a far-away country in order to avoid war; the British public was not expected to make any material sacrifices. All that Duff and those who thought like him could offer was an appeal to honour, and public opinion shared Falstaff's view:

> What is honour? a word. What is that word, honour? ... Who hath it? he that died o' Wednesday.... Therefore I'll none of it: honour is a mere scutcheon.*

Duff and the others were also hampered by the fact that they thought Chamberlain a good Prime Minister – and far preferable to an Opposition which hankered after disarmament.

Duff thought that Hitler was bluffing and that his bluff must be called. In Cabinet on 12 September he pointed out that intelligence reports indicated that Hitler would be unable to go to war before 22 September and argued in favour of delivering a firm warning. But Chamberlain felt, then and later, that any such warning would actually

* *Henry IV, Part 1*, Act 5, Scene 1.

cause a war. This remained the essential difference between Duff and his leader.

Chamberlain had his own plans, aimed at outflanking both his critics and Hitler. In Cabinet on 13 September he seemed to agree with Duff that a dramatic gesture was needed. But he did not intend the sort of action Duff imagined. The following day it was announced that the Prime Minister was going to fly to Berchtesgaden to meet Hitler and put to him proposals for a solution of the Czech crisis. Duff, and those who thought like him, were caught off-guard. Duff feared lest the Germans, by accepting a plan which the Czechs might reject when they saw it, should gain a moral advantage; but there was no gainsaying Chamberlain's pluck.

While the Prime Minister was meeting Hitler and offering him Britain's support in persuading the Czechs to hold a plebiscite in the Sudetenland, his critics had a chance to mull over the implications of his dramatic *démarche*.

Winterton thought that they should all resign. Stanley, increasingly dejected, was 'much occupied as to what was the minimum we could stand upon'. Duff expressed his views thus, in a letter to Kakoo Rutland on 15 September:

> There are now only three horses left in the race: 1. Peace with Honour; 2. Peace with dishonour; 3. Bloody war. I don't think that no. 1 has an earthly. The other two are neck and neck. If I were betting I should transfer my money continually from one to the other – and I'm not quite sure which I want to win. But if no. 2 wins the Derby you can safely back no. 3 for the Leger.[7]

In the meantime, as the 'world tumbles into ruins', he determined to 'try to keep a gay heart and enjoy what is left of it'.

When the Cabinet met on 17 September to hear Chamberlain's report, it became apparent that his tactic of personal diplomacy carried risks as well as promising political dividends. It was one of his supporters, Inskip, and not Duff, who recorded in his diary:

> The impression made by the PM's story was a little painful.... The PM said more than once to us that he was just in time. It was plain that Hitler had made all the running: he had in fact blackmailed the PM.[8]

Duff, and others, concurred with Inskip. Chamberlain had not even put the pre-arranged proposals to Hitler and seemed ominously impressed by Hitler's threats of violence if the British could not get the Czechs to agree to his demands.

The relative failure of the Prime Minister opened the way for a prolonged debate in the afternoon's Cabinet; a debate in which he received little support. Lord Maugham, the Lord Chancellor, tried to argue that it was an essential principle of British diplomacy never to intervene unless she could bring overwhelming force to bear. This met with an angry response from Duff, who contended that Britain had to maintain the balance of power in Europe – by force if need be: 'if we held to the Lord Chancellor's doctrine of defeatism it meant that we could never intervene again, that we were in fact finished'. But although Duff criticized Chamberlain for trusting Hitler's promises, he was not willing to go so far as to reject the proposal that the Government should try to persuade the Czechs to accept the German ultimatum.

Chamberlain, who had been expecting Duff to follow his argument to its logical conclusion, was surprised. But, as Duff explained, war was such an horrific prospect that he was willing to go along with the Prime Minister's scheme, if only as a means of postponing conflict. It might be, he said, that in the interval 'some internal event' would 'bring about the fall of the Nazi regime'. But Duff warned that there were 'limits to the humiliation I was prepared to accept', and he insisted that Hitler should be brought to hold a plebiscite 'under fair conditions'. When Inskip said that he 'doubted whether there was any essential difference' between Duff and Chamberlain, Duff responded that he 'hoped this was so'. But he argued that a strong line ought to be pressed on the French who should be told that 'we would fight rather than agree to an abject surrender'.

Duff feared that Chamberlain intended to encourage the French in their obvious desire to shuffle out of their obligations towards Czechoslovakia. In fact, as he soon discovered, things had got beyond even that.

When the Cabinet met on 19 September, after Chamberlain had had a chance to talk with the French, its members were told that Daladier and Bonnet were clearly looking to Britain as a future scapegoat, seeking to make the British responsible for persuading the poor Czechs to give in to Hitler. Chamberlain said that he had avoided falling into this trap, but had suggested that Britain might join France in a guarantee of Czech territorial integrity once the Sudeten question was out of the way. With some grumbling and reluctance, Duff and his associates accepted the idea. They would have agreed with the Permanent Under-Secretary at the Foreign Office, Sir Alexander

Cadogan: 'We must go on being cowards up to our limit but *not beyond*.'[9]

For the moment, Duff's money was on 'peace with dishonour'. But this meant that the decencies of international behaviour should be observed. When Chamberlain saw Hitler to give him the news of the Cabinet's decision, he must make clear to him that German troops could not be allowed into most of the Sudetenland until after a plebiscite had been held. As he said in Cabinet on 21 September when taking part in a discussion about what Chamberlain should say to Hitler:

> He should say he had done all and more than all that he had undertaken, that he was bringing him Czechoslovakia's head on a charger, and that in order to do this he had incurred charges of surrender, betrayal and cowardice. Further he could not go. He would prefer, if it were necessary, to go to war.

There were no dissentient voices.

While Chamberlain flew to Bad Godesberg, all differences of opinion could be submerged in the hope that he would be successful. This proved impossible upon his return. Once more Chamberlain's report shocked even his supporters within the Cabinet. He told his colleagues on 24 September that Hitler had been totally intransigent: if the Czechs did not unconditionally agree to all his demands by 28 September, he would take what he wanted by force. To Duff's horrified amazement Chamberlain proposed that they should accept this, saying that he had won Hitler's respect and did not think he would 'deliberately deceive a man whom he respected'.

Duff told his colleagues that in place of the two options he had thought open to them there now appeared a third – 'war with dishonour'. He foresaw 'the boot of public opinion' kicking the Government into war 'when those for whom we were fighting had already been defeated'. He warned Chamberlain that they would all have to answer for the failure to mobilize the armed forces, a course of action already suggested by the Chiefs of Staff. The Prime Minister replied angrily that that advice had been given only 'on the assumption that there was a danger of war with Germany in the next few days'. Astonished by this, Duff riposted that 'it would be difficult to deny that any such danger existed'.

It had been with some reluctance that the Cabinet had swallowed the proposal to persuade the Czechs to agree to Hitler's Berchtesgaden proposals; it became clear when its members reassembled on the morning of 25 September that the dictator's new demands stuck in the throat.

Throughout the crisis Chamberlain had been able to rely on the support of his senior colleagues, but now the most important of them broke ranks. Lord Halifax, the Foreign Secretary, said that he 'thought he could not advise the Czechs to accept the ultimatum'. 'This', Duff recorded, 'came as a great shock to those who think as I do.' To an exhausted Chamberlain it came as a 'horrible blow'.[10]

Where Halifax led, other Cabinet Ministers followed. Chamberlain held the view that the crisis had to be decided around the military realities of the situation; if Hitler attacked the Czechs, there was nothing Britain could do to help. For Duff it was a moral issue. If Hitler's overt aggression won the day, that would be the end of the rule of law in international relations. In such a situation there 'was no time to weigh out one's strength too carefully'. It was no longer a matter of whether the Sudeten Germans should have the right of self-determination, nor even of how that right was to be exercised – 'it was the honour and the soul of England which were at stake'.

In the face of what might easily become a Cabinet revolt, Chamberlain reacted with great skill. He took his stand on the fact that Britain had no obligations to Czechoslovakia and could, therefore, bring no pressure to bear. He 'admired', he said, 'the logic' of Duff's view, but did not agree that they should tell the Czechs to reject Hitler's proposals. He argued that Britain could give the Czechs no advice; all that could be done was to place the 'full facts' squarely before them.

In Duff's view this was sophistical gerrymandering. It was important to get together with the French to concert policy. He deplored the fact that those who 'thought as I do' never seemed to be a party to conversations with the French. He said that it seemed as though his dissent only prolonged argument and 'I therefore felt that it was better that I should go, because my continued presence in the Cabinet was only a source of delay and annoyance to those who thought differently from me.' The official Cabinet minutes contain no mention of Duff's offer; it was not accepted; nor was it rejected.

The Cabinet met for the third time that Sunday at 11.30 p.m. to hear what Daladier and Bonnet had had to say to Chamberlain. Duff was disgusted with Chamberlain's refusal to stiffen the French by telling them that, if they found themselves in a war because they had advised the Czechs to reject Hitler's demands, they would receive the support of Britain. He was 'pretty offensive' to Chamberlain, who hotly denied any such intention.

Duff prepared to resign. To his amazement Chamberlain, instead of saying that Hitler's demands must be accepted, concluded with the remark that he intended to make one last personal appeal to the dictator. He would send a letter by means of his chief adviser, Sir Horace Wilson. In it he would propose that a commission should be set up to decide the details for the transference of the Sudetenland to Germany. He would authorize Wilson to tell Hitler that unless this demand was accepted France would go to war – and where France went, Britain would follow.

Duff was stunned; it was 'a complete reversal of what the Prime Minister himself had advised. Yet none of the "yes men" who had supported his policy all day said a word of criticism on its reversal.'

When the Cabinet heard on the following morning that Daladier was entirely satisfied with Chamberlain's policy, Duff felt that he could now withdraw his offer of resignation as he was 'in entire agreement with the policy now adopted'. He had felt sorry for Chamberlain the previous night, so tired had the Prime Minister looked. Now that there was no question of 'war with dishonour', Duff felt able to apologize for his 'forcible' presentation of his own case. He told Chamberlain that if, after discussions with the leaders of the Labour Party, it was felt desirable to 'broaden the basis of his Government, I, for one, should be very glad to serve him in any subordinate position or to continue to support him as a private MP'.

However, the events of 26 and 27 September gave rise to renewed doubts in Duff's mind. In the first place, despite what he had said in Cabinet, Chamberlain did put pressure on the Czechs to give in to Hitler. Then there was his broadcast on the evening of the 26th when he spoke about Czechoslovakia as a 'far-away country', and the quarrel over the Sudetenland as one between 'peoples of whom we know nothing'. Duff agreed with Churchill that 'the whole tone of the speech showed plainly that we were preparing to scuttle'. He had been cheered by news that Chamberlain intended to accept his advice and announce the mobilization of the Fleet; but no such thing happened. Worse was to come.

During the Cabinet meeting on the evening of 27 September, Sir Horace Wilson reported that he had not delivered his message to Hitler at once, and even when he had done so, it had been bedecked with caveats. Duff was furious and spoke up before any of the senior

Cabinet Ministers could do so, this on the ground that they would agree with Chamberlain 'and thus influence the "yes men" who are the majority of the Cabinet'.

Duff attacked Chamberlain's whole attitude: his defeatism in placing credence only in depressing reports while rejecting any hopeful signs; his depressing speeches and his pharisaical policy of saying that although we could put no 'pressure' on the Czechs, we could 'put before them' the suggestion that the best way of avoiding bloodshed was to announce that although they would not accept Hitler's demands, they would offer no resistance to his armies. For Duff it was a matter of honour: 'If we were now to desert the Czechs, or even advise them to surrender, we should be guilty of one of the basest betrayals in history.' If the Cabinet gave way now:

> I was going to say that it would be the end of England and of democracy, but I didn't really believe that. What I did believe was that it might be the end of the Government and that it would certainly be the end of my connection with it.

But Duff's anger could do little to influence Chamberlain. Once more it was Halifax who did that. He said that he had already secured French consent to a new plan which was being put forward in Berlin and Prague. Under these proposals, the timetable of the German occupation would be brought forward, which would at least preserve the illusion that the Czechs were not yielding to force. In the face of Halifax's opposition Chamberlain backed down; there now seemed no alternative to war.

By the end of the meeting Duff had calmed down enough to apologize to Chamberlain for criticizing his speeches; he had done so, he explained, because of his disappointment that the mobilization of the Fleet had not been announced. Chamberlain agreed that there was no longer any point in keeping it secret. The moment Duff got out of 10 Downing Street he dashed home to telephone the news to the press section of the Admiralty. It was in all the papers on the morning of 28 September – the day Hitler's deadline expired.

15

Resignation

The mood in the chamber was tense when the Commons assembled on the afternoon of 28 September; many expected to hear that war had been declared. Chamberlain embarked on a long explanation of his policies and said that he had done all that any man could to avoid war. As he approached his peroration, Duff saw a commotion to the side of him as a piece of paper was passed to the Prime Minister. There was a brief pause as Simon said something to him, and then Chamberlain made the announcement which brought most Members to their feet as they waved their order papers and cheered: 'I have now been informed by Herr Hitler that he invites me to meet him at Munich tomorrow morning'; war was off. 'Thank God for the Prime Minister,' shouted one back-bencher, and most of the House concurred. Even Duff felt, for the first time since the crisis began, that 'there will not be a war'.[1]

At the time, and later, there were many, including Duff himself, who attributed Hitler's action to the news of the mobilization of the Fleet. But it seems clear that Hitler could not have received this information until after he had despatched his letter and that he was, in fact, responding to Wilson's warning.[2] Either way, it is a vindication of Duff's belief that Hitler could be brought to see reason only by standing up to him.

Early on the morning of 29 September Duff joined his colleagues at Heston to see Chamberlain off to Munich; it was his last act of solidarity with them.

By evening, the tensions of the day had built up to a point where men who disagreed with Chamberlain could scarcely talk to those who agreed with him. At a meeting of the Other Club at the Savoy, tempers raged to the point at which even the 'rancour and asperity of party politics' passed the bounds of civilized behaviour.[3]

News from Munich was eagerly sought, but what little there was of it depressed Duff, who reflected that 'we might as well have accepted the Godesberg ultimatum and have done with it'. It seemed to him as though the honour of England was being sold – and the price was a paltry one. Sir Colin Coote, who was at the Other Club that night, wrote that nobody could forget it as long as he lived. Duff was 'choleric', and well he might have been, as Churchill denounced the Government of which he was still a member. There were arguments in Chamberlain's favour, and Duff used them; but his heart was not in it; temper bursting out he

> insulted Professor Lindeman, Bob Boothby and I insulted Garvin so that he left in a rage. Then everybody insulted everybody else and Winston ended by saying that at the next General Election he would speak on every Socialist platform in the country against the Government.

Boothby felt that the crisis was, in its 'simplest, crudest and ultimate form', a conflict between 'Reason and Force, Civilization and Barbarism' and he sympathized with Duff in his predicament. The argument raged until the early editions of the morning papers were brought in: they contained the terms of the Munich agreement; Boothby recalled that 'Duff Cooper flushed, but said nothing until he whispered in my ear: "I shall resign tomorrow morning."'

In fact Duff did not finally make up his mind until he was dressing later that morning, but he had felt 'at first sight' that he 'could not agree' to the Munich terms. They maintained the 'principle of invasion'; the Czechs were not to be allowed to depart under cover of the fiction that they did so of their own accord. It was a victory for force and for barbarism. Duff went to the Cabinet on 30 September determined to resign.

By the time the Cabinet met that evening, Duff knew that if he resigned he would go alone, and he was content that it should be so; as he told Elliot, who made a half-hearted offer to resign with him: 'It would be better for me to go alone, as I had no wish to injure the Government.' De La Warr and Stanley both decided that they could do better work inside the Cabinet than outside.

As he pushed his way through cheering crowds to Downing Street, Duff felt 'strangely lonely', unable to share in the general rejoicing. Like Sir Robert Walpole, he felt that 'They are ringing the bells now, but tomorrow they will be wringing their hands.'

After listening to Chamberlain's exposition of the differences between Godesberg and Munich, Duff began to waver in his resolve. The differences seemed to be greater than he had thought, but he still felt uneasy, fearing that this would be merely the prelude to further German aggression. He said that while he agreed with those who wanted more time to study the terms and was willing to 'defer a final statement of his position' until then, 'he had come to the meeting prepared to resign and that he still felt it was his duty to offer the Prime Minister his resignation'. Chamberlain said that they could discuss the matter privately, and when Stanley and Hore-Belisha tried to raise a discussion, Hoare

> intervened rather crossly. He said it was most improper and quite without precedent to discuss private matters of this sort in Cabinet, and he hoped the discussion would not be prolonged. It was odd that he should have said this, considering that last February we spent two days discussing whether Anthony should go or not.

Duff thought that it was 'because he hates me, is anxious to get rid of me and fears that further discussion might lead to my staying on'.

The question of whether or not Duff did try to 'stay on' when he saw Chamberlain on the Monday morning is worth raising only because at least one reputable historian has been misled by a statement to the contrary in A. J. P. Taylor's biography of Lord Beaverbrook.[4] Mr Taylor quotes a 'reminiscence of Duff Cooper's resignation' provided for Beaverbrook by Mike Wardell, one of his minions.* According to Beaverbrook's account Wardell said that

> Duff stayed on at the end of the meeting at Chamberlain's request. Duff was quite conciliatory and said he supposed his threat of resignation would be forgotten. Chamberlain refused saying: 'I am afraid that at this stage that is impossible.' Duff was out.

It would have been very odd if Duff had chosen to repeat this damaging story only once, and then to an employee of a man he detested. Neither Lady Diana nor Lord Boothby believes it; indeed the latter considers that his recollection of the Other Club dinner 'disposes of the story that he tried to remain in the Government'. The story which Duff told in his memoirs was the one that is in his diary. He called on Chamberlain on the morning of 1 October to repeat his offer:

> He had no hesitation in accepting it. He felt as I did that I had long been out of harmony with the direction of foreign policy, and that I was likely

---

* Business manager of the *Evening Standard*.

to continue to be so. We were in complete agreement that I was taking the right course. I was not with him for more than ten minutes.

Mr Taylor has been challenged on several occasions to produce any supporting evidence for his statement, but has always been unable to do so; it is not surprising for there is none.[5] The story sounds like a garbled version of Duff's withdrawal of his resignation on 25 September after Chamberlain backed down over accepting the Godesberg terms, transposed to 1 October in order to do maximum damage to Duff's reputation. It is not one which historians would be well advised to accept. As we have seen, Duff resigned at the end of a long struggle with his own conscience; he would like to have remained in the Government, but he could not.

His letter to the Prime Minister was published in the evening papers on 1 October:

My dear Prime Minister,

It is extremely painful to me in the moment of your great triumph to be obliged to strike a discordant note. For reasons with which you are acquainted and which I propose to explain to the House of Commons in due course, I profoundly distrust the Foreign Policy which the present Government is pursuing and seems likely to pursue. Feeling as I do I have considered that I should offer you my resignation. I do so with profound regret because I have been so proud to hold my present office, the one I envied beyond all others in the state, and I have been so grateful to you for having placed such confidence in me and for having shown me such invariable kindness and patience.

Yours very sincerely
Duff Cooper.[6]

In his reply, Chamberlain expressed the hope that 'differences over public policy will make no breach in our personal relations'; the two men scarcely exchanged another word.

Those who admired Duff and who hated appeasement praised his courage: 'That is fine of him. He has no money and gives up £5,000 a year plus a job he loves', was Harold Nicolson's comment. Those who did not admire Duff, like Alec Cadogan, were more pithy in the expression of their feelings: 'Good riddance of bad rubbish.'

For those who felt that their country's honour had been sullied, Duff's action provided the one source of comfort. As Bob Boothby wrote on 2 October, Duff's resignation 'has already brought a gleam of hope to thousands who have hitherto believed in the fundamental decency of British public life, and who were beginning to despair'.

Oliver Lyttelton, writing the following day, expressed similar sentiments:

> Thank God someone has been found to take a stand against this nerveless folly; some of us who now feel largely humiliation and fear take heart again because we shall have a spokesman. Damn it, peace at this price is not worth buying and retribution will be awful and probably speedy.

Even those who, like Leo Amery, found their 'sentiments and instincts' 'painfully in dispute' with their 'reason', wrote to congratulate Duff. He became a symbol to all those who felt sullied at buying peace with someone else's freedom.

A large number of his White's Club cronies wrote to Duff. Brendan Bracken thought that 'nothing can sully the lustre of your example and sacrifice'. Another staunch anti-appeaser, Lord Lloyd, wrote that

> I can well appreciate how poignantly you will feel this divorce from the direction of almost the greatest office in the state: all the more are those grateful to you for making this stand against what I believe to be a disastrous foreign policy.

Even before Duff made his resignation speech, everyone who opposed Munich, for whatever reason, attributed their own motives to Duff.

The speech which Duff made in the Commons on the afternoon of 3 October left no one in any doubt as to why he had resigned. It was a difficult moment for Duff. The House wanted to hear Chamberlain's report on Munich, and most of its members felt only irritation at the delay. Thus it was that Duff began by asking for the forbearance of the House, assuring his listeners that he had not resigned in order to damage the Government. He outlined the circumstances in which he had resigned, saying that Chamberlain had received the news with 'relief'. Having thus secured a hearing, Duff moved on to his main theme.[7] Bearing in mind the lessons of 1914, he told the House:

> I have always felt that in any other international crisis that should occur our first duty was to make plain exactly where we stood and what we would do. I believe that the great defect in our foreign policy during recent months and recent weeks has been that we have failed to do so.

Indeed, he said, we had done the opposite.

Dealing with the allegation, often repeated during the crisis, that British public opinion would never sanction a war over Czechoslovakia, he attempted to demolish the insularity of the House as he had that of the Cabinet. Britain had not gone to war in 1914 for Belgium or Serbia:

> We were fighting then, as we should have been fighting last week, in order that one great Power should not be allowed, in disregard of treaty obligation, of the laws of nations and the decrees of morality, to dominate by brutal force the Continent of Europe. For that principle we fought against Napoleon Buonaparte, and against Louis xiv of France and Philip ii of Spain. For that principle we must ever be prepared to fight, for on the day when we are not prepared to fight for it we must forfeit our Empire, our liberties and our independence.

One could not ask for a better statement of the classic principle of traditional British foreign policy.

Although it was true that both Chamberlain and Simon had, at different times, warned Hitler that if there was a European war it would be unwise of him to count on British neutrality, Duff did not feel that this was 'the language which the dictators understand'; they spoke the language of 'the headlines of the tabloid press' and such 'guarded, diplomatic and reserved utterances' probably meant 'nothing to the mentality of Herr Hitler and Signor Mussolini'. Whenever he had pressed for the use of more appropriate language Duff had always been told that 'on no account must we irritate Herr Hitler', but:

> It seems to me that he never makes a speech save under the influence of considerable irritation, and the addition of one more irritant would not, I should have thought, made a great difference, whereas the communication of a solemn fact would have produced a sobering effect.

Duff instanced the effect which he thought that the mobilization of the Fleet had had in prompting Hitler's letter to Chamberlain; even if we can now discount this, the substitution of Wilson's message instead makes Duff's point even more valid. This business of how to deal with Hitler had been

> the very deep difference between the Prime Minister and myself throughout these days. The Prime Minister has believed in addressing Herr Hitler through the language of sweet reasonableness. I have believed that he was more open to the language of the mailed fist.

He admitted that he had been prepared to accept the Berchtesgaden terms as a means of avoiding the 'final disaster', but he had always insisted that the territory to be transferred should be done so in a 'normal, civilized manner'. All that Chamberlain's 'sweet reasonableness' had met with was the Godesberg ultimatum. When he had seen that, 'I said to myself, "if these terms are accepted it will be the end of all decency in the conduct of public affairs in the world".'

Although the Munich agreement was, according to the Prime Minister, a great improvement, it was not good enough:

> I spent the greater part of Friday trying to persuade myself that those terms were good enough for me. I tried to swallow them – I did not want to do what I have done – but they stuck in my throat.

To Duff, however much those terms modified Godesberg, they still meant that Czechoslovakia was 'to be invaded' – and that, at least, she should have been spared.

He moved on to deal with Chamberlain's famous piece of paper. Not only had Chamberlain signed it without any consultation with anybody, not only did it bear the signature of a man who had shown that he would dishonour his word whenever it suited him, it was positively dangerous. As part of the Munich settlement Britain had undertaken a commitment to defend Czechoslovakia; to be able to make that effective a 'tremendous quickening up of our rearmament schemes on an entirely new basis' would be necessary. The Continental army which Chamberlain had always opposed would be essential. But how was the Government going to justify the increased expenditure to a country which had just been assured that Hitler would not go to war? Chamberlain thought that Hitler could be trusted; Duff saw nothing in the man's previous history to warrant such optimism.

He had now been speaking, without any notes, for nearly three quarters of an hour. With a slight lowering of the tone of his voice, visibly moved, he reached his peroration:

> The Prime Minister may be right. I can assure you, Mr Speaker, with the deepest sincerity, that I hope and pray that he is right, but I cannot believe what he believes. I wish I could. Therefore, I can be of no assistance to him.... I should be only a hindrance, and it is much better that I should go. I remember when we were discussing the Godesberg ultimatum that I said that if I were a party to persuading, or even to suggesting to, the Czechoslovak Government that they should accept that ultimatum, I should never be able to hold up my head again. I have forfeited a great deal. I have given up an office that I loved, work in which I was deeply interested and a staff of which any man might be proud. I have given up association in that work with my colleagues with whom I have maintained for many years the most harmonious relations, not only as colleagues but as friends. I have given up the privilege of

serving as lieutenant to a leader whom I still regard with the deepest admiration and affection. I have ruined, perhaps, my political career. But that is a little matter; I have retained something which is to me of greater value – I can still walk about the world with my head erect.

As he sat down he received a note from Churchill: 'Your speech was one of the finest parliamentary performances I have ever heard. It was admirable in form, massive in argument and shone with courage and public spirit.'

Following Duff, Chamberlain excused himself from replying to his speech, saying that there would be plenty of time later in the debate; he never answered Duff. As Venetia Montagu wrote on 4 October:

The coroner very wisely said he wasn't going to answer you. I don't believe that he could give one to any single point you made. His faith in Hitler's word would be pathetic if it were not so full of tragic consequences.

Whatever effect Duff's speech had, no one else resigned. Harry Crookshank, who had actually sent in a letter of resignation and then, under pressure, agreed to defer his action, eventually withdrew it after Chamberlain's speech on 6 October.[8] So Duff was the solitary hero of Munich.

For the next month the letters arrived at 90 Gower Street in mailvans; he received well over four thousand from all parts of the world and from all sorts and conditions of men. With a few exceptions they all applauded his action. So heavy was the burden of correspondence that Duff was forced to take on an extra secretary, and John Julius was drafted in to help, soon becoming adept at forging his father's distinctive signature.

Thus it was that Duff severed his connection with the Chamberlain Cabinet. He had not ceased to think that it was a good Government, and he was sure that it was better than any of the probable alternatives; but he could not stomach Munich and its implications. The difference between his position and Chamberlain's was not large, but it was decisive. Duff's action gave Englishmen something to look back to with pride when 'peace with honour' became war with dishonour; this assured him of his place in history.

Lord Cranborne, who had resigned with Eden in February, wrote from his sick-bed to congratulate Duff. Raising the question of timing, he said that there was probably 'no right time to resign', and that choosing to do so 'when the crisis is over and the Government has wriggled through its difficulties' was 'as near a right time as there can be'; he had stood by the Government during the darkest hour and cut the painter only when calm waters had been reached. In so far as the Munich crisis can be said to have had a hero, Duff deserves the title.

～ 16 ～

Seeking Employment

Resigning from the Cabinet is rather like committing suicide; it does not leave much scope for future action. Chamberlain was the hero of the hour and his political position was impregnable. No one, including Duff, wanted to appear in the guise of his enemy; and those who had in any wise opposed him, found themselves facing chill political winds that winter.

Conservative Central Office put pressure on chairmen of local party associations to show their displeasure with potential rebels. Churchill, Lord Cranborne, Richard Law and Duff, all had trouble from their 'local blimps'.[1] Duff had a harder time than most: the 'blimps' were thicker on the ground in St George's; and he was the chief heretic.

His Executive Committee questioned him for over an hour on 11 October, finally passing a resolution recognizing his right to resign, but stating that they were 'in complete agreement with the actions of the Prime Minister' and that as long as Duff remained their MP he was bound to 'direct his efforts and ability to the preservation of unity in the party, and will support the Government, especially in the strengthening of the defences of the country'. They left themselves free to select a new candidate at the next election; Duff was on probation.[2]

This was one of the reasons why he did not come out as a leading opponent of Chamberlain. In retrospect it is clear that, had he done so, his future would have been made, in much the way that Churchill's was. But the most notable feature of the post-Munich political landscape was Chamberlain's dominance and the quietism of his opponents; including Churchill.

Eden, as a former Foreign Secretary, was the chief dissident, and his group, which Duff joined in November, was known to the Whips as 'the glamour boys'; they had taken its measure. Its members decided that we should not advertise ourselves as a group or even call

132

ourselves a group'. It is not thus that a Prime Minister with a parliamentary majority of nearly 300 is toppled. But then there was no intention of doing 'anything rash or violent', and they were careful to distance themselves from Churchill who gave the impression 'of being more bitter than determined, and more out for a fight than for reform'.[3]

If Churchill's stand against appeasement seemed, in retrospect, a solitary one, it was because he was shunned by these more cautious anti-appeasers. After all, they were young enough to have political futures ahead of them and did not want to upset the Party bosses; Churchill was a 'busted flush' with his career behind him and nothing to lose by bitterness. That this would make him Prime Minister in 1940 was a development none could foresee.

The distance between the respectable anti-appeasers and Churchill was quite clear when he attacked the Government in the House on 17 November over the failure to set up a Ministry of Supply. A three-line whip went out, ordering all the Government's supporters to rally to the cause. Duff expressed the dilemma which the 'glamour boys' found themselves in:

> It is quite possible to be a more loyal supporter of the National Government even than ... Mr Churchill ... and yet think that a Ministry of Supply might possibly help them carry out that policy. But if anyone evinces that opinion tonight ... he has immediately committed a crime against the party, the Government and his constituents, and renders himself liable to all the pains and penalties that inevitably ensue.[4]

Which remained true until May 1940 and explains why neither Duff nor Anthony Eden made a good rebel chieftain.

Churchill had been far from happy with the tone of Duff's references to him and wrote to ask if they had been prompted by 'the desire to isolate me as much as possible from the other Conservatives who disagree with the Government?'; which was, despite Duff's denials, not far from the truth.[5]

The *Evening Standard* became the forum for Duff's criticisms of the Government, and very moderately phrased they were too. He was shocked when, in early 1939, two of his former colleagues declined to address a meeting in his constituency, and he went out of his way not to appear contumacious. On 23 December 1938 he had written to Chamberlain:

> It happens that we have not met since I said goodbye to you in Downing Street on October 1st. I don't want this season to pass without wishing

you and Mrs Chamberlain a very happy Christmas. I have tried since I left office, to say and write nothing which would make your heavy task more difficult and would be in any way offensive. If I have failed, I hope you will attribute it to my constitutional lack of discretion which you know so well.[6]

Nor was he the only anti-appeaser anxious to remain on the right side of the Prime Minister. It was with evident satisfaction that Chamberlain told his sister Ida on 12 March:

All the Prodigal Sons are fairly besieging the parental door. You may have seen Winston's eulogies as reported in the Saturday press. Anthony loses no opportunity of letting me know how cordially he approves the Government policy. Duff Cooper is loud in his praises.[7]

It was not until after the Germans occupied Prague on 15 March that Chamberlain's position began to look at all vulnerable, and even then he moved quickly to strike the right note of warning. The resources of Birmingham diplomacy were far from exhausted; Chamberlain was a formidable politician and, whatever fury Duff and others felt, they had neither an alternative to offer nor a hope of getting into office.

Duff's thinking on foreign policy underwent, however, some interesting changes under the impact of these events; changes pregnant with consequence for his post-war career. In the first place he came to see the importance of both the Soviet Union and America. Writing to the British Ambassador in Paris, Sir Eric Phipps, Duff expressed the view that 'If, in the face of the real and terrible German danger, all our efforts are to be paralysed by the imaginary Bolshevik bogey ... then indeed I feel inclined to despair.'[8] And as his policy towards Russia shed any ideological bias, so his policy towards Italy acquired one. He wrote to Halifax in March 1939 stressing the need to present British policy in 'moral terms' in order to win American support; this meant, he thought, abandoning the *realpolitik* approach he had thus far favoured towards Mussolini.[9]

If, in this respect, his thinking was becoming geared to what would prove to be the demands of war, other aspects of it reveal even greater foresight. In his articles in the *Standard* (published in 1939 by Cape as *The Second World War*), in speeches in Paris, and in a pamphlet co-authored with that curious half-Austrian, half-Japanese visionary, Count Coudenhove-Kalergi, Duff propounded the merits of 'pan-Europism'.[10] He advocated an Anglo–French alliance not merely as a way of stopping Nazism, but also as the first step towards the union of Western Europe; only in this way would the countries of Europe be able to maintain their influence in a world that was bound to be dominated by the burgeoning power of America and Russia. It was an idea that had few takers in 1939, but one with which Duff persevered and which became the central theme of his political life as well as the inspiration behind his most constructive diplomatic achievement.

The outbreak of war in September found him still without gainful political employment. Churchill, in the Cabinet as First Lord of the Admiralty (but dispensing with Diana's dolphin furniture), wrote to Chamberlain on 29 September suggesting that Duff might be made Chairman of the British Council, adding that 'he is very unhappy at being without any task at this time of general effort'.[11] But the Prime Minister rated Duff's abilities no higher than he had done three years before, and no post came his way.[12]

It was in these circumstances, after toying with the idea of rejoining his old regiment, that Duff decided to take up a long-standing invitation to lecture in America. He was aware that there would be those who would accuse him of running away, but, with the 'phoney war' in full swing, there did not seem much to run away from. He consulted Churchill and other political friends, who all urged him to go. Chamberlain sent a message asking him to refrain from making 'propaganda' – a request he found no difficulty in ignoring.[13]

Duff and Diana set off on their American tour in September 1939. For her it was an opportunity to revisit old haunts; for him, a chance to put Britain's case to the most important neutral country: for both it proved a successful trip.

His first speaking engagement was on 28 November in New York City. There he spoke about the causes of the war and the necessity of civilization defending itself from barbarism; it was a constant theme in his lectures. In quick succession he visited Boston, Toronto, Cincinnati, Chicago and Ohio, speaking at a series of dining-clubs, universities and civic forums. Addressing New Yorkers at the Brooklyn Hall on 13 December he spoke about 'The survival of liberty', while outside protesters demanded he be returned to England. Duff's response to them was crisp: 'No doubt those stupid young people were well paid for carrying the banners,' and he added that he could not help but recall occasions in Russia and Germany and Italy when young persons carried bludgeons and weapons to 'prevent free expression'.

135

Such protests were, however, uncommon. Both Duff and the organizers of the tour were delighted with the generally favourable reaction, which was evidenced in requests for extra lectures. Few of these requests could match the eloquence of the 'Lord Mayor of Amarillo':

> Amarillonians all worked up over your visit with us tomorrow evening and I as Lord Mayor (please understand folks here usually say 'My God here comes the Mayor') respectfully extend to you a Panhandle welcome – than which there is no other quite so hospitable. And the large crowd who will gather for your talk here will contain the highest *per capita* of intelligent Americans of any similar number in any other spot on the North American Continent or Europe too for that matter, so I extend to you and your gracious help-meet a goodwill that I know will be exemplified here tomorrow evening in such a manner that Amarillo and the Panhandle will always hold a favourable position in your memoirs.[14]

Alas, the Amarillo Knife and Fork Club provided only another rubber-chicken dinner – as well as the inevitable reporters.

As Duff and Diana were in America to fly the flag, publicity was welcome – but they could have wished that American journalists were other than they were. The variations on Duff's name became progressively weirder the further west he went. Greeted in New York as 'Former Sea-Chief' Lord Duff-Cooper, or as 'War Lord in City', he became 'Albert Duff-Cooper' in Ohio, and 'Lord Alfred Duff-Cooper' in Topeka. Then there was Diana – who was always said to be knitting socks for the soldiers. Worst of all was the reporting of their arrival. New York had 'Widely-known Britons pass through City' as the headline with a report which began, quite unbelievably:

> How about this gent Hitler, anyway? Is he going to twist the Lion's tail? 'Pfoof ... pfoof!' So emitted no less an authority than the Right Honourable Alfred (Duff to the press boys) Cooper ... when he stepped off a New York gas train ... and ran smack into a Siegfried line of local reporters and cameramen.

The reporter described him as 'groomed almost to the point of severity' and went on to retail his ordeal by flash bulb. So it was in every town and city. The *Seattle Sunday Times* had a picture of 'Ex-War Lord and wife' being greeted by the local British consul which would have done service in any police 'wanted' posters: Duff, looking as though he is suffering from terminal toothache is shooting a crooked smile at his hosts who are grimacing back, while Diana is looking at them as

though she does not believe what she is seeing. A Santa Barbara
newspaper had Diana, in floppy hat, summer frock and mink, with a
'come-hither' look on her face and Duff, seated beside her in pin-
stripe suit, looking lost. But the prize for the most intrusive photograph must be shared between the *South Bend Tribune*, which had
'British Lord and Lady in South Bend' holding hands and smiling
sweetly, and the *Kansas City Star*, which has Duff in his dressing-gown
looking (unsurprisingly) coy, and Diana, with her knitting, looking
winsome. She was, the *Star* assured its readers, 'a devoted wife', and
Duff's testimonial as reported will bear quotation: 'She does all the
packing, knows where everything is, is the best business manager I've
ever heard of. I guarantee I'd leave shirts and cravats from coast to
coast if it weren't for Di.'

The compensations for all this were considerable. The same papers
that published gushing accounts by their gossip columnists also
printed Duff's speeches. He developed on this tour the ideas about
European federation which had been such a feature of his articles in
the *Standard*; the Americans gave them a warm welcome. He also had
the satisfaction of feeling that, in preaching the British cause, he was
being a sight more useful than he would have been sitting on the
back-benches of the Commons: he also made $15,000. It was this last
point, one suspects, which prompted British criticisms.

Alfred Edwards, Labour MP for Middlesborough East, called Duff
a 'menace' and said that Chamberlain 'ought to bring him back and
put him in a concentration camp'. The Foreign Office, while less
inclined to totalitarian measures than socialist MPs, did find the idea
of Duff telling the Americans that Hitler would launch an offensive
into Belgium in the spring too much, especially when accompanied
by the forecast that Churchill would then become Prime Minister:
'The sooner he comes home the better for us. But how pleasant to
earn so many dollars with so little effort,' minuted one official in
January.[15] The hostess, Mrs Ronnie Greville, wrote to the Chairman
of the St George's constituency organization to protest about Duff's
absence and his dereliction of duty. His response, when he learnt that
it had been read at a meeting of the executive, was pugnacious: 'I am
doing far more useful work addressing sixty meetings than by asking
questions in the House of Commons.' As for Mrs Greville, not only
was she not a constituent, she was not even a Conservative, having
refused to help in the 1931 by-election; she was, moreover, a German-
ophile and was thus 'naturally disappointed at the turn of events and

feels resentment against those like myself whose prognostications proved correct'.

Duff was longing to serve England and was glad to have something to do, but there were times when his frustration at being excluded from the real war effort showed. The *Boston Evening Transcript* noted on 28 November 1939 that he looked 'a little weary', and when asked what he would do when he returned to England he 'murmured something about its being twenty years since the last war and his being nearly fifty. The subject was dropped.' What he heard from England was no encouragement.

Bobbety Cranborne, one of the staunchest of anti-appeasers, described the parliamentary scene in early February 1940: 'The House of Commons goes on very much as usual. The black sheep still seem to be regarded as rather black, though Winston and Anthony are white as driven snow.' Any criticism of 'the leader', who was (according to the Chief Whip) 'the most open-minded of men', was frowned upon, although there were hopes that 'hatchets are being buried'. Cranborne's impression was that the Government would alter the Cabinet 'as soon as they could do so without anyone suggesting that they had taken advice from outside': 'They are getting more and more Japanese. Their faces have continually to be saved – though alas only too often at the National expense.'

Churchill, whom he had just seen at The Other Club, had seemed 'dreadfully tired' by his triple burden of the Admiralty, the Cabinet and the Commons, but had 'picked up under the influence of dinner'. The latest 'Winston story' was that: 'he is said to have sent for his typist the other evening and said to her: "I shall want you all night tonight – I'm feeling very fertile."' But he and Eden had been taken in as individuals. There was still no place for other dissidents. As Brendan Bracken reported, although 'the coroner' (Chamberlain) was 'gout-ridden', his *eminence grise*, Sir Horace Wilson, was well: 'So our affairs remain in sound hands.' As long as they remained in those hands there was no place for Duff.

He returned to England in early March to find that Bracken had been correct when describing London as 'fast becoming the Non-conformist's dream' with 'Jermyn Street deserted', 'Bond Street a distressed area', the theatres 'near bankruptcy' and 'good booze' becoming 'as scarce as radium'. Thus it was that, in Bracken's words: 'A peace and pleasure-loving generation' braced themselves 'to a brave endurance of sufferings and to the acceptance of what is almost as

bad, a long period of life without grace or amusement'.[16] Duff longed
to do his proper part.

The only task which fell to him was to deputize for Churchill at
the annual dinner of the Royal Society of St George on 23 April: 'To
substitute for Mr Churchill proposing the toast of England is almost
too much for any man', he told his audience – thus breaking the ice
caused by the non-appearance of the great man. It was one of his best
speeches. He did not hide his feelings: 'My love of my country admits
of no limitations, makes no concessions, allows of no exceptions.' His
voice became a little husky as he confessed that his love of England
was 'not a calm, cool, rational emotion – it is what true love should
be – blind, prejudiced and passionate'. The audience loved it – but
applause was no substitute for action.[17]

It was not until the Commons met to debate the failure of the
Norwegian campaign on 7 May that it became clear that 'the
Coroner's' days were numbered. The Government which had survived
so many storms found itself facing one of unparalleled vigour. Lloyd
George at last paid off old scores by telling Chamberlain that, having
talked to the Nation about making sacrifices, his best sacrifice would
be to surrender the seals of office. Most devastating of all was the
speech made by Chamberlain's fellow Birmingham MP, Leo Amery,
who hurled at him Cromwell's words to the Long Parliament: 'You
have sat too long here for any good you have been doing. Depart I
say, and let us have done with you. In the name of God, go.'

Neville Chamberlain responded with that appeal to party loyalty
which is the last refuge of the Prime Minister who has run out of
arguments. He appealed to his 'friends' to support the Government.
Much ink has been spilt by his apologists purporting to prove that he
did not mean what he said, but Duff, who spoke straight after him,
had no doubts. He resented Chamberlain's appeal and declared that
though he did not relish voting against the Government, this was no
time to imitate Pontius Pilate. He announced his intention of voting
against Chamberlain. He would have agreed with a later speaker
who, quoting from a sermon deploring the respectability of Christian-
ity, said: 'What we want are some more cads like the Apostles.'[18]

But, when the Government majority sank to only eighty-one on
8 May, and when Chamberlain finally left 10 Downing Street on
10 May, 'the cads like the Apostles' failed to come into their own.
Churchill came to the highest office, but he did so trammelled by the
fact that the largest party in the Commons, the Conservatives, still

supported Chamberlain as leader. Moreover, he came to power at the head of a genuinely national government, and Labour ministers had to be given jobs. Thus it was that there was little in the way of potage to be doled out to those who had been 'black sheep'. Eden went to the War Office and Duff was offered the post of Minister of Information. At the time it seemed like the answer to his fervent wish of nine months – he was at last able to serve his country. But those whom the gods wish to destroy they first grant them their wish: he could have said, with the Ancient Mariner, 'The albatross around my neck was hung.'

～ 17 ～

Minister of Morale

With queens, ambassadors and Kenneth Clark
Reith sank dishonoured to the outer dark,
And Duff interprets all that England means
With Kenneth Clark, ambassadors and queens.

Thus Sir Maurice Bowra 'On the reform of a Ministry'.[1] If this is taken to imply that all that had changed was the person who was Minister of Information, it is accurate, as well as witty. Reith was moved because Churchill had little time for him, and Duff was given the job on the assumption that as a good speaker and a man of letters it was the sort of thing he would do well. This was not altogether inaccurate. He made an impact as a radio broadcaster and did his best to 'interpret all that England means'; but his efforts, although excellent, were inevitably thrown into the shade by the inspirational speeches of Churchill. But there was more to the job of Minister of Information than boosting morale. The Ministry of Information (MOI) was a new creation and lacked both direction and clear functions; Duff attempted to deal with these problems, but administration was never his strongest suit.

He came to his new post just as the war was turning badly against the Anglo–French alliance, which made his task all the more difficult. It is easy enough to be propaganda supremo when things are going well and all the news is good; telling the people good news is one sure way of enhancing a political reputation. Alas for Duff, during the period he occupied that position, he had nothing but a diet of almost unrelieved gloom to offer; the hungry sheep looked up and were fed stones.

His bellicose nature was, however, well suited to rally morale at such a dark hour. In his very first broadcast on 13 May he struck

141

what were to be the characteristic notes of his style: praise for Churchill; condemnation for those 'locust years' of appeasement; and an appeal to the great historic traditions of the English race:

> Now once again Great Britain is facing a fearful danger; but our hearts are firm and our courage high. We have defeated more formidable foes in the past though we have never fought with one so barbarous, so brutal, so utterly bereft of humanity, decency or honour. In English history the hour has ever brought forth the man.... The present crisis has already produced Winston Churchill, who the people of this country believe will prove equal to the high task which awaits him now.

It was in like fashion that when the news of the fall of France came he went to the microphone and read Macaulay's *The Armada*. His deep sense of history combined with his robust patriotism to make him sure of victory, but it may be doubted whether reading Macaulay was of very much use in arousing the morale of the mass of the public, many of whom can have had little idea what he was going on about. Perhaps this was the sort of thing Kenneth Clark had in mind when he wrote that 'with his graceful intelligence and his low opinion of the "common man"', Duff was almost less qualified than Reith for his post.[2]

But if he was occasionally guilty of being too 'literary', if his style sometimes had too much of *The Times* flavour about it for a mass-audience, Duff could switch quite effectively to a more populist tone; the problem was that when he did so he was accused of being 'vulgar'; and when he was more 'elevated', he was said to be 'out of touch'.

When Italy entered the war on 10 June, Duff gave full vent to the indignation which many people felt at these 'jackal-tactics'. He called Mussolini a coward and prophesied that the only result of Italian intervention would be 'to increase the number of ruins for which Italy has so long been famous'. There was, he told his listeners, something rather cheering about the news, for whatever qualities the Italians possessed, these did not include martial prowess: 'we know we can never fail to defeat them soundly on the field of battle'. This piece of 'Eyetie-bashing' went down well in the popular press and with public opinion. Other, more elevated circles were not so happy.

The Queen of Bulgaria protested to the British Ambassador about the use of such language by a Minister of the Crown, and Lord Simon, the Lord Chancellor, complained to Churchill.[3] The Prime Minister wrote to Duff on 12 June to chide him gently – and received a strong answer. The Queen of Bulgaria was, after all, an Italian, and Lord Simon, although not an Italian, had, as Sir John Simon, been one of the 'men of Munich'; Duff was not going to accept rebukes from such quarters as these.

Duff warned Churchill that 'the Munich spirit is not dead in this country'. It was, he thought, significant that the only Labour MP who had protested about the broadcast, Mr McLaren, had also been the solitary socialist who 'definitely and violently supported the Munich Agreement'. The 'Munich spirit' at its worst 'degenerates into treason', Duff wrote, but was more commonly manifested in the belief that 'you can defeat your enemies by kind words and courtesy'. If, he concluded, they had to tailor their remarks to suit the Queen of Bulgaria, 'the outlook would be dark indeed'.[4]

The outlook was, by any standards, quite black enough. The collapse of the French Army and the evacuation from Dunkirk left Britain awaiting invasion. Unlike so many Francophiles, Duff did not react to these events by condemning the French; he adjured his listeners to remember the heavy losses which their allies had borne in the common struggle and told them that:

> If anyone says to you, 'The French have let us down', you ought to reply, 'Either you are a paid agent of Germany, if you say that, or else you are an unpaid one doing German propaganda for nothing. In either case your mouth should be shut and silenced because you are an enemy ... to the Allied cause.'

He was always a faithful friend; nor was his love of France shown solely in words.

Duff warmed to the spirit displayed by a relatively unknown Brigadier-General, Charles de Gaulle, who in a broadcast on 18 June declared that although France had lost a battle, she had not lost the war; this was his own opinion. Like Churchill, Duff approved of de Gaulle. The Foreign Office, under Lord Halifax, did not, worrying about the effect he would have on Britain's relations with the Vichy regime. Halifax wanted to stop de Gaulle's broadcasts, but Duff stepped in to save them – thus playing a vital role in the creation of *Le Général Micro*. At the time he, like Churchill, saw in de Gaulle the leader of a French Army; neither of them had any inkling of the Frenchman's political ambitions and there must have been times, four years later, when they must have wished that they had let Halifax have his way.

Duff was also involved in attempts to rally other and more prominent Frenchmen to the common cause. On 25 June he set off with Lord Gort in a flying boat, bound for Morocco. They tried to establish contact with former French ministers who had been taken there on the SS *Massilia*, but had no success.

If his beloved France had suffered, his even more precious London was about to follow suit. Once the bombing started Duff saw with sadness and horror the destruction of much that he had loved; his morning drive from the Dorchester Hotel, where along with other members of the Government he was lodged, to the Senate House of London University where the MOI had its headquarters, took him through the parts of the capital he knew best; it was a melancholy experience. But even before the bombing started, open season had been declared on the Minister of Information.

If Duff's time at the MOI was generally considered one of the less successful periods of his career, the events of June to August 1940 are to blame. The storm which descended on him was partly his own fault, partly the product of misunderstanding, and, it must be added, partly the result of Beaverbrook's malice.

In early June Churchill asked the MOI to investigate the question of government control of the press; a number of schemes were examined and the idea of a Censorship Board was mooted. Duff put this scheme to the newspaper editors in early July. They, fearing that the MOI wanted to 'muzzle' the press, were swift to hit back. Unfortunately for Duff, there was plenty of ammunition to hand.

Those who liked to allege that the MOI was a haven for intellectuals with no instinct for propaganda could draw support for their view from the first campaign to emerge under the new minister. This was 'The Silent Column'. Designed to stop the spread of alarmist rumours by 'Mr Secrecy Hush Hush' (a seedy gent with a trilby and a five o'clock shadow which made him look positively sinister), 'Miss Leaky Mouth', 'Mr Knowall' and a host of similarly unlovable folk, the campaign had the unfortunate effect of giving the impression that almost any exchange of information about the war was tantamount to treason; something the press were quick to point out. On 24 July, after less than a month, it was 'discontinued'.[5]

Scenting blood, the press campaign against the MOI was pursued with a skill which suggested that its originators should have been running the Ministry themselves. A harmless attempt by the MOI to gather information on the state of popular morale by sending out teams of investigators, reached the headlines as 'Cooper's snoopers' intruding on harmless folk.[6]

Then there was the helping hand given to the press by Duff himself. Diana was anxious about John Julius's safety, a feeling shared by mothers all over the country about their own children; unlike most of them, she had a chance to send her son away. The American Ambassador, Joseph Kennedy, organized the evacuation of some British children by American ships; Diana wanted to send John Julius. It is impossible to be certain what Duff's reaction to this was; it is possible to state what it should have been. As Minister of Morale, giving speeches on the radio about 'we can take it', he was setting the worst of examples by allowing Diana's pleas to prevail. Off to America went John Julius; and on to Duff's back leapt the press, with pictures of his son sitting waiting to be carried to safety.

Beaverbrook reported, with obvious relish, to Sam Hoare in Madrid on 14 July that

> Duff Cooper's situation is at present not a comfortable one. He is in trouble with the newspapers who suspect him of a desire to marshal all the press into an obedient legion under his orders. And he is in trouble with the public because he has sent his son to New York on an American ship. It is felt that as our Minister of Morale, in effect, he should display more personal faith in our ability to beat off attack and stand together as a united race.[7]

The 'political stockbrokers' were, as R. A. Butler told Hoare, 'selling Duff Coopers'.[8]

Beaverbrook's role in this movement on the political stock exchange was not merely that of an amused observer. Diana wrote to John Julius on 25 July:

> Papa is still attacked daily with great malice by my oldest demon-friend Lord Beaverbrook. He announced at a dinner-party of his own adherent yes-men, and to two outsiders who blabbed, that he was not going to stop until he got Papa and the Minister for Air (Archie Sinclair) out of office.

Hugh Dalton, the Minister for Economic War, who wanted more say over propaganda himself, dined with Beaverbrook at Stornaway House on 31 July and recorded in his diary that 'much of the conversation consisted in running down various Ministers, particularly little Mr Cooper, whose days Beaverbrook thinks are numbered'.[9] He suspected that Beaverbrook hankered after the MOI for himself.

Harold Nicolson, Duff's number two, detected a 'conspiracy' among 'the whole press', 'pro-Munich Conservatives' and Beaverbrook to 'pull Duff Cooper down';[10] nor was he the only one. As the assault on the Senate House of London University grew in force, so did theories of conspiracy. Lord Davidson, a former Chairman of the Conservative Party working with the MOI, saw enemies within the gates and, in a 'secret and very personal' letter written on 17 July, gave Duff the warning. The letter was headed 'please burn'; the fact that this injunction was ignored allows us to recapture something of the atmosphere within the MOI in those heady days between the end of the Battle of France and the beginning of the Battle of Britain. It also acts as a reminder that inter-departmental squabbles do not stop merely because the country is at war; assuming anyone ever thought that they did.

Davidson saw Kenneth Lee, the Director-General at the MOI, as being behind 'the campaign which was started against you personally'; which made a change from people seeing Beaverbrook there. He could offer no proof, only the 'verb sap': 'I have studied his methods. The time has come to act quickly. He has served two Ministers – I need say no more.'

Diana described Duff's reaction to the 'rough passage in the press' to John Julius on 21 July: 'Papa weathers it well but it makes me sick and ill.' She hoped that the appearance of Beaverbrook in the Cabinet as Minister for Aircraft Production would remove the driving force behind the campaign.

Whether for this reason, or because of the disappearance of Kenneth Lee in a reorganization of the MOI at the beginning of August, the press attacks became less powerful. Duff's own counter-attacks may even have had more effect than the removal of the chief conspirators.

Speaking in the Commons on 1 August Duff made a 'most spirited defence' of his activities; perhaps too spirited. As his friend Euan Wallace noted in his diary:

> With his usual honesty and courage, he attacked the Press pretty strongly and, in particular, reminded them of their revolting activities in ringing up bereaved persons for news. His remarks as to the limited value of MPs in a moribund Parliament, though perfectly true, will also earn him continued enmity in powerful quarters.[11]

Duff clearly felt no reservations about having scored 'a triumph' – he took Nicolson round to Pratt's Club for a champagne celebration.

If his speech in the Commons had been a little tactless, he showed 'skill and patience' according to Euan Wallace, when he addressed the 1922 Committee on 4 August[12] – qualities which were also in evidence the following day when he dined with the editors of Fleet Street. He assured them that the Government had no intention of bringing in compulsory censorship. On 6 August he wrote to Beaverbrook, telling him of the success of his meetings and expressing the hope that his relationship with the press would now improve: 'I know how much you can help me in this respect.'[13]

The eye of the storm had been traversed. Beaverbrook told Hoare in mid-August that:

> You may be interested to hear that the newspapers have let up the attack on Duff. He has done some things to put himself right with the editors after making a bad-tempered speech about them in the House. He gets some support here and there, in the *Manchester Guardian* for instance.[14]

It was no use Duff looking to the *Express* for support. But at least it did not go as far as the *Sunday Pictorial*, which, as Diana told John Julius at the end of July, had held a 'Duff Cooper ballot':

> There is a picture of Papa as a debauched criminal and the coupon says: 'He gets £5,000 a year for being Minister of Information. Do you think he should hold the Office?' Now only cross people who hate you or are indignant fetch a pair of scissors, cut it out and buy a stamp and send it off, and those women who are in love with you, but they are very few.

Diana bought a job lot of 240 copies of the paper at St Pancras Station and sent them to friends 'scissored and enveloped', but by that time the furore had died down.

The following months were crucial ones in Britain's history. 'The Few' held off the German assault and Churchill was loud in their praise; but there was not much here for the MOI: the margin of survival was too narrow and the heroism of the fighter-pilots self-evident; small pickings for the propagandists.

Duff and Diana continued to live at the Dorchester, crowded though it was, as the blitz began. Their suite was on the top floor, which gave a magnificent, if worrying, view of London. 'It's not really the place to sleep,' Diana wrote. Duff's total indifference to danger occasionally led to quarrels. One night in early September the sirens went and the anti-aircraft batteries started up. Diana had made her preparations:

I said that we must go down to the basement. I had meant to all that day, and had taken precautions to stop arguments such as 'I haven't got a suitable dressing-gown' by buying him a very suitable shade of blue alpaca with dark red pipings.

He still refused to move: 'I think you're too unkind', she said, pulling off a stocking. 'We *can't* go down, I'm too tired', was his response, 'besides, it doesn't make any difference where you are'. The appearance of a warden saved Diana further tears: 'You are advised to take cover.' Duff 'donned his Tarnhelm outfit with the slowness of a tortoise, and down we went'. On another occasion, when she was visiting him at the MOI and the sirens went, she was ushered down to the basement where she found Duff 'sitting in a sound-proof room with his big shots round him and fifty telephones, maps, signals, lamps and gadgets'; he might, she thought, 'have been conducting a war from GHQ Armageddon'. If courage and patriotism had sufficed, then Duff would have been a run-away success as Minister of Information; but they were not enough.

Lord Davidson, writing in August 1940, thought that the real problem for Duff was 'lack of any political guidance'; his diagnosis made sense. He pointed out the weakness of the Minister's staff: Harold Nicolson may have been a nice man with the right views, but he 'was not reliable and has the outlook of a journalist'; Lord Hood, Duff's young Principal Private Secretary, had 'no political experience'; and as for his Parliamentary Private Secretary, Ronald Tree, the man who should have been the Minister's eyes and ears in the Commons: 'he is possibly the most unpopular Private Member and certainly the most unpopular PPS in the House'. The real threat came from Duff's critics in the Conservative Party where his position, thanks to his pre-war record, was 'weak'; the Party may have accepted Churchill, but it still loved Chamberlain. There were, moreover, 'several of your non-Tory colleagues who are waiting for your shoes'.

Certainly Dalton sought to expand his own activities on the Political Warfare front at the expense of the MOI,[15] which also had to cope with obstruction from the Foreign Office and the Service departments. Duff's failure at the MOI was as much a function of the fundamental defects in the organization as it was of any lack of interest he is alleged to have shown in propaganda. The first Minister of Information, Lord Macmillan, put his finger on the root of the matter when he complained in September 1939 that 'The Minister of Information is a mere postman, and has no discretion or power.'[16]

Duff found the blitz easier to bear than he did the sense of 'dyspep-
tic ineffectiveness' which others noted he gave. He was, Diana told
Conrad Russell in late September, 'both bored and worried and dislikes facing doom'. He thought that 'Winston hates him now'. She
began to worry about him: 'All these weaknesses are frighteningly
unlike Mr C.' He could not get any interest out of Churchill in his
struggles to create a role for the MOI, and was, himself, increasingly
unable to whip up enthusiasm for being a Whitehall warrior.

When Lord Lothian died in December, Diana hoped that Duff
might be chosen to succeed him as Ambassador to Washington, but
Lord Halifax went instead.

Tired and frustrated, Duff fell prey to colds and influenza. He was
ill with a temperature of 103 degrees just before Christmas, and,
unusually for him, was dogged by minor illnesses throughout the next
few months. Diana, who fretted if he had so much as a snuffle, was
seriously concerned. She wrote to John Julius in March 1941:

> Papa says he is tired, a thing I've never heard him say before. He some-
> times used to say, with a view to upsetting me: '*Ich bin so müde, Weibchen,*'
> which is what the Prince Consort said to Queen Victoria when he began
> to die, but the way he says it now wrings me.

He was tempted to resign, but thought that would be unpatriotic, so
there he stayed.

In March they moved out of the Dorchester. Diana determined to
turn West House at Bognor into a smallholding. She delighted in her
goats and beehives – and in the absence of bombs. Duff commuted
up to London, where things were moving to a climax in his reign at
the MOI.

It was noted by some that he arrived late at the office most mornings and was content to take long weekends at Bognor.[17] Nicolson
thought that he had given up any idea of pressing reforms on the
Prime Minister and 'hopes to live from day to day without trouble
and authority'.[18] It was the Director-General at the MOI, Walter
Monckton, who tried to spark him back into his old fighting
form.[19]

In mid-May he went down with flu. While recovering at West
House he received a letter from Monckton dated 21 May urging him
to press for the MOI to have control of all propaganda, and warning
that unless this was done, he and others would resign rather than
carry on 'wasting our time on a penny-in-the-slot machine'.[20] On 24

May Monckton wrote again, resigning.[21] Duff's reply on 28 May is redolent with his frustration:

> I have long known that the MOI is a misbegotten freak bred from the unnatural union of Sir Horace Wilson and Sir Samuel Hoare (considering the progenitors I wonder the offspring is not even more revolting) but I have tried to strengthen the freak's limbs and make it serve some useful purpose, as the only alternative was to scrap it and begin again from the beginning, which was hardly practicable.[22]

He asked Monckton to stay and help, proposing that 'we should go on gradually asserting our rights and improving our position'. After further argument, it was agreed that Duff should put the reforms suggested by Monckton and Cyril Radcliffe to the Cabinet.

Once aroused, his final effort was a forceful one. On 6 June he opened the batting by writing to Churchill suggesting the time had come to make important decisions.[23] A few days later in 'an amazing harangue to the lobby correspondents', he made it plain that he would resign unless he was given a place in the War Cabinet and full control over information.[24] He pressed Churchill for a definite decision before the House debated the subject on 25 June.[25] On 24 June he put his case to the Cabinet:

> The broad issue ... is whether the Head of the Ministry of Information is to be a very important Cabinet Minister charged with the conduct of political warfare and therefore having control of all propaganda and publicity, or whether he is to be a high official with the duty of carrying out the directions of other departments and maintaining liaison between those departments on the one hand and the Press and the BBC on the other.[26]

But Duff lacked the weight and Churchill the interest to get what the MOI wanted. The Service departments retained their right to issue communiqués without being subject to the MOI; nor was control over political warfare given to the Ministry.

Hugh Dalton, whose department had survived Duff's attempts to emasculate it, recorded in his diary at the beginning of July that in the face of the MOI's defeat, it was rumoured that its leading officials had handed in their resignations:

> It is also said that Duff Cooper, screaming with anger, flings their resignations back in their faces and refuses to accept them. He is said to have told the PM that he does not think Ministers should resign in wartime, otherwise he would have gone.[27]

Armistice Day in Paris, 1944: Churchill and de Gaulle with Duff and Eden
in the background

Duff in his magnificent
library at the Embassy in
Paris, 1945

Outdoing the French for style: Monsieur l'Ambassadeur and Lady Diana, 1945

The statesman at work, Paris, November 1945

Period piece at Chantilly, late 1940s

Duff and Louise de Vilmorin,
late 1940s

Louise at the Embassy taken by
Cecil Beaton

In relaxed mood with Susan Mary Patten, late 1940s

Democratizing the Paris Embassy: Low's view in 1946

With Bevin (centre) in Paris in 1947 at the Quai d'Orsay

Caroline Paget's wedding, 1949. Left to right: Micky Renshaw, David Herbert, Juliet Duff, Liz von Hofmannsthal, Michael Duff and Caroline, Octavian and Arabella von Hofmannsthal, Duff, Cecil Beaton, Diana, Raimund von Hofmannsthal

The Château de St Firmin at Chantilly

Left: On the eve of retirement: at the presidential shoot at Rambouillet, December 1946

Below: Before the final cruise: Duff and Diana, 1953

On the face of things, Duff's failure seemed surprising. He was an excellent speaker and an effective broadcaster; he had a wide range of contacts in Fleet Street and was known to be a friend of Churchill's: but none of these things was enough. In part, his task was thankless – building bricks of morale without the straw of victory; in part, his failure stemmed from his own limitations. Francis Williams, an experienced journalist who worked at the MOI, wrote of Duff and Nicolson: 'Both were belated Edwardians. They treated the Ministry of Information as if it were a branch of Belles-Lettres'; with them and Ronald Tree, the MOI seemed like 'an annexe of White's or the Beefsteak'. Of Duff, Williams wrote: 'He was a curiously inbred political figure and had by now become also rather an idle one. He preferred talking over lunch to doing anything.'[28]

This is not altogether fair; Duff had tried to make the Ministry work, but it was a new creation; it fitted uneasily into the normal bureaucratic structures of Whitehall and it was filled with talented amateurs. It was not until the colourful and ruthless Brendan Bracken, who was an intimate of Churchill's, took over that the MOI began to work: and when offering Bracken the post, 'the PM had the hardihood to say that it was worse than manning a bomb-disposal unit!'[29]

Duff was in a curious position at the beginning of July; known to have been defeated in the Cabinet, with rumours rife as to his desire to leave the MOI, he was a lame-duck minister. But, as he waited for the Cabinet reshuffle which he hoped would take him to fresh pastures, he was to find himself involved in what has become known as 'the Wodehouse affair'.[30]

The broadcasts made by the novelist P. G. Wodehouse from Berlin in 1941 are now generally acknowledged to be pretty harmless stuff. Read at a distance of forty-four years from that grim summer of 1941, they even raise a smile. This was far from being the case at the time. The popular press, vulgarly untouched by the remnants of what Duff had called 'the Munich spirit', condemned Wodehouse's actions; not even his warmest admirers have argued that broadcasting on Nazi radio at such a time was a wise move. Questions were asked in the Commons.

The matter came up at one of Duff's lunches with journalists in early July. Francis Williams dates the lunch as being after the German invasion of Russia, which Lady Donaldson, in her official biography of Wodehouse confirms: 'A good deal of brandy and vodka had been taken.' William Connor, 'Cassandra' of the *Daily Mirror*, complained about the favouritism shown to American journalists by the MOI and said that they did not dare let him broadcast for 'fear that he might attack some of their pets'. Williams, who was at the lunch, recalled: 'Duff-Cooper [*sic*], who by now had consumed a good deal of brandy, denied having any pets and was thereupon attacked by Cassandra for doing nothing about P. G. Wodehouse.' The argument ended, according to Williams, with Duff inviting Connor to broadcast on Wodehouse but, according to Charles Graves, who was also there: 'Cassandra then offered to broadcast to America himself, knocking Wodehouse for his tax evasion. I regarded this as silly but Duff Cooper jumped at it.'[31]

When Cassandra's script was submitted to the BBC on 14 July it caused consternation. The verdict of the corporation's legal adviser was unequivocal: 'It is clearly libellous and, if broadcast, slanderous as well.'[32] Connor was asked to amend his script. He refused to do so and appealed to Duff. He thought it 'wholly admirable' and ordered the BBC to broadcast it.[33] When the question of libel was raised, Duff's response was: 'That's nothing to do with you or the BBC.'[34] In his diary on 4 July, Harold Nicolson had recorded that one of the MOI's objectives in the near future should be to 'get control of the BBC';[35] this was doing so with a vengeance.

Cassandra's broadcast went ahead on 15 July. It was a scurrilous, vulgar, cheap and nasty piece of character assassination, written in his usual venomous style. But that style was usually inflicted only on those who chose to read the *Daily Mirror*; those unfamiliar with it were shocked. Members of Parliament (in the Conservative interest) and journalists writing for the *Spectator*, *The Times* and other 'quality' papers, condemned it as 'vulgar', 'poisonous' and 'unfair'. They were, of course, right, just as they had been about Duff's broadcast on Italy's entry into the war.

However, there was quite a different reaction from the popular press. The *Star* praised Duff for having the guts to allow the broadcast; the *Daily Herald*, the newspaper of the Labour Party, commented that it showed 'that if the MOI had a free hand over propaganda something might happen'; and Cassandra himself lectured *The Times* on its 'holier-than-thou attitude'. His postbag showed that 'the working classes' approved of his words, and like another socialist he did not give a 'tinker's cuss' about the rest. He proudly boasted that his readership was ten times more than that of *The Times* and in answer to the charge of vulgarity commented: 'I would remind you that this is a vulgar war in which our countrymen are being killed by the enemy without regard to good form or bad taste.'[36]

As an attempt to demonstrate that this was a 'People's war' and to show that not even famous novelists were exempt from the rules which governed the lives of ordinary people, the broadcast seems to have worked.

Duff took the view that at such a point in the war 'plain speaking' was more desirable than 'good taste'.[37] His patriotism could not encompass the idea that, in the middle of a war which was going badly, there was no harm in broadcasting on Nazi radio. The aptest contemporary comment on the whole sorry business was that of the *Picture Post* on 19 July 1941:

> Lovers of Wodehouse may think there is nothing very harmful in what he says. The Nazis would not use him unless his words were harmful to our cause. It is harmful that any Englishman can speak of the Nazis with anything but firm hostility.

It is a point usually ignored by the great novelist's admirers. He was, himself, more conscious of his folly. In a letter to the Foreign Office in November 1942 he apologized for his 'inexcusable blunder' and called the broadcasts 'an insane thing to do'.[38]

Wodehouse was never prosecuted for his actions which were, in truth, more foolish than anything else. He refused to take legal action against Cassandra, wisely letting sleeping dogs lie. Williams recorded that Duff 'regretted the broadcast as soon as it was made'.[39] There is no evidence to show that this was so. In public he defended his conduct, but it is perhaps significant that he did not mention the incident in his memoirs; it was no one's finest hour.

It was Duff's swan-song as Minister of Information. In early July he was sounded out by Churchill as to his willingness to go on a special mission to the Far East; he accepted the post unhesitatingly. As he wrote to Lord Wolmer on 22 July: 'I cannot pretend that I am very sorry to leave the MOI and I am looking forward to my new job.'[40]

18

Singapore

On the evening of 21 July Duff celebrated the end of his last day at the MOI by dining at the Dorchester with Sir Robert Bruce Lockhart,* who had watched, with interest, the progress of the battle for control of propaganda. Lockhart recorded that he 'was drunk again', and that he 'showed me his charter for Singapore; it was very vague. Might mean much or nothing at all.'[1] The vaguenesss of his mission was an inevitable consequence of the circumstances of its genesis.

With Russia's entry into the war Britain at last had an ally, but the chances of ultimate victory still seemed slender. Diplomatic relations with Japan were deteriorating and the British Empire in the Far East offered the Japanese a tempting and vulnerable prize. In early June the British Ambassador to China suggested that a Minister of State for the Far East might be appointed. Churchill toyed with the idea, but the opposition of Eden at the Foreign Office and Lord Cranborne at the Colonial Office prevented such an appointment being made. Instead, it was decided to send someone on a tour of investigation.[2] Duff was sounded out in early July and the only possible hiccough was news that the press was planning an 'extensive campaign' against the MOI, which might make it look as though Duff had been removed to appease the Press Lords. Churchill sent for Beaverbrook.[3] There was no press campaign and, on 21 July, Duff was appointed Chancellor of the Duchy of Lancaster. It was also announced that he would proceed to the Far East on a special mission.

The Duchy of Lancaster is reserved for politicians in transit: young men on the way up and failures on the way down are its usual inhabitants. Churchill himself had held it in 1915 when he had been moved from the Admiralty after his part in the Dardanelles fiasco, at which time *Punch* had run a picture of him with the caption: 'What

---

* 1887-1970, diplomat and writer, working for the Political Warfare Executive at this time.

is a Duchy and where is Lancaster?'; so might Duff have felt. That he did not is an indication of how much he had hated the MOI.

His main problem was how to break the news to Diana. She was engrossed in the bucolic delights of Bognor: haymaking, keeping pigs and taking her cow to its 'bull bridegroom'; what did she want with the Orient? She took the news well. That she would go with him was a foregone conclusion. The Far East was not a war zone and, in any event, he did not want to leave her behind. His courage had sustained her through the darkness of the blitz and without him her spirits might fail. Her main fear was that his absence from England might deprive him of the chance of getting the post of British Ambassador in Washington. The Embassy was currently occupied by Lord Halifax, but she could not think that the old appeaser would stay there long. She wrote to Beaverbrook asking him to use his influence in Duff's favour should the job become vacant in the near future;[4] nothing came of this.

The Chancellor of the Duchy of Lancaster and his party left England on 6 August; it took them over a month to get to Singapore. Diana was the most nervous member of the group; she hated flying. Duff's calm composure was positively irritating. He sat there, quite oblivious to his surroundings, reading *War and Peace*, sighing, laughing and crying as he lost himself in Tolstoy's masterpiece; for Diana it was the eighth floor of the Dorchester during the blitz all over again. They were accompanied by Martin Russell, the nephew of Diana's friend Conrad Russell, who came along as Duff's private secretary.

Their journey gave Duff the opportunity to get through *War and Peace*. First stop was Lisbon, where they were delayed for three days. Then, via the Azores and Bermuda to Diana's beloved America, made all the more so by the fact of being able to see John Julius. There they spent a happy week: Diana and John Julius enjoying the sights, Duff seeing President Roosevelt and making speeches. Lord Halifax, who did not find him 'a particularly attractive speaker', thought that he went over well at a Press Club lunch on 14 August: 'He has got a good capacity for making points with vigour.'[5]

In San Francisco they picked up an addition to their party in the form of Tony Keswick, the Far Eastern expert of Jardine-Matheson: 'the man Duff most wanted to poach', according to Diana.

San Francisco was followed by Hawaii. Diana enjoyed the exotic scenery and surfing with Tony Keswick. Duff's feelings were less happy. As he told the Duchess of Westminster, he did not care much for Hawaii: 'You can have it so far as I'm concerned. I infinitely prefer Bognor.' This jaundiced view was the result of being stuck there for eight days: 'It was maddening being detained there when every day one expected the war in the Far East to break out.'⁶

They arrived in Singapore on 11 September. Before leaving London Duff had had a chat with the Secretary of State for India. Leo Amery. He had said that he thought he would find sufficient work in the East to keep him out there some time; this Amery had doubted.⁷ Both men were right: there was plenty of work to do, but Duff did not stay in Singapore for very long.

During the flight Martin Russell had, with the enthusiasm of youth, started 'getting out a report on how he thinks the Far East should be co-ordinated'; Duff was less precipitate. He spent his first month travelling and receiving visitors at his base at 106 Jervois Road. Writing to Loelia Westminster on 22 September he commented on progress thus far:

> Archie Kerr has just arrived from Chungking to see me – and I may go to Burma next week to see Dorman Smith. I have already flown to Batavia and back – and seen the beauties of Java – the scenic beauties I mean, because there are none other.

India provided, in the form of Jack and Mary Herbert at Calcutta, the delight of being 'once more with people to whom one could talk about all one's friends and understood all one's needs'. After that it would be Australia, New Zealand and, he thought, perhaps Hong Kong:

> And then I believe my labours will be over. But what lies beyond I cannot say – nor how soon I shall come back to you. The future is so uncertain and so dependent on the little yellow gentlemen who, in my opinion, have not yet made up their own minds on what to do next.

Duff wrote this in the interstices of composing his report. He had this ready for 29 October and sent it back to London with Tony Keswick. It was a percipient document and diagnosed not only what was wrong with the organization of the British Empire in the Far East, but also what was likely to happen in the future.⁸ He foresaw the Far East becoming the workshop of the world and doubted whether 'vast populations of industrious, intelligent and brave Asiatics' were likely forever to acknowledge 'the superiority of Europeans'. There would need to be changes if Britain was to maintain her position in this increasingly important part of the world; the most urgent ones would have to be in the machinery of government which had 'undergone no important change since the days of Queen Victoria'. The overlapping and stultifying jurisdictions of the Foreign Office, Dominions Office, Colonial Office, India Office, Burma Office and other Departments of State, needed to be sorted out. The long-term solution was to have a Minister for the Far East; in the short run it would suffice to appoint a High Commissioner with executive powers. All this was very true. Alas, Duff was reporting at the eleventh hour.

In a private letter to Churchill on 31 October, he made it plain that he did not want the job himself, suggesting for it the former Australian Prime Minister, Sir Robert Menzies.[9] Diana feared lest 'Winston thinks Duff comfortably out of the way' and gave him the post; she was right to do so. Churchill minuted on the bottom of the letter: 'I am against Menzies, I think DC should be told to stay there and do it himself.'[10] Thus he wrote on 29 November. The problem, as Tony Keswick told Duff on 2 December, was that although the report had been printed quickly:

> The PM is sitting on it. But today I suggested ... that it should go to the Cabinet without more ado. Ministers are beginning to ask about it and show interest and surely the situation is hot enough for action.

Just how hot was soon to be revealed.

Duff spent an impatient month waiting for even Keswick's letter, with no sign of a response from Whitehall. November was passed in the Antipodes: 'I enjoyed my visit although I never had a moment's peace. You can have New Zealand but I have formed quite an affection for Australia – especially Sydney.' Bridge at half-a-crown a thousand points, when he had been promised a 'good gamble', and social chat such as 'Do you and Mr Eden play much Chinese chequers?', help to explain his dislike of New Zealand which he found parochial and provincial. On the way out:

> We had one intoxicating night at Bali.... It far surpassed the best I had heard of it. We might live there after the war. We got the right information beforehand and instead of going to the big Dutch hotel we went to the local Cavendish kept by the local Olga Lynn.

There he and Diana 'dined in a bower of jasmine, waited on by beautiful creatures of uncertain sex and fed on lobsters and sucking pig washed down by real burgundy and followed by strange aromatic liqueurs'.[11] An unexpected, and therefore all the more delicious, moment of peace.

Until the Government got round to considering his report, Duff's position was an odd one. He hoped that he would soon be allowed home: 'Although in this peaceful, warm, sunny and plentiful land it seems mad to want to be in England. But mad I am.' He was, Diana reported to Conrad Russell, 'very restive', even if he would not admit it: 'He is such a one for pleasure. Old English ones, girls, champagne, bridge, clubs, weekends, libraries and a spot of sport. None of them here.' In early December he told Loelia Westminster that he was hoping to be instructed to return home: 'If war breaks out on this side of the world it will complicate everything and diminish, I fear, my chances of return.' At three o'clock on the morning of 8 December he and Diana were woken by the irruption into their bedroom of an excited Martin Russell shouting, 'The Japs have landed on the north-east coast of Malaya.' That, as it turned out, put paid to the idea of Christmas in England.

The Singapore campaign was one of the greatest disasters in British military history. Duff's part in the sorry business came only in the final act and yet, like almost everyone else associated with the fiasco, his reputation was damaged. The irony is that, had his report been ordered and produced a year earlier, some of the damage might have been averted.

His first reaction was to ask London for instructions. He was, he said, willing to perform the co-ordinating duties suggested in his report 'pending the appointment of a successor'. In order to do so he asked for powers similar to those enjoyed by Oliver Lyttelton, the Minister of State in the Middle East: 'My present role of spectator is most uncongenial.'[12]

Brendan Bracken suggested to Churchill that they might send the Permanent Under-Secretary at the Foreign Office, Sir Alexander Cadogan, out to Singapore, but the Prime Minister determined to appoint Duff.[13] In a telegram on 9 December he was made Resident Cabinet Minister at Singapore for Far Eastern Affairs. Like those of his original mission, the terms of appointment were vague enough to mean everything or nothing.[14] He was to be directly responsible to the War Cabinet and was to form a War Council for the Far East. His 'principal task' was to 'assist the successful conduct of operations' by relieving the Commanders-in-Chief of 'those extraneous responsibilities with which they have hitherto been burdened' by 'giving them broad political guidance'; he also had the power to 'settle emergency matters on the spot where time does not permit of reference home'. Duff's position was to be broadly similar to Lyttelton's but 'did not affect the existing responsibilities' of the Colonial Governors on the spot. The ambiguity was fatal, or would have been had the Empire not already been mortally stricken by its incapacity to respond to the speed of the Japanese attack.

Lyttelton wrote of his own post that 'If I am the highest authority on the spot, in the strict interpretation of these words, I am no authority at all',[15] this because of the multiplicity of local authorities. He managed to secure the co-operation of local representatives of other Ministries; Duff was not so fortunate.

It is clear from Colonel Montgomery's biography of the Governor of Singapore, Sir Shenton Thomas, that the local representative of the Colonial Office was determined to stand on his own dignity; it would also seem as though he took against Duff from the start. Thomas regarded him as a 'tough snooper', sent out to interfere and, from the very start of his mission, had 'little enthusiasm' for him.[16] But it was not until the entry of Japan into the war that Duff reciprocated.

Colonel Montgomery's book presents Thomas's unflattering portrait of Duff with no comment. There are in it odd distortions which read like gossipy afterthoughts. The idea that Duff and Diana arrived with 'some 100 suitcases' is palpable nonsense.[17] Martin Russell estimates that the true figure may have been as high as ten.[18] Diana habitually travelled light, although no doubt those who saw her as a frivolous society lady imagined that such an array of paraphernalia should have accompanied her. Thomas also imagined that Duff kept the dinner-tables at Jervois Road rocking with laughter by giving impersonations of himself; an allegation denied by Martin Russell and which certainly accords ill with what one knows of Duff.[19]

These complaints, and others, stemmed from the ambiguity about Duff's role in Singapore. At the first meeting of a hastily assembled War Council for the Far East on 10 December, Thomas and the Commander-in-Chief, Brooke-Popham, told him firmly that they intended to take their orders from their respective masters in Whitehall (the Colonial Office and the Chiefs of Staff); neither of them saw any use for a War Council. Duff asked Brooke-Popham (known locally as 'Old Pop-off') if he could let him have a list of military requirements, but was informed that such a list had already been despatched to London, where the Chiefs of Staff had turned it down. Duff offered to intercede with Churchill but was told by Brooke-Popham that he could not 'be guilty of disloyalty to the Chiefs of Staff'. Not surprisingly, Duff lost his temper:

I told him that if he thought loyalty to the Chiefs of Staff was of greater importance than winning the war I could not agree with him, and that if he really believed that the supply of certain weapons was essential there were no methods which he should not adopt to secure those weapons.[20]

Thomas found such aggressiveness in bad taste: 'A revelation'. He saw nothing wrong in Popham's attitude.[21] No wonder the campaign went the way it did.

The meeting ended with Duff offering to telegraph London asking for a precise definition of his functions. Unfortunately he let Brooke-Popham persuade him that there was no need to do so.[22] It was a pity, but probaby mattered little; by this stage there was little that could have been done.

But Duff did feel increasing disquiet with the local administration in Malaya. This he expressed in a letter to Churchill on 18 December. Colonel Montgomery, for reasons best known to himself, calls this an act of 'impropriety' and arraigns him for not showing it to Thomas first.[23] As one of his duties was to report to his old friend, it is hard to see any 'impropriety' here; and as one of the main thrusts of the letter was criticism of Thomas and the local set-up, it is hardly surprising that it was not shown to him.

There is little in the behaviour of either Brooke-Popham or Shenton Thomas to belie Duff's pen-portraits of them. The former was 'a very much older man than his years warrant' who 'sometimes seems on the verge of nervous collapse'; the latter 'one of those people who find it impossible to adjust their minds to war conditions'. Lord Cranborne, Thomas's chief at the Colonial Office, wrote to Duff in early 1942:

> From the Governor downwards they seem to have been incapable of dealing with an abnormal situation. This, more than any inherent rigidity in the system, seems to be the real cause for criticism. Clearly the Governor should have been replaced earlier.

In Cranborne's view, the fact that Thomas had been called to England in 1940 for seven months' leave 'ought to have convinced the Office that he was not the man to tackle a situation demanding energy and enterprise'.

It was, as Martin Russell observes, 'a shame' that Thomas never realized that 'the presence of a man with the experience of Duff, who had direct access to the Cabinet, was an asset and not a liability'.[24] Instead he stood on his dignity.

When Duff suggested on 13 December that, as it seemed unlikely that Malaya could be held by four divisions and three squadrons, all troops might be withdrawn to Singapore Island, Thomas dismissed this as 'defeatist' and 'expected every serviceman everywhere to exhibit courage, guts, stamina and determination to win';[25] it may have been magnificent, but it was not war – or at least not the way to win a war.

Thomas was equally scathing about the evacuation of women and children from Penang, which he thought would have a 'bad effect' on the Asiatics; he was particularly critical of Duff's insistence that Europeans should be evacuated first. But to Duff, to have done otherwise would have been a crime: 'The first time in the history of the British Empire when it had been our policy to evacuate the troops first and to leave the women and children to the tender mercies of a cruel Asiatic foe.'[26] Again what is striking is Thomas's inability to adapt to changed circumstances.

But even had he and Duff co-operated like blood-brothers, it would not have stemmed the tide of defeat. During the inter-war years the Far East had had a low priority when it came to defence spending and, with Britain so hard-pressed in Europe, this state of affairs had not changed after 1939. British power in the region was little more than a façade; the Japanese hurricane blew it away.

In Washington, Roosevelt and Churchill were making their own plans to defend the region by setting up what became known as the ABDA (American–British–Dutch–Australian) Command with General Wavell as Commander-in-Chief. The news of this appointment prompted Duff to suggest that he should now return home as his duties were at an end.

Wavell himself had other ideas. His Chief of Staff wrote to Duff on 7 January 1942 to say that he had 'been thinking hard over the situation here, as the result of what he has heard and seen since his arrival'. General Pownall told him that Wavell had drawn up a telegram to Churchill and enclosed the text. It stated that as a result of his 'preliminary examination' of the 'military and civilian situation' he did not 'consider that the defence of Malaya is being inspired by sufficient drive and determination in some quarters'. He exempted Duff from this category and asked for the order that he should return to London to be cancelled. Wavell thought that he had 'done much to improve defence situation in Singapore from a civilian point of view' and that 'his resolution in present crisis' was 'most valuable'.

161

But, despite this weighty testimonial to set against the irrelevant carpings of Shenton Thomas, Duff decided to go. There was, he thought, no role for a civilian in a theatre of operations. As Diana told Conrad Russell: 'The argument against Duff remaining here is that in his present position he is powerless ... and that nothing short of being Governor would give him authority.' Of this there was no chance.

On 13 January Duff and Diana, following orders from London, left for home. By the time they arrived the island had fallen. The journey was a long and tiring one, which included almost being stranded in Cairo, but their problems were nothing compared to the ones faced by Thomas and those left in Singapore.

Shenton Thomas's courage in captivity was the reverse and the noble side to his obstinacy. He clearly later came to believe that Duff had set out to discredit him in London. This was not so. His report to the Cabinet was critical of the whole machinery of administration in the Far East; he had no personal animus against Thomas. He thought him unsuited to his post in wartime and said as much to Churchill; to have done otherwise would have made him culpable. The campaign to discredit Thomas which his biographer professes to find, existed only in the mind. To imply, as Colonel Montgomery does, that Duff prepared a speech which would have cast a slur on Thomas's reputation, and that he helped to cast the mould for the version of the fall of Singapore given in the official history, is to show the signs of incipient paranoia.[27] It also demonstrates why Duff's job was so difficult.

He had been sent to Singapore because it was a means of utilizing his talents and of getting him out of the MOI. The appointment, and the manner in which it had been made, say much about why the Empire in the East collapsed with such rapidity.

When Duff and Diana arrived back in England it was mid-February and the political winds were as chill as those of the winter frosts.

$\sim\!\!\sim\!\!9$ 19 $\epsilon\!\!\sim\!\!\sim$

Out of Favour

'It is damaging to be associated, however distantly, with failure'; thus noted Duff in the aftermath of Singapore. He wrote his reports, corresponded with colleagues and provided material for an inquest into the disaster; but no one really wanted to rake over the mess, not yet. Leo Amery, with whom he and Diana lunched on 25 February 1942, noted in his diary:

> Duff was cheerful and in good form, hoping, or professing to hope, that WSC wouldn't send him to Cairo. I confess I don't quite know what Winston is going to do with him and I don't think he means to drop him altogether.[1]

In this, Amery was quite correct.

Churchill had, in fact, been considering sending Duff to Cairo in place of Oliver Lyttelton, but dropped the idea when it was opposed by Eden.[2]

There were those ill-natured souls who asked why Duff was being paid a ministerial salary for work which must have taken all of an hour a week. This was somewhat unfair. As Chancellor of the Duchy he was also head of the Security Executive – a fact which could not be stated in Parliament. He was concerned with such matters as the detention of enemy aliens, the development of germ-warfare, and the planning of operations designed to mislead the enemy. It was in this last capacity that he became privy to the details of the deception operation involving the planting of faked documents on a corpse which became the germ of his only novel, *Operation Heartbreak*.[3]

It was, for the most part, a quiet and frustrating life. He and Diana lived down at West House, the beach disfigured with rusting barbed wire, and the garden by Diana's rustic habits. Chips Channon, who went down there in April 1942, found himself driving pigs and feeding rabbits 'still in my London clothes'. Diana, 'a dream of golden beauty' still, 'showed me her poultry and the swill for the pigs. The world's most beautiful woman showing off her swill.' On another visit in October he was driven into Bognor 'in her dirty, disreputable-looking car, with a trailer full of swill behind'.[4] She was totally bound up in her farming.

Duff had no such absorbing pastime. In June 1942 he began to write a book on which he had long meditated: the life of the Old Testament figure, King David. It kept him occupied for a few months. Writing to Rupert Hart-Davis on 15 September, he said that 'the end is in sight'. Glad that his nephew liked what he had read, he hoped 'your colleagues will share your view and come down handsome'; they did. *David* was published by Jonathan Cape in May 1943. Duff received a handsome advance – a not over-frequent occurrence where Cape was concerned – and the book sold well. Leo Amery, who found it 'ridiculous' at first, thought it improved as it went on: 'He certainly has made an effective story and emphasized the politics underlying the simpler, and in itself finer, Bible story.'[5] At a lunch which Duff gave for Wavell at Buck's in May, Channon told him how much the Field Marshal had enjoyed the book, 'which pleased him'.[6] It could, however, scarcely be argued that *David*, enjoyable though it is, was an adequate use of Duff's talents.

He was not wholly inactive politically, and his two most notable interventions during this barren period show him arguing the case for the civilized and the honourable against the expedient. When Eden proposed recognizing the Russian conquest of the Baltic States, Duff protested at once. In a strong letter written in April 1942 he said:

> There was no more brutal and indefensible act of aggression than Russia's occupation of Estonia, Latvia and Lithuania. Germany's interference in Czecho-Slovakia, where there was a large German population, and with Poland, where the Corridor created an extremely difficult position, were far more excusable actions than that of Russia against the Baltic States.

He told Eden that recognition of Russia's frontiers of June 1941 'would tear into ribbons the Atlantic Charter and brand us as the arch-hypocrites of the world'.[7] As Churchill and Roosevelt took a similar view, Eden's plan failed.

Duff was less successful when, in July 1943, he argued against proposals to bring Fascist war-criminals to trial. Not only did such prosecutions usually create martyrs out of the 'criminals', they were of doubtful legality: 'By what code and before what tribunal' could a Head of State be arraigned? There was also a moral question: 'Could we, as allies of Marshal Stalin, go into court with clear consciences and spotless hands?' The Russian presence at the Nuremberg trials provided an ironic commentary on this last theme.

Commuting up from Bognor, weekending at West House, Duff seemed 'in the gentlest of moods', according to Channon.[8] Diana's friend, Evelyn Waugh, who stayed with them in August 1943 had 'only one row with Duff and that a mild one'.[9] The fact was that he was bored.

The ministerial reshuffle that was to bring him out of this state of affairs came in September 1943 when the Chancellor of the Exchequer, Sir Kingsley Wood, died. Churchill suggested to Eden, who had long been complaining about his double burden of the Foreign Office and Leader of the Commons, that Duff might become an 'Assistant Minister at the Foreign Office'. Suddenly the work-load did not seem all that bad. Eden had no wish to lose any of his authority to another Conservative. The Permanent Under-Secretary, Alec Cadogan, and Eden's secretary, Oliver Harvey, also evinced little enthusiasm for Churchill's bright idea, telling Eden: 'We liked Duff but that he was far too lazy and indeed incapable now of hard work at the Foreign Office.'[10] Attlee's desire to have the post for the Labour Party finally put paid to Duff's prospects of a job which he would have enjoyed. went to a Labour MP, George (later Viscount) Hall; it is not recorded that he had a great influence upon British diplomacy.

Churchill was, however, determined to 'get Duff some job of this sort'.[11] On 28 September he suggested to Eden that the post of Ambassador to Italy might be suitable. This too met with a frosty response. Eden, who had resigned over the appeasement of Italy, was hypersensitive on the subject. Remembering Duff as one who had been 'soft' on Italy, he did not want him in Rome. He suggested that he might go to Algiers as British Representative to the French Committee of National Liberation (FCNL).[12]

The FCNL had been created in June 1943 as the body which represented all those French resistance groups opposed to the Nazis and the Vichy regime. The British had been its main sponsors, seeing in it a way of ridding themselves of the problem which General de Gaulle had become. Churchill, following the lead of President Roosevelt and exasperated by de Gaulle's behaviour, had turned against his former protégé. He would have been glad to see him removed from his position as head of the Fighting French. This view was not shared by Eden or by the British Minister Resident in North Africa, Harold Macmillan. They had worked tirelessly for a union between de Gaulle's movement and the regime of General Giraud based in Algiers. Churchill and Roosevelt had extended limited diplomatic recognition to the FCNL in August, but it had been with a bad grace.

Eden and the Foreign Office feared that Churchill was too prone to see Anglo–French relations through the prism of his own dislike of de Gaulle. The Foreign Office wanted a strong post-war France and, convinced that de Gaulle would play a crucial part in this, wanted good relations with the FCNL. It was necessary to appoint an Ambassador to the Committee and Harvey, in conversation with Eden on 30 September, outlined the many advantages of appointing Duff:

> The PM's affection for him which would enable him to stand up to the PM over French policy far better than any professional. Duff knew France and the French well. He was stout and Gaullist. His lack of activity would also be something of an advantage. He would leave the French alone.[13]

Given the difference of opinion between Churchill and Eden, adding to this the unbending character of de Gaulle and the American dislike of him, the post of Ambassador to the FCNL was clearly going to be a bed of nails. In these circumstances Harvey felt able to waive his own claims to it and Eden overcame his dislike of appointing outsiders to diplomatic posts; as he told Harvey, 'He didn't always want to be standing in Duff's way.'

Although not privy to Harvey's advice and the reasons for it, Churchill was not blind to the implications of such an appointment. He wrote to Eden on 3 October.[14] His letter merits extended quotation – as an example of Churchillian prose, and as a testimonial to Duff:

> When you remember that he has been a Secretary of State and resigned the office of First Lord of the Admiralty over Munich, I cannot feel that stepping into Macmillan's shoes, or one of them, at Algiers, would be an offer which I could make to him.

He wanted Duff to go to Rome as Ambassador; 'the other alternative I could not contemplate'. He warned Eden that:

> We must not underestimate Duff Cooper because he has had bad luck in the war. He has great qualities of courage. He is one of the best speakers in the House of Commons. He has the root of the matter in him. He has made as great a sacrifice as anyone has made for the ideas which we served before the war. He is a man of great culture. He might easily

become a formidable voice and figure in right-wing Tory politics in the future. This last is a consideration which should have more weight with you than me.

This is indeed a weighty paean of praise to set against the chorus of denigration encountered elsewhere. The spectre here evoked, of Duff as a Churchill-like rebel to Eden's role as Baldwin of the future, is an intriguing one; but it is only a simulacrum. Duff lacked Churchill's insatiable appetite for political life.

But Eden chose to ignore Churchill's advice. In Duff's words:

> On 6 October 1943 Anthony Eden asked to see me at the Foreign Office and, when I went there, he offered me, much to my surprise, to go either to Algiers as British Representative with the French Committee, having the rank of Ambassador and with the prospect of becoming Ambassador in Paris, or, alternatively, to take on the position which they thought would soon be vacant, of Ambassador to Rome.[15]

Duff's reply was immediate and firm. He 'was not politically interested in Italy' and he thought that his broadcast at the time of Italy's entry into the war would make him *persona non grata* to the Italians. He did like the idea of going to Algiers and asked Eden 'for a little time to think it over'. This he was given.

That evening he dined at Claridges at a big party which Churchill was giving in honour of Field Marshal Wavell who had just been made Viceroy of India. Duff sat next to Bracken, who embarrassed him by talking about his proposed appointment; he was, however, strongly in favour of Duff accepting it. After dinner he went to Pratt's Club where he met Macmillan, who was spending a few days in England: 'He was most welcoming, and said that he thought it would be an excellent thing.'

With such encouraging comments, Duff had made up his mind by the time he travelled down to Bognor the following day. He told Diana that he had decided to accept the post. She was reluctant to leave her rural pursuits but, as ever, put his interests first. Dinner that evening almost brought the whole scheme to a premature end.

Their guests for dinner were H. G. Wells's former mistress, Moura Budberg, and a young journalist, Alastair Forbes. During the meal: 'We had a somewhat heated discussion about General de Gaulle, both Moura and Forbes denouncing him very violently and I standing up for him.' Duff thought nothing of this until he dined with Churchill on 11 October.

The only people present on this occasion were Beaverbrook, Clementine Churchill and the Prime Minister; but after dinner Churchill's daughter Mary came in, accompanied by Alastair Forbes, who lived near Churchill's country home at Chartwell. The conversation again came round to de Gaulle:

> Forbes had, I found afterwards, already informed the Prime Minister that I was violently pro-de Gaulle, which was not true. The Prime Minister had to leave suddenly after dinner to go to a meeting, and he left me with the impression that he had grave doubts as to whether I ought to go to Algiers, seeing the views that I held.

Two days later Duff wrote to Churchill to try to clear up the situation. He said that he had understood from Eden that 'the offer of the post had been a firm one which I accepted', but that 'if he now thought that I had better not go there, I should be glad if he would let me know as soon as possible, because I would have to make my arrangements'.

The following day a letter arrived from Churchill, it was dated 'October 1943':

> My dear Duffie,
>
> I did not authorize the Foreign Secretary to offer you this post but only to find out what your general views and wishes were between remaining where you are in the Government, or going to Algiers to work with the French or going to Italy. However, I quite understand that the conversation [may have given that impression]....
>
> It would be disastrous if one of your high standing and powerful personality were to go to a post in which he would be conscientiously pursuing an absolutely different policy from that which I, as Head of the Government, deem necessary. This would only lead to collision after a little while with a lot of trouble to all concerned.

In his letter Duff had said that 'if I were appointed' he would 'loyally carry out the policy of His Majesty's Government'. Churchill replied that he was glad to know that, but that he wanted to make sure that Duff was 'doing no violence to your convictions' by taking the post. He sent Duff a copy of a long Cabinet paper on British relations with de Gaulle and put at his disposal all the Foreign Office files dealing with the subject. He left Duff in no doubt as to his own views and the reasons for them:

> The help of Britain and the United States is essential to the building up again of a strong France which we both agree is a prime British interest.

De Gaulle, I fear, has contracted a deep antipathy to both these countries. He is a man Fascist-minded, opportunist, unscrupulous, ambitious to the last degree, and his coming into power in the new France would lead to great schisms there and also to a considerable estrangement between France and the Western Democracies.

Churchill added that he did not

want to bring about a situation where the President will think of France primarily in terms of de Gaulle. I see very grave dangers in the future. I am sure de Gaulle, having failed to split Britain and the United States, will try to split them both from Russia. I am therefore most anxious to build up an impersonal and collective unit to symbolize France and to avoid the dangers which I have mentioned above.

Duff could have no excuse for not knowing what Churchill's policy was. The Prime Minister stuck to these views until the end of the war. He told Duff that, if he should change his mind after reading the relevant files, 'this would in no way weaken our friendship or my great desire to see you in a station adequate to your political standing and the sacrifices you have made for our cause'. When Duff had read all the papers, they could, Churchill said, have a private talk:

My difficulties are very great and I do not want to add to them by putting a friend in a position where he would feel it his duty to take a line entirely different from the one I am following. It is not simply a question of carrying out instructions. There must be a foundation of agreement such as exists between ministers who join a Government for a common and definite purpose. If ... we find we cannot work together in this field, I will exert myself to find some other sphere which would be agreeable to you.

It was a kind and a generous letter, but it did not deter Duff. During a weekend spent at Bognor he wrote to Churchill to thank him for his letter and the Cabinet papers, either of which

is quite sufficient to convince me of the soundness of your view that General de Gaulle is a potential source of mischief and a standing menace to Anglo–French and, what is even more important, to Anglo–American relations.

In defence of what he now said were his former opinions, Duff pointed out that he, like the general public, had no idea of the various objectionable things which de Gaulle had done. In view of this fact, Duff suggested that:

It might be worth considering whether it would not be wise to allow some of this information gradually to leak out in order to correct the impression that the struggle is between de Gaulle the democrat on the one hand and the reactionary State Department on the other, HMG inclining towards the latter.

Duff went on to argue that any British Ambassador should aim to build up the power of the FCNL at de Gaulle's expense. He suggested that 'an individual who had the reputation of being pro-de Gaulle and no longer deserved it' would make 'a very suitable envoy'. 'I cannot but think', Duff concluded, 'that our views will agree on this subject, and I am glad to remember that they have never differed on any point of foreign policy.'

Duff had, perhaps, slightly overdone the imitation of a zealous convert to Churchill's position on de Gaulle. Certainly Churchill's reply on 19 October emphasized that:

I do not wish in any way to overlook the good qualities of de Gaulle, and I certainly do not underrate the smouldering and explosive forces in his nature or that he is a figure of magnitude.

Churchill advised Duff to 'make every effort to win his confidence and to cultivate friendly relations with him'. He also emphasized his determination to try to build up the FCNL as a collective body which the Allies could deal with. But he tacitly conceded the main point; Duff would go to Algiers, but the final decision would have to await Eden's return from a conference in Moscow.

Why did Duff want the job so much? Its main attraction was that it would give him the reversion of the Paris Embassy; it was a way back into diplomacy. The decline of interest in politics which had set in with Baldwin's departure had reached its nadir in the aftermath of Singapore. It was clear that with Eden having almost a sitting tenancy, the Foreign Office would remain closed to Duff. Politics had lost their attraction. The chance of exerting some real influence in a sphere in which he had so much interest was irresistible.

From Eden's point of view it was an ideal appointment. As Harvey confided to his diary: 'Great knowledge of France. A compliment to the French.... Takes our view of FCNL and de Gaulle. Would be of great help with the PM.'[16] Even the final announcement of his appointment on 22 November improved Anglo–French relations. Because the FCNL was not a Government it did not merit the appointment of an Ambassador, but Duff was given that rank, as a 'personal compliment', thus pleasing the French while not annoying Churchill. The French were delighted at the appointment of such a distinguished politician to the post, seeing it as a compliment to France – which indeed it was.[17]

It was with a light heart and buoyant spirits that Duff left England, accompanied by Diana, on 2 January. He was conscious that a new phase of his career was opening. His interests and his training suggested that he was well-matched with his new post – but not even Duff can have expected quite the political Indian summer which followed.

~~~ 20 ~~~

Between Two Millstones

Had the 'gamble' been worth it? Back in 1924 Duff had asked whether it was worth giving up a gentleman-like career which might lead to an Embassy, for a career in politics. Here he was, almost twenty years later, an Ambassador after all. He had no security of tenure: as a political appointee he could expect nothing from any future Labour Government. But that did not worry him. Ever since Baldwin's departure from politics Duff had been increasingly inclined to look elsewhere for employment. Politics under Chamberlain had done nothing to re-awaken his appetite, and the experience of the Ministry of Information had been almost the final straw. Having reached the end of the political road, Duff was glad to escape back to his first love, diplomacy. But the road to the Embassy in Paris was neither smooth nor comfortable.

Instead of the grandeur of that Embassy, the new Ambassador found himself sharing a villa with his number two, Kingsley Rooker, and in place of state banquets and comfort, he found himself making do with scratch meals, no hot water and damp sheets. Diana, who had been idyllically happy farming at Bognor, was plunged into the deepest depression: no social life, no parties, no bucolic pursuits, no Conrad Russell – nothing, in fact, save the Rookers and a lot of squabbling Frenchmen.

It took two weeks before hot water was available, and a little longer to create a social life, but Duff scarcely had time to notice these unaccustomed hardships. From the very first he was plunged into the task which was to dominate the first period of his mission – trying to bring Churchill and de Gaulle together.

On the day they arrived in Algiers, 3 January 1944, Duff lunched with Harold Macmillan, who had spent the last year as Minister Resident at Allied Forces Headquarters. One of Macmillan's jobs had been to look after the French, and he was able to tell Duff how difficult his new assignment would be. The main problem was that Churchill thoroughly distrusted de Gaulle, a fact of which Duff was already only too well aware. In order to bring the two men together, Macmillan had arranged for them to meet at the villa at Marrakesh where Churchill was recovering from pneumonia. Duff watched with some dismay as the prospects of that meeting faded as first de Gaulle, and then Churchill, decided that his *amour propre* had been offended.

It was only on the morning when de Gaulle was due to arrive, 12 January, that Duff, with the help of Clementine Churchill, finally persuaded Winston to see the Frenchman; and even then it was with the caveat that it should be a purely 'social' call.

It was equally characteristic of the way the Churchill–de Gaulle relationship worked that the Prime Minister should, once the ice had thawed a little, have mellowed and asked 'Why can't we be friends?', while de Gaulle became, if anything, more frosty. The Frenchman objected to the fact that Churchill had invited *him* to Marrakesh which was, after all, *French* territory; while Churchill, as we have seen, held a whole catalogue of sins against de Gaulle. The latter did, however, unbend enough to ask the Prime Minister if he would like to review French troops on the morrow. Churchill, who was always susceptible to personal compliments, accepted the invitation with pleasure. Reporting the meeting to Eden on 21 January, Duff hoped that 'this may be a fresh start, provided further unpleasant incidents can be avoided'; but, of course, they could not be avoided.

Diana described Duff as 'the oilman', and it was in pouring the stuff on troubled waters and into the wheels of diplomacy that he was to spend the next few months; indeed, in one sense the rest of his public career was spent in this fashion.

De Gaulle, or 'Charlie Wormwood' as Diana called him, did less than nothing to help this process. On almost every occasion when Duff asked him to do something to help Anglo–French relations, he contrived to make them worse. Churchill was keen to secure the release from house-arrest of a number of French politicians, including the former Prime Minister, Pierre-Etienne Flandin. He thought they had been the victim of de Gaulle's spite and regarded their fate as an indication of how he would behave if ever he ruled France. He constantly urged Duff to take the matter up with de Gaulle and suspected that he did not press him hard enough. Duff was aware of Churchill's feelings, but also of how de Gaulle would react to suggestions that

Britain was interfering in French internal affairs.[1] All his efforts to pour oil on these troubled waters met with no co-operation. Churchill became convinced that de Gaulle and his 'vindictive crowd' must not be allowed to become the 'sole monopolists of official power';[2] de Gaulle bristled at Churchill's interference; and Duff despaired of getting either of them to see sense.

So it was to prove in every sphere. It may be that, as some of his critics alleged, Duff was inclined to take a broad view of diplomacy and neglect the minutiae, but in Algiers this enabled him to concentrate his efforts on what was really important – restoring Anglo–French amity. Churchill, with his habit of regarding Anglo–French relations as an extension of his relationship with de Gaulle, often forgot the wider dimension; and as for de Gaulle, his diplomatic objectives were not the same as Duff's.

De Gaulle's main efforts in the early months of the year were directed towards securing his own hold on power so that, by the time the Allies landed in France, they would have no alternative but to work with him. Churchill and Roosevelt clung to the hope that by refusing to recognize the French National Committee as the Provisional Government, they were keeping some hold over de Gaulle. Duff tried to point out, as in mid-March, that this was a doomed policy, but all he got for his pains were stern telegrams from Churchill rebuking him and calling into question his loyalty.[3] The problem for Duff was that every step which de Gaulle took to secure his own position further alienated Churchill and Roosevelt. In March the French Committee allowed a former Vichy Minister, Pierre Pucheu, to be shot. Churchill called it 'judicial murder'.[4] Duff tried to explain that de Gaulle had had to allow the execution in order to ensure that there would not be a host of vigilante trials once France was liberated; he had to convince the wilder elements in the Resistance that he would be firm with 'traitors'.[5] Duff was right, but Churchill refused to listen.[6]

Macmillan had warned Duff that French affairs were marked by monthly crises, which turned out to be no more than the truth. In April de Gaulle manœuvred his co-president of the Committee, General Giraud, out of office. Diana, who was on a visit to London at the time, reported Churchill's reaction: 'Charlie had done himself no good.' The more de Gaulle engrossed power to himself the more did he encourage Churchill's tendency to personalize Anglo–French relations – and the more difficult Duff's job became.

Because of the fact that he was based in Algiers, Duff was deprived of most of his home comforts. There was no White's, no Beefsteak and a dearth of pretty women. Given the state of Anglo–French relations social intercourse was not very easy, and the wheels of diplomacy often became clogged. De Gaulle was not the easiest of dinner-guests, nor was Duff the most loquacious of hosts, his natural disinclination for small talk being increased by his shyness of trying to make it in French. It was an unpromising beginning.

Duff had to contend with another, and far more intractable problem: that of his fellow MP, Louis Spears. Spears, who had brought de Gaulle to England in June 1940, had been the British Minister in Syria and Lebanon since 1942, and everyone to whom Duff talked in Algiers thought that he was a major carbuncle on the neck of Anglo–French relations.

Duff had known Spears for twenty years; indeed, he was the stepfather of Rupert Hart-Davis's wife, Comfort. When Rupert had asked his uncle for his opinion of Spears, Duff had replied: 'He's a shit and he'll do you down in the end',[7] which was an accurate prophecy.

It was soon clear to Duff that so deep were the French suspicions of Spears and his designs that they cast a shadow over the whole of Anglo–French relations. Reporting this to Eden on 20 January, Duff wrote:

> If it is our policy to impede the restoration of the French Empire, and to oust the French from Syria and the Lebanon ... he should certainly be allowed to continue on his way, but if, as I believe, our policy is something quite different, I would suggest for him either of Nelson's alternatives – a peerage or Westminster Abbey.

Eden had long ago reached the same conclusion, but the protecting hand of Churchill had kept Spears from the Foreign Office.[8] As the Prime Minister had written to Duff in October:

> The French have an intense dislike of Spears because he fights for British interests in French which is more French than theirs. I have always sustained Spears and there is no doubt at all that he has shown great force of character in Syria.

It was hardly likely that Churchill would have changed his mind about Spears, but Duff thought that an attempt had to be made to remove him.

Questions in Parliament about MPs who were unable to perform their normal duties gave Duff the chance to raise the question of his own future – and that of Spears. In a letter to Churchill on 21 February he applied for the Chiltern Hundreds and told the Prime Minister that he could implement the request at once if it would help. He went on to raise the problems which had been created by the state of relations between Spears and the French, and concluded by suggesting that 'consideration could be given to the three years' disfranchisement that has befallen the burghers of Carlisle'. Churchill replied that there was no need for Duff to resign his seat and that there was 'nothing doing about burghers of Carlisle'. Duff was sure that Spears would do much less harm back in his constituency.

The most that Churchill would agree to do, even under constant pressure from Eden, was to tell Spears not to 'overegg the pudding'.[9] But Spears defended himself hotly and Churchill rallied to his support.[10] He told Eden on 2 April:

> I am not prepared to throw Spears over at the present time. I hope he will take my warning seriously. Duff Cooper has set himself to discredit him in every way, and runs some risk himself in the line he takes.[11]

The Foreign Office more than shared Duff's view that Spears was a first-class blot on the landscape and that he was quite right to tell Eden that Anglo–French relations could not improve while Spears remained in Beirut. In early March the French intercepted a letter from Spears intended for Duff; it was full of the most virulently anti-French sentiment. Duff wrote to Eden on 22 May to tell him of this mishap:

> No more unfortunate document could possibly have fallen into French hands, and I fear that nothing that Spears can do or say in the future can remove the impression which they have that he is their sworn enemy.

Eden drew Churchill's attention to this on 1 June,[12] but the moment was hardly propitious; Anglo–French relations were about to reach their nadir.

Because of Churchill and Roosevelt's refusal to deal with the FCNL, the Allies approached D-Day without any understanding with any French authority. Not unnaturally the French resented this. Churchill reminded Duff at the end of April that there 'is a great deal more in France than is represented by the Vichy Government or the FCNL'. But Duff thought that this was to miss the point; after all, as he minuted on his copy of the telegram: 'there is a great deal in the UK that is not represented by HMG and a great deal more in the USA not represented by FDR'.[13]

When Churchill invited de Gaulle to London at the end of May, the General churlishly refused when he realized that he was not being asked to take part in discussions with the British and Americans about the future of France. After annoying both Duff and Churchill, he was prevailed upon to go but, in a gesture reminiscent of Churchill's in January, de Gaulle made it clear that he was going purely in a military capacity.[14] Thus it was in the company of de Gaulle that Duff set off for London at the start of June; neither of them knew that they were going to have ringside seats for D-Day.

Duff wrote to Diana from the Dorchester on 4 June to say that he had been 'looking forward to a day divided between White's and the girls', but that such was the pace of diplomatic activity that it was straight down to work. But before setting off for Churchill's head-quarters near Portsmouth, he did manage to have ten minutes at White's, 'to remind myself of the taste of port' – he was to need it.

In the circumstances both Churchill and de Gaulle were bound to be tense, but things went badly from the moment the latter arrived at Portsmouth. Churchill was, in Duff's words, 'playing at soldiers and living in a train to everybody's inconvenience'. What de Gaulle thought as they were taken to this railway siding is unknown, but when he saw that Field Marshal Smuts was with Churchill his re-action was predictably frosty; Smuts was regarded with great dis-favour by the French for having pronounced France's obituary as a Great Power, and his presence was hardly tactful.

As a headquarters, the railway carriage left everything to be de-sired: its one bath and only telephone seemed permanently in the possession of the Prime Minister and General Ismay. One of the staff commented to Duff that 'he intended to lead a reformed life in the future because he now knew what hell was like'. Duff was soon to sympathize.

At first things seemed to go well. Churchill explained that the Allies were soon to land in Normandy and went out of his way to be nice to de Gaulle, trying to persuade him to come to an agreement about the governance of liberated France. But de Gaulle was at his most prickly. He turned aside suggestions that he should visit Washington and referred with some asperity to the fact that he had always been willing to talk whereas the Allies had always refused to deal with him. Churchill, under this sort of treatment, became, as he always did with de Gaulle, angry and resentful; after all, he had helped de Gaulle in 1940 and wanted to help him now, but the fellow insisted on going his own way. Shouting, he told de Gaulle that nothing he could do would break the Anglo-American alliance which he, and he was sure the House of Commons, regarded as of paramount importance. De Gaulle responded icily that 'he quite understood that in case of a disagreement between the United States and France, Britain would side with the United States'. Bevin and Eden tried to repair the damage, but to no effect.[15]

Talking with Duff later, Churchill said: 'Well Duffie, I see you flew over in the same aeroplane as your friend the General.' Duff replied: 'He's not my friend. You put me with him, and I do my best to get on with him, but I detest the fellow.' But Churchill was in no mood to bear contradiction: 'No, no, Duffie. He's your friend, this wicked man, this implacable foe of our country.'[16] Nothing would ever shift this notion from Churchill's mind, and he seemed unable to see that what Duff was trying to do was to preserve some basis for an Anglo-French alliance; the fact that he 'got on' with de Gaulle was to be rather important in the major crisis which was brewing.

Duff spent the evening with Eden at Binderton where, united by their common battle with Churchill, he found that he had 'never liked Anthony so much'.

The day before D-Day, 5 June, was spent getting back into the gossip of London life. After having his hair cut at White's, he wandered to Claridges for lunch with two female American journalists. The only cloud on the horizon was that: 'Everyone says "How well you're looking. Bronzed and thin. Diana said you were enormously fat."' He dined with Diana's niece, Caroline Paget, at the Savoy, where his only problem was the usual one of trying to decide whether she really was prettier than her sister Liz; it was something he was quite prepared to leave undecided.

Ernest Bevin, the Minister of Labour, presented quite a different problem when Duff saw him at 11 o'clock on 6 June; there had been, it seemed, fresh and ominous developments with 'Wormwood'. At the Foreign Office he was told by Eden that there 'had been terrible scenes the night before'. Churchill had been told that de Gaulle would neither broadcast on D-Day nor allow French liaison officers to accompany the Allied armies. Eden had tried to explain that the former was due to a misunderstanding, but Churchill had seen the poor French Ambassador, Pierre Viénot, and 'insulted him in the most violent way ... telling him that he was a blackmailer'; he had then 'written a letter to de Gaulle telling him to go back to Algiers immediately'. Fortunately, Brendan Bracken had persuaded him not to send it, but the situation was extremely grave. After talking to Viénot and the diplomat most concerned with French matters, Oliver Harvey, it was agreed that only Duff could persuade the General to change his mind.

Duff saw the General at 3 o'clock and managed to wring from him, as a special favour 'to please *me*', the concession that *some* officers would be allowed to go. Getting back to the Foreign Office with the good news, Duff found he had won a 'great diplomatic triumph', and was greeted with cries of 'only you could have done it'. As he put it in a letter to Diana: 'Wormwood seems to like me. Nobody can understand it. I least of all.' In his official report of the conversation, Duff noted that de Gaulle had said that 'he was always making concessions but ... nobody ever made them to him'. This piece of effrontery prompted Churchill to minute, 'Good lord!'[17]

One thing which reassured Duff from the point of view of the future was that everybody he spoke to – Bracken, the Cranbornes, Bevin, Eden, Victor Rothschild, Attlee, and no doubt the barber at White's – was 'sound on France'; it was a pity that the one man who wasn't was Churchill, who was the one who really counted. Before going to a dinner party which was being held for de Gaulle at the Connaught Hotel, he went to see Clementine Churchill. She had asked to see him and Duff thought that 'Winston had asked her to find out what I was thinking'. He 'left her in no doubt on that subject, but found her violently prejudiced against de Gaulle'.

Dinner was a frosty affair. De Gaulle was, even to Viénot's eyes, '*odieux*', responding scarcely at all to Eden's efforts to persuade him to open talks over the governance of liberated areas of France.[18] He unbent only so far as to allow such conversations between civil servants. It was little wonder that Duff left before the end, announcing that he had an engagement elsewhere. Eden, who felt that he had been left in the lurch, commented to his private secretary, Pierson Dixon: 'Lecherous little beast!'[19]

During his visit to London Duff did what he could to smooth the path of Anglo–French relations. As well as talking to politicians, journalists and newspaper proprietors, he actually dictated a pro-French leader which appeared in the *Daily Mail* on 10 June. But Churchill remained adamantly hostile.

Duff went round to see the Prime Minister on 9 June to tell him that the French had agreed to open conversations, albeit at the lowly level to which de Gaulle had reduced them, and found himself listening to a long 'fulmination against de Gaulle'. Churchill was particularly incensed at de Gaulle's claim that the 'military francs' used by the Allied troops would not be accepted; after all they had British and American backing. Duff told him that this was not so, and Churchill summoned the Chancellor. As Sir John Anderson was unavailable, it was left to a Treasury official to confirm Duff's statement. Churchill responded huffily: 'What did it matter, every country would be bankrupt after the war', only to be told that the French would not because they had 'vast gold reserves' in America. Duff came away from the meeting 'disturbed by the levity' with which Churchill treated the 'whole matter'.

In spite of the success of the Allied landings, Duff still found himself ground between the two great millstones of Churchill and de Gaulle. Even the final scene of the visit went off badly. De Gaulle sent Churchill a very polite letter of farewell, only to receive a reply which was 'a good deal cooler in tone'. Duff recorded in his diary on 16 June, the day he left with de Gaulle for Algiers, that it was 'impossible' to get Churchill 'to take a really reasonable view of the situation'.

Just how unreasonable Churchill was prepared to be had been shown by his reaction to the various efforts made to persuade him to remove Spears from Beirut. He told Duff that 'Massigli had no right to open the letter' which Spears had written, to which piece of moralizing he received the reply that 'if the same thing had happened to anybody in the service of HMG, the only difference in our procedure' would have been that 'after reading and copying it, we should have put it back in the envelope and sent it on' without letting on that it had been opened. But Churchill was unimpressed. Writing to Eden on the subject on 11 June, he said:

> I hope you will not encourage Duff Cooper in his hostile attitude to General Spears.... Both these men are friends of mine, but I should certainly not allow my friendship for Spears to be affected by the attitude of Duff Cooper.

He looked forward, he told Eden, 'to the day when we shall see the representatives of a clean and honest France, decent, honest Frenchmen with whom we can work, instead of the émigré de Gaullists'.[20]

However, Eden's patient diplomacy began to pay dividends once de Gaulle left England on 16 June. The negotiations with the French over the question of civil affairs were both speedy and successful; by the end of June five agreements had been drawn up. Churchill was impressed by this – and even more impressed by the welcome which Roosevelt extended to de Gaulle when the Frenchman visited Washington in mid-July. Eden persuaded Churchill that it would help Anglo–French relations if Spears was recalled to London for 'consultation'.

Duff, who had been pessimistic after the visit to London, was much cheered by the news about Spears. Writing to Eden on 26 July he said that it would be 'difficult to exaggerate the satisfaction with which the French' had greeted it. Duff hoped that Spears would not return:

> You will know I have no private or personal animus in the matter, as I have been on the best of terms with Spears for some twenty years and usually in political agreement with him, but I consider his removal from his present position of such importance that there is little I will not do to secure it.[21]

Eden, who heartily agreed with Duff, told him that he would hold this letter in reserve against the possibility of Churchill wanting Spears to return.

The slow improvement in Anglo–French relations gave Duff some grounds for optimism; if only de Gaulle and Churchill would keep out of things, there was every chance that his real objective, an Anglo–French alliance, would become a possibility. But, of course, the two leaders would not and could not stay out of things.

Churchill's more benign mood was in evidence in early August when, during a tour of the Mediterranean theatre of operations, he proposed to drop in to Algiers and see de Gaulle. As Duff should have learned to expect by now, this friendly gesture only served to produce a boorish response from de Gaulle; he sent a letter saying that he did not wish to disturb the Prime Minister. This produced a fresh outburst of gallophobia on Churchill's part and an exasperated response from Duff: 'it is incredibly stupid on his part, one of the most foolish things he has yet done'.[22]

Paris was liberated on 11 August and there was dancing in the streets of Algiers; everyone began to look forward to getting back to the capital. For Duff there would be changes for the better, not least the proximity to London and to the culture of France; but one thing would not change – he would still have to act as a buffer between Churchill and de Gaulle.

~~~ 21 ~~~

The Future of Europe

In Algiers Duff and Diana had been 'wonderfully unambassadorial'. Evelyn Waugh, who, along with Randolph Churchill, stayed with them in early June 1944, told his wife that he had had an amusing time:

> French & Americans & jews in & out all the time clearly enjoying it very much, D & D very popular & happy, good food, one lavatory, one bath, everyone in pyjamas all the morning, like Venice before the war.[1]

Things had changed for the better since January and the early discomforts had been replaced by a curious life-style which might be called Bohemian-ambassadorial, if it was not for the fact that the two adjectives consort together so ill.

The Bohemian aspect of life reflected Diana's influence. Those who saw her as any sort of *grande dame* could hardly have been wider of the mark. One of the reasons she had so enjoyed her acting career was that she had been able to live among eccentric actors and producers whose love of the bizarre and the unorthodox matched her own. Life at the villa could, however, occasionally become too much, even for her tastes, as she told John Julius in a letter at the end of July:

> It's like a madhouse these days. Randolph stumbles in at 8.30 when Papa is still in his bath and says: 'Can I have my breakfast here?' I say yes. A few minutes later Victor* lollops in, tray in hand and plunks it on the bed. When Sweeny† arrives with Papa's tray there is no place to put it. Papa leaving his contiguous bathroom gives one look, renounces his coffee and leaves the house.

It was little wonder that Duff's temper should sometimes have been, as Waugh and 'Bloggs' Baldwin‡ found out, somewhat short.[2]

---

* Lord Rothschild, b. 1910, biologist, businessman and bomb-disposal expert.
† The Coopers' soldier-servant, now with Lord Rothschild.
‡ Wyndham Baldwin (1904-78). He succeeded his brother as 3rd Earl.

Diana, who had dreaded Algiers, having found herself a rural idyll at Bognor, now had the same feelings about going to Paris. There, surely, the ambassadorial style would have to predominate?

That this never quite came to pass was partly because of Diana's own style; it also owed something to the unusual circumstances in which they began their time in Paris.

Instead of the entry into the great house on the Faubourg St Honoré, the home of Pauline Borghese purchased for Britain by Wellington, they found themselves lodging in the Berkeley Hotel. This small, informal hotel suited Diana; it was not so congenial to Duff, and it was quite unsuitable in the eyes of the Foreign Office. They arrived in Paris on 13 September 1944 and spent their first week in these informal surroundings. The Embassy itself was like some vast rubbish-dump:

> It was stuffed to its closed doors with all the paraphanalia [sic], and treasure, the chattels and junk of Commonwealth diplomats' families and exiled Parisian residents: pianos, hatstands, bureaux, bath-mats, sponges, bottles, good and bad pictures, boxing-gloves and skates, clouds of moth, powder of woodworm.

Such was the first impression of the new British Ambassadress of the house she was to make her own.

On 24 September they were moved to the more impressive surroundings of the Hotel Bristol: 'We have more rooms and more space and I like it better than the Berkeley, but Diana prefers the latter.' Thus wrote the Ambassador, who rather hankered after ambassadorial grandeur. There was one problem thrown up by the change of residence: staying on the same floor was P. G. Wodehouse. The local MI5 man told Duff that he was

> afraid that if the Press got hold of the story it might cause some difficulties here and at home. If the English people were told that Wodehouse was living in luxury on the same floor of the same hotel as the British Ambassador, they might not be best pleased; and the French people might also say that if he were a Frenchman he would have been locked up long ago.

In a city that was seething with accusations of collaboration with the Germans, the British had to be careful of appearances; Wodehouse was moved. This solicitude to avoid charges of harbouring 'collabos' was not always so evident, as we shall see.

Duff found Paris oddly unchanged, especially compared to blitz-scarred London. The diplomatic situation resembled London rather than Paris. During the Munich era he had not so much recanted his earlier faith in the nostrums peddled by the League of Nations, as fallen back on the view of British foreign policy current when he had joined the Foreign Office: Britain's function was to correct the balance of power in Europe. In 1939 and 1940 he had argued the case for a union of Western European states to meet Nazi aggression. The failure of June 1940 and the rise of American and Soviet power had, to him, strengthened the arguments in favour of Western European union.

If the first part of his embassy was dominated by the Churchill–de Gaulle problem, he never let that blind him to its real purpose which was the promotion of an Anglo–French alliance as the first step towards Western European union. These ideas he had propagated before the war and they remained with him. Others too showed signs of thinking similar thoughts. But they were not British. When the Belgian Foreign Minister, Paul-Henri Spaak, raised the question with Eden in early 1944, there seemed little enthusiasm for it. Such lukewarmness and lack of vision suggested to Duff that the time had come to put his thoughts down on official paper. For much of late April and May he collected his ideas and, in a twenty-nine paragraph despatch which was completed on 29 May, he set out his 'political testament'. It is one of the last great state papers of British diplomacy.[3]

Duff's thinking on diplomacy was cogent and eloquent. He wanted British foreign policy to have an architectonic theme; and he wanted Britain's allies to know what it was. Living from hand to mouth, calling it pragmatism and making a virtue of it, would not, he thought, suffice in the post-war era.

He had not totally lost faith in the idea of a League of Nations-type organization. Britain should join any such body; but it would be 'imprudent to stake the whole future of mankind on its success and to make no provision for its failure'. He took it as axiomatic that the mistakes of the inter-war years would be avoided and, in particular, that care would be taken to keep Germany disarmed and harmless. But this would not be a solution to the new problems which Britain was likely to face: 'Throughout her history as a Great Power it has been the policy of Great Britain to prevent the domination of Europe by any one too powerful nation.' In accordance with that policy Britain had fought Philip II's Spain, the France of Louis XIV and Napoleon, and the Germany of the Kaiser and Hitler. This policy had preserved Britain's independence and helped her to build an empire: 'it may therefore be assumed that that policy will be maintained, for to abandon it would be to sign our death-warrant'. In which case: 'The ineluctable logic of events compels us to acknowledge that in the period that follows the war Great Britain must beware of Russia.'

Duff was sensible of the risk of being labelled a right-wing scaremonger who wished to cancel the Anglo–Soviet alliance of 1942, and he was careful to try to avoid it. He stressed that his argument had nothing to do with Russia's politics, except in so far as Communism gave the Russians a 'fifth column' in every democratic nation. It was based upon solid facts. After the war Russia would have the largest army in Europe; she would have the potential to become master of Europe. Now it might be that she would be exhausted by the war, or else genuinely anxious to co-operate with Britain, and Duff would be only too happy if these things came to pass. Certainly she used honeyed words at the moment: 'But two world wars should have sufficed to convince us that the safety of the British Empire should be based on more solid foundations than kind words and scraps of paper can provide.'

Duff thought that the most 'solid foundation' upon which to guarantee freedom from Russian aggression was a union of 'the nations situated on the western seaboard of Europe'. Such a union might start off with a Franco–British alliance and then gather momentum; starting off as a military union, it could become, in time, a political and economic one. This would, Duff thought, make sound sense, given the common economic and political interests of the nations concerned. Such a union would wield enough international influence to speak on equal terms with the twin colossi of Russia and America.

This then was Duff's 'vision splendid'. This was what he hoped to play his part in creating. It would not come in a day. But an Anglo-French alliance, the corner-stone of the edifice, could be had, and had fairly quickly given the will to achieve it. This Duff could press for, would press for, and did press for. And he urged Eden to let Britain's prospective allies know of this plan. The fund of goodwill towards Britain in France, Belgium and other Continental countries was enormous; it would not always be so; let Britain capitalize on it. By maintaining a stony reserve Britain might drive these other nations to make their own accommodation with a Russia bent on expansion.

It was not until July that Eden replied. An initial letter dated 11 July seemed to presage a favourable response. It was 'refreshing that at any rate one of our diplomatic representatives should have found time to try to distinguish the wood from the trees in such a constructive fashion'. All the more bitter was Duff's frustration with the considered reply dated 25 July. It damned Duff's ideas with faint, indeed almost inaudible, praise; and, an ironic touch, it was signed, in Eden's absence, by that future advocate of European union, Gladwyn Jebb.

Eden did not 'of course suggest that there is no danger of the Soviet Union pursuing a policy of aggression in Europe'. But he felt that Duff's suggested policy would 'increase that danger (if it exists) rather than diminish it'. Although Eden went on for several more pages, this was the kernel of his objection. He wanted to base Britain's foreign policy upon the Soviet alliance and the United Nations organization. A Western European defence union might seem to the Russians to be directed at themselves, which would mean that by creating it 'we should be throwing away the considerable chances' of Russia 'pursuing a policy of collaboration after the war'. It might also prompt Russia not to collaborate in creating the United Nations, and, as a consequence, imperil the peace of the world. It might also divide Europe into two armed camps. Was it, Eden wondered, really worth risking all this for an idea which might very well prove impractical?

Duff's frustration showed in his marginalia and, at the bottom of the despatch, he wrote bitterly that Eden was, in fact, saying to him:

> Yours is a very good idea but there are two insuperable obstacles to it – (1) It is difficult; (2) It is dangerous. It might irritate Russia and not wholly please the USA, therefore we prefer to wait and see what policies these countries intend to favour – and meanwhile do nothing.[4]

Duff replied on 16 August, pointing out to Eden how similar were his arguments to those used by the pre-war appeasers. Then it had been said that the democracies must not co-operate against Germany or Italy for fear of annoying the dictators; now Eden was saying the same thing about the Russians: 'this specious fallacy paralysed our foreign policy, for rather than risk doing the wrong thing, we preferred to do nothing'. It was, he told Eden, essential that the smaller states of Europe should be aware that Britain was willing to commit herself to the maintenance of the balance of power on the Continent.

Duff was quite prepared to agree with Eden that a European federation was not going to be achieved easily, but that was

> no reason why we should shut such visions from our horizon. The bottom on which I proposed to build was an alliance between those western

European democracies which had fought together in the war, which was surely not too broad or idealistic a base of construction.

There was, after all, little sense in Britain helping to rearm France and starting staff-talks without being sure that the states of Western Europe were willing to co-operate with her, and 'no useful defence scheme can be concluded' between those powers 'prior to a political agreement'.

Duff's ideas on foreign policy were unashamedly Eurocentric. The great problem in the post-war era would be how to prevent a renewal of German aggression and it would be, he argued, unwise of Eden to rely upon America breaking her long tradition of isolation 'in order to prevent what will always appear in its early stages to be a purely foreign war'. He did not share Churchill's diplomatic priorities.

Finally, Duff turned to the problem posed by the fact that Russia and America might not approve of such a pact. Could we, he asked,

allow the formation of our European policy to wait upon the ukases of the Kremlin or the votes of the American senate. We shall emerge from this war with greater honour than any other country ... the only country that took up arms of its own will at the beginning and remained undefeated until the end. The leadership of Europe will await us, but we may miss the opportunity of acquiring it if we hesitate to adopt a positive foreign policy through fear of incurring the suspicion of Russia on the one hand, or the disappointment of America on the other.

Duff's vision was a bold one, but it was not unrealistic; the materials existed for the construction of a united Western Europe, but someone had to act the master-mason.

But Duff was not wholly disappointed with the response to his despatch. One advantage of being a politician turned diplomat was access to the political world, and Duff had sent copies of his letter to Eden to many other colleagues; the response was overwhelmingly favourable. Oliver Stanley at the Colonial Office, Oliver Lyttelton at the Ministry of Production, Harold Macmillan and Lord Halifax, all replied in laudatory terms. Halifax's letter cheered Duff: he was, after all, Ambassador in Washington and if he thought that the Americans would not necessarily be hostile to a Western European union, who was Eden to say that they would be? Most pleasing of all was the letter which he received in March 1945 from Lord Cranborne. He had resigned with Eden in 1938 and had been far more outspoken than his chief. In him was preserved something of the Cecilian genius for foreign affairs shown by his grandfather, the great third Marquess of Salisbury, and it is to be hoped that, one day, justice will be done to the fifth Marquess. His letter to Duff enclosed a copy of a document upon which he had been labouring which expressed similar views. He was scathing in his opinion of the Foreign Office reply which he stigmatized as 'utterly futile. It is just our old friend appeasement over again, and we can't build a positive foreign policy on that.' He pointed out that Halifax in Washington and Clark-Kerr in Moscow both reported that the governments to which they were accredited had no a priori objections to such a scheme as Duff proposed, and that even if they had: 'we really mustn't let ourselves be bullied into the position of a second-class power'. He did not agree with Eden's claim that 'there is plenty of time'. Like Duff, Cranborne feared that 'if we continue to snub the Western European countries they will begin to look elsewhere, and the chance may be lost'. But even before he had received Cranborne's support, Duff had begun to write a further epistle to doubting Eden. And there was certainly sufficient reason for Duff to take up his pen again.

France played a pivotal role in Duff's scheme. He had feared that the Churchill–de Gaulle feud would so damage Anglo–French relations that it would be impossible to conclude an Anglo–French alliance; his fears seemed, as ever, to have been correct.

When Duff arrived in Paris on 13 September 1944 he found de Gaulle installed in power along with his Provisional Government; but still Roosevelt and Churchill refused to acknowledge him and it. In early October 1944 Duff lamented to Harold Nicolson:

> These personal misunderstandings are really very unhappy, because they spoil the wonderful opportunity that exists of forming a firm and lasting friendship between the two countries. Never have the English been so popular in France as they are today, and the most popular of all of them is the Prime Minister, who would get a delirious welcome if he came here. ... But he cannot come until we have recognized their Government, and the longer we put off doing so now, the more foolish we appear, and the less thanks we shall get when we eventually do so.[5]

He warned the Foreign Office that they would have to face the fact that 'the time has come when we cannot expect any gratitude in return for recognition'.[6]

Duff's fears were well founded. The Americans, having through their influence with Churchill, held the British back, got in ahead of them with their decision to recognize the Provisional Government. The manner in which they did so caused considerable annoyance to Duff and the Foreign Office.

When Duff saw the American Ambassador, Jefferson Caffery, on the morning of 20 October, he was told that Roosevelt had taken no final decision about recognizing de Gaulle's Government. This was the usual American line, and Duff went away sighing over their obtuseness. He spent the evening at a show and learnt only in the early hours of the morning that his staff had been hunting all over Paris for him. Charles Peake, the diplomatic liaison officer with General Eisenhower's headquarters, had discovered that the State Department had, earlier that day, told Caffery to inform the French that recognition would soon be granted. All that Duff and the Foreign Office could do was to mutter under their breath and follow suit. Roosevelt's lame excuse was that it was all the fault of the State Department, but Duff, who had laboured so hard in vain, could not help feeling that the Americans were not averse to gaining a diplomatic advantage at the expense of their British allies. The fact that Caffery had a reputation as an Anglophobe confirmed him in this suspicion.[7]

On 23 October the Ambassadors of the three Great Powers conveyed the news of the formal recognition of the French Government to the Foreign Minister, Georges Bidault. Had this come when Duff had wanted it might have given an impetus to an Anglo–French entente. Now it seemed superfluous – even a little insulting. When Duff dined with de Gaulle on the following evening he found that all his forebodings had been only too correct:

> France, he said, was now determined to go ahead for herself without regard for the Allies who seemed to take no interest in her future. The result would be that Russia, to whom the continent of Europe was being abandoned, would in due course, when she had absorbed the other countries, pick up France who would be unable to resist her.

He also told Duff:

> The three Great Powers were trying to settle Europe without Europe being consulted. The result would be that later the settlement imposed by the Powers would be torn up and Europe would settle her own future. In that final settlement France, as being the most important purely European continental Power, would play the principal part.

As Duff commented in his report of this conversation for Churchill:

> Although the General displayed throughout a singularly dreary evening his usual reluctance or inability to say anything pleasant, I, nevertheless,

came away with the feeling that he had enjoyed himself more than any of his guests.[8]

De Gaulle's attempts to assert France's position as a Great Power added a fresh difficulty in the way of the fulfilment of Duff's vision. He hoped that some headway might be made in early November when Churchill was due to visit Paris. It took Duff several days of hard work to convince Churchill that Paris was a safe place for him to visit. But in spite of Duff's success and the apparent cordiality of the meeting, nothing was achieved. Churchill was determined not to have a 'serious conference' with de Gaulle, while the latter, chagrined at this snub, looked towards Moscow for consolation. Duff's warning that the European nations might look elsewhere was not a hollow one. De Gaulle's visit to Moscow in December 1944 only served to chill Anglo–French relations further.

Churchill was thoroughly sceptical about 'these ideas of what is called a "Western bloc"' and rather wished to hit them on the head. Eden was not so dismissive. Since his reply to Duff's despatch, the Foreign Secretary had been delving deeper into the question of European union and saw some merit in it. He was particularly anxious that de Gaulle should not conclude a bilateral Franco–Soviet pact, as he looked forward to linking the Anglo–Soviet alliance of 1942 with an Anglo–French pact which would form a tripartite diplomatic entente. He persuaded a reluctant Churchill to put the idea to Stalin.[9] De Gaulle took this as a sign that the British did not want a Franco–Soviet pact and insisted on signing one. This merely served to convince Churchill that all talk of an Anglo–French pact was premature. It also helped to get Duff in hot water.

The lack of progress towards any Anglo–French entente, despite a year of effort, merely prompted Duff to try to give things a little 'encouragement'. He saw de Gaulle on 5 January 1945 and tried to dispel his suspicions of Britain's reaction to the Franco–Soviet pact. He also tried to deal with the wider aspect of Anglo–French relations. Duff told London that he thought de Gaulle did not 'want to give the appearance' of being in favour of an Anglo–French pact for his own reasons. The two outstanding problems between the two countries were the future of the Levant and the future of Germany; Duff thought that de Gaulle wanted to link an Anglo–French treaty to a settlement of these questions, hence his reticence. Duff more than made up for this, telling the Foreign Office that he was in favour of an Anglo–French treaty and did not think de Gaulle's reluctance to take the initiative should 'form an obstacle'.

'It is these kind of telegrams from Mr Duff Cooper', Churchill wrote to Eden on 11 January, 'that make me doubt his wisdom and sense.'[10] The Prime Minister remained inflexibly opposed to any attempt to court de Gaulle, refusing even to invite him to the Yalta conference.

Only one opportunity seemed to present itself for Duff to make any progress in the aftermath of this setback. At the end of February he took part in talks at Eden's country home, Binderton, when the Foreign Secretary met Bidault and the head of the French Foreign Office, Jean Chauvel. But this time it was the turn of the French to place spokes in the wheel of progress.[11] Bidault (fuelled, Duff feared, by Eden's brandy)

> did not distinguish himself. He got excited, rhetorical and noisy ... adopted a threatening attitude, saying that if there were another meeting of the Big Three without France, France would put herself at the head of all the discontented powers – a *fronde* of nations.

This was hardly encouraging. Duff would have agreed with Oliver Harvey's verdict on the talks: 'I'm afraid the Anglo–French treaty is down the drain forever.' He was, however, less despairing than Harvey – or more willing to persevere.

It had been a request from the Belgian Foreign Minister to Eden in March 1944 which had persuaded Duff to write his original despatch on the future of British foreign policy; it was a telegram from the British Ambassador in Brussels, Sir Hughe Knatchbull-Hugessen, in March 1945 which prompted him to return to the theme and compose its successor.

In early March Sir Hughe informed Eden and the Foreign Office that the Belgians were fearful of French ambitions in the Low Countries. Duff, writing on 11 March, told the Foreign Secretary that, while it was early days to be worrying about such things:

> The freedom of the Low Countries from French interference is one of the oldest and soundest principles of British foreign policy, and the answer to this problem would seem to me to be the formation of a group of Western European democracies which I have been urging on the Foreign Office for the last twelve months.

He also took the opportunity to point out that whereas Russia had taken many steps to consolidate her influence in Eastern Europe, the

British had done nothing. He warned that France might indeed become so discontented that she would lead a *fronde* of nations; such a league, 'under the benign patronage of Russia, would present a very grave menace to Great Britain'.

Nor was Duff content with mere despatches. He sought, as he ever did, to find an opportunity of giving British policy a shove in the right direction. Thus it was that when, at the end of March, he found Bidault speaking favourably of the prospects of an alliance, he followed up the subject when he next saw de Gaulle on 5 April. He was unwise enough to send a detailed report of the conversation to London.[12]

His conversation with de Gaulle ranged over the whole area of Anglo–French relations, with Duff offering comments upon ways of dealing with particularly contentious topics like the Rhineland and the Levant. De Gaulle referred to the forthcoming San Francisco conference at which the organization of the United Nations was to be discussed. Duff said that it was 'unfortunate' that the Russians seemed so unhelpful, insisting upon a seat for all the Soviet Socialist Republics, to which de Gaulle replied that he thought the Russians had always intended to sabotage it. Duff then

> mentioned the possibility of an Anglo–French pact. He said that there was nothing he desired more, and that he had always desired it, but that he wanted it to be something more than the Anglo–Soviet or the Franco–Soviet pacts, he wanted it to be an alliance, in which all outstanding questions between France and England should be definitely settled.

When Duff suggested that a pact could be concluded before the San Francisco conference, de Gaulle said that there was no hurry. Duff thought that de Gaulle was now 'conscious of a new menace looming up from the East' against which it was 'more than ever necessary for the two greatest Powers of Western Europe to stand together'.

Later that day Duff saw Chauvel, who told him that Bidault had been so impressed by de Gaulle's mood that 'they were now all in favour of trying to conclude a real alliance before San Francisco'. In view of de Gaulle's caution on this subject, Duff should perhaps have quizzed Chauvel a little more closely as to whether Bidault's view was shared by his master. But he did no such thing; instead he telegraphed a 'most immediate' message to London proposing that Chauvel should be allowed to come to England with drafts of agreements on the Levant, the Rhineland and an 'all-in alliance'. Duff thought he had good reason to feel both pleased and optimistic as he set out for a visit to Lyons on 10 April; he would not have remained so had he known how Churchill had reacted to all of this.

Duff's telegram of 5 April brought forth a grand Churchillian explosion. In a minute to Eden on 6 April he roundly castigated Duff for his *démarche* in raising the question of an alliance with de Gaulle – and for his comments on the Levant and the Rhineland:

> It crosses my mind that de Gaulle rushed precipitately into the arms of Russia and has been, for the last two years, ready to play Russia off against Great Britain, but that after making an alliance with them he was somewhat disappointed with the result.

The Frenchman was now trying to draw closer to Britain, but he should be left alone until he asked for an alliance. Churchill thought that all Duff's attitudes

> are entirely contrary to our policy as you and I have agreed it.... Why on earth can he not remain passive and be wooed, instead of always playing into de Gaulle's hands and leaving him the giver of favours when he has none to give? This telegram emphasizes very clearly in my mind the very great differences between Mr Duff Cooper and His Majesty's Government. Why can you not give him clear instructions that he is not to press for any engagements with France?

Churchill thought that 'we shall only be snubbed and blackmailed'.[13]

Eden and the Foreign Office actually approved of Duff's conduct, and defended him against Churchill's accusations of indulging in unauthorized initiatives by pointing out that it was Chauvel and Bidault who had suggested signing an alliance before San Francisco. Churchill did not care; 'the essence of diplomacy is right timing', he told Eden on 8 April, and Britain, being in a 'stronger position', could 'afford to wait'. He was eventually persuaded to let Chauvel come to London, but only on condition that no commitments were entered into.

Unfortunately for Duff, Churchill's fears turned out to be quite justified. Eden's offer to receive Chauvel was met with a snub. On 19 April Bidault replied that he had been thinking of taking a draft pact with him to San Francisco, but was now unlikely to do so, since de Gaulle had not made up his mind on the content of the notes that would need to be exchanged about the Rhineland and Levant questions. It was, Bidault concluded, unlikely that Chauvel would go to

London. Churchill was not slow to point out to Eden that this was what he had forecast, and he sent a rebuke to Duff:

> I was sorry that you indulged in a *démarche* towards de Gaulle about a Franco–British treaty ... the only result has been what I foresaw from the beginning – that this man has had another opportunity of inflicting a slight upon the Western Allies.[14]

Duff thought Churchill's allegation unjust and pointed out, as Eden had done, that it was the French who had made the *démarche*.[15] He later discovered that Bidault and Chauvel had gone beyond what de Gaulle had authorized, and the General himself denied that there had been any intention of snubbing Britain; but Anglo–French relations were hardly cordial enough to bear the burden even of a misunderstanding.

This was, as things turned out, the last missed opportunity for Churchill, whose period of office was drawing to a close. There was one last, and major, crisis to come, as though to ensure that Duff's mission under Churchill would end as it had begun, stormily.

~~~ 22 ~~~

His Proper Profession

Visiting Duff in November 1944 Harold Macmillan found him

> in capital form, much enjoying the 'Empire' splendour of the apartments
> as well as his great diplomatic success. It is quite clear that Duff has now
> really found (or returned to) his proper profession. But he has returned
> immensely strengthened and developed by his experience in politics.[1]

It was a shrewd assessment.

Diplomacy was Duff's 'proper profession' and Paris the ideal place
for him to practise it. He was a diplomat of the old school. He belonged to the Service he had joined in 1913: politics enthralled him,
economic policy bored him. He saw that Europe would lose power
over its own destiny unless its statesmen did something about it, and
he knew what should be done. No doubt there were economic and
other obstacles in the way – there were always problems; but given
the will and the vision they could be dealt with. Someone had to take
the first step and, in default of anyone else doing so, he would.

He did not enjoy the formal aspects of his mission – the pomp and
protocol – but they were a small price to pay for doing an important
job in the city he loved most. It had been with a sense of relief that
he had noted that Paris 'has all changed very little'. Paris was to him
the home of civilized living, the city of Napoleon and Talleyrand, a
place to feel at home; this feeling communicated itself to the Parisians,
which helped make him a popular Ambassador.

But if the external appurtenances of the city had changed but little,
there were other things which had altered. Brilliant Parisian Society
took some time to revive, and even when it did, accusations of col-
laborationism were rife. That it did revive so quickly was due in no small
measure to Diana, who quickly gathered round her that circle of actors,
artists and writers which usually sprang up in her wake: Christian

(Bébé) Bérard, Jean Cocteau, and the poetess Louise de Vilmorin, were at the heart of what Diana christened '*La Bande*'; and visiting Britons, such as Evelyn Waugh, Stephen Spender, Peter Quennell and Harold Nicolson, were also among those who thronged the *salon vert*. No doubt the fact that warmth, food and drink were to be found in plentiful supply there accelerated the process by which the Embassy became the centre of Parisian Society, but Diana's personality was the catalyst without which it would never have happened.

The informal parties gave Diana great delight, but the social prestige enjoyed by the British Embassy was not to everyone's taste. *The Times* was to observe in its feline way that Duff's 'range of contacts was too small to make him the ideal ambassador'; which was one way of saying that too many 'collabos' and too few trades unionists attended Embassy functions. Massigli, now Duff's opposite number in London, spread stories that too many collaborationists frequented the *salon vert*, and there were parts of the Labour Party where such rumours were easily accepted as the truth. Such stories did him some harm, and Duff constantly denied them. What his critics overlooked was the ease with which the label 'collabo' could be fixed to anyone who had actually spent the war in France.

In one sense the only people who could plausibly claim to be free of any taint of collaborating with the Germans were those sea-green incorruptibles who had been in London with de Gaulle; but these were few in number. Duff was well aware of the problems posed by the charges and countercharges that so and so was a 'collabo'. He and Diana used de Gaulle's Chef de Cabinet, Gaston Palewski, to adjudicate in all doubtful cases. He was their 'pilot fish'; but it may have been that his standards were not those employed by harsher judges.

Lord Rothschild tells a splendid story about the time when the French authorities asked him to warn Duff about the company he was keeping. No sooner had he acquitted himself of this delicate task than his host had one of his famous 'veiners', which resulted in the suspension of their friendship for several days. It is a nice story. Duff's diary bears no trace of such a meeting, but it has the ring of authenticity. Certainly the French authorities were not averse to the indirect approach. At the beginning of 1945 Duff was approached by his friend Victor (Toto) de Lesseps with a list from the *Sûreté* accusing many of those who frequented the *salon vert* 'of being pederasts and collaborationists'. Duff was indignant. No doubt Jean Cocteau was a queer, and others too – Diana had always found the company of such folk amusing and restful – but he was damned if he was going to be told who could and could not come to the Embassy. If the French wanted to tell him something, let them do so officially: 'I rather frightened Toto by saying that I must have an explanation or an apology'; he received the latter. He also wrote to the Foreign Office to ask them to warn Massigli to stop giving currency to such stories. The presence of Louise de Vilmorin at the Embassy ensured that the rumours would continue.

Duff had first met her at a party given at the Russian Embassy in early November 1944. He had found her attractive and had been annoyed to be called away before the end by busines. His disgruntled mood did not last. Louise went with him to the door and he 'found myself kissing her and falling in love'. Thus began an affair which was to last for most of his remaining years in Paris. Diana admired her as much as Duff did. They found her intelligence, wit, stories and dazzling conversation irresistible. There were those who found her too precious by half, but to Duff, at the budding of their affair, she could do no wrong. She was tall, very lame and rather frail; adept at love-making she was a grand passion – for a while.

His ardour was largely physical, and with familiarity came boredom. Love-making was a diversion, a delicious relaxation, not a commitment. Duff liked sensual women, those who, like him, took their pleasure where they found it with no nonsense about love. Nothing killed passion more quickly than too great a seriousness.

Louise, or 'Loulou' as everyone called her, first moved into the Embassy in early 1945 when she fell ill; thenceforth she was seldom out of it. But too close a proximity brought problems. Duff began to find her something of a trial. His passion lessened, and her possessiveness, her anti-Americanism and anti-Semitism, all led to quarrels. By the time he said good-bye to her before going on his trip to Lyons in April 1945, he was afraid that she was a good deal more upset by their parting than he was: 'I am very fond of, but not madly in love with her.' A nadir was reached in May when his old temptress, Daisy Fellowes, came to stay at the Embassy. Her masculine attitude to love affairs always made an appeal to Duff's senses even when, as on this occasion, he found her rather unattractive. She was the one mistress whom Diana resented, having made herself available to Duff soon after their wedding. Diana did not like the way Duff paid so much attention to Daisy on this occasion. Equally discontented was Loulou, who fled the dining salon without even a cavatina. Duff and Diana pursued her back to her house where, in Duff's words:

> We found her in bed, poor darling, very unhappy. We had a great many tears, but she was fairly calm before we left. It was charming, if rather odd, to see Diana trying to comfort her and assuring her that I really loved her.

It must indeed have been 'odd'. Diana correctly diagnosed the problem: 'Duff belongs to the sense school, she to the sensibility. I fear she is on his nerves, he probably prefers bitchy women and cannot carry the weight of her adoration.' As Duff put it when speculating on the reasons why he did not find a 'perfectly nice young lady' very arousing: 'That's the trouble – she's perfect. I like 'em a bit spoilt.'

His affair with Louise continued for most of the time he was in Paris, and whatever it may have done for his reputation in London, it did his prestige in Paris 'some good as she is acknowledged to be the most remarkable and attractive woman' in Society. And whatever the truth about her wartime career, the French authorities did not scruple to use her as an unofficial contact with the Ambassador. During the Levant crisis in June 1945 Palewski saw Loulou and

> solemnly informed her that he was instructed by General de Gaulle to ask her to convey to me his assurances, in which Palewski joined, that they both regretted that owing to recent events their relations with the British Embassy could not be what they had been in the past, but they wished me to know that they still had nothing but the friendliest feelings towards me personally.

Duff thought this 'a most extraordinary procedure' and wondered that de Gaulle lent himself to it.[2] Maybe he did not. Palewski could well have been giving free rein to his own penchant for intrigue as he had a few weeks earlier when he had offered Louise money ('he almost produced a cheque-book') to spy on Duff. Channon did not know the half of it when he wrote: 'Duff's career resembles Talleyrand's more closely every year.'[3]

The glamour which attached to the British Embassy during this period was never recaptured after the departure of Duff and Diana. They provided a rare mixture of the grand diplomatic style and the Bohemian intellectual. To outsiders their marriage seemed as odd as ever it had. The Ambassador's latest *amour* was a source of gossip which could be guaranteed to fill awkward gaps in con-

versation at diplomatic cocktail parties, and the activities of his
wife were an endless subject of rumour and speculation. The
prophecies of imminent divorce which had been part of such tales a
decade earlier now seem to have stopped; the obvious success of this
odd marriage made them otiose. Diana had long given up worrying
about Duff's women. No longer jealous, she had convinced herself
that she never had been. She loved Loulou and felt no challenge from
any of Duff's more fleeting attachments. Only Daisy Fellowes remained capable of arousing her ire – and that was more a matter of
habit than of anything else. She was happy with her poets and actors.
And Duff? Women were as essential and peripheral as ever. He 'loved
the sex' as much as ever he had done, finding, like MacHeath, that
'nothing unbends the mind like them'. There was no decline in his
vigour or potency and he still found no reason for believing in platonic
friendships. He loved the company of pretty women and needed the
diversions provided by clandestine love affairs, but that was all there
was to it. They moved into their mid-fifties, in Duff's mind at least,
as a latter-day Darby and Joan. It was not an image which com-
mended itself to Diana, who dreaded advancing age and did all she
could to ignore it. He was as stoical as ever. There was no use lamenting the inevitable so it was only sensible to make the most of it.
Autumn was his favourite season. He strove to inculcate something of
this into her, but without success.

If he was thus a considerable figure in the diplomatic and social
world of Paris, he was also one in the eyes of his staff.[4] At first most
of them stood in awe of him, or rather of what they had heard about
him. It did not take long for awe to cede precedence to admiration,
particularly with his private secretaries. In Algiers he had been served
by Eric Duncannon, the heir to the Earldom of Bessborough. Well-
born, well-bred, half-French, young and handsome, Duncannon was
well-fitted to win the confidence of the Ambassador. He was succeeded
in his post by another young aristocrat with French blood in his veins,
George Mercer-Nairne, who had just become Lord Lansdowne. The
fact that he was a descendant of Talleyrand told in favour of his
appointment; that he proved efficient and discreet were added bon-
uses. His dark good looks made him a welcome figure at Embassy
parties – and the beau of the female staff. Duff found him congenial
and was sad when he decided to leave in early 1945 for personal
reasons. Lansdowne wrote to him to say: 'You have taught me a lot
and I enjoyed the work enormously.'

Eric Duncannon proved willing to step back into the breach, helped by John de Benden, whose beautiful wife attracted Duff's attention. Duff felt happier with non-professional diplomats, finding many of the regular Foreign Office men 'dull dogs'. He made an exception for some of the younger men assigned to his staff such as Brooks Richards and Robin Hooper, and had great respect for Ashley Clarke who joined him as minister in 1946. Those who worked with him in Paris are lavish in their praise. He was a demanding chief – a firm believer in delegation and its virtues – and he liked his subordinates to pull their weight; but once his trust had been won, he was generous with praise and willing to give his juniors their head.

Those who imagined that the Ambassador's social activities left little time for work underestimated him. Eric Duncannon found him an astonishingly quick worker who would 'rip the heart out of a despatch' almost at once, before settling down to *The Times* crossword while awaiting drafts from Chancery. Shoddy drafts met with short shrift and explosive comments; the young men found this insistence on only the best an exhilarating introduction to diplomacy. Once the Ambassador had formed the opinion that a young man was to be trusted he would give him a great deal of freedom. The most important documents, particularly those dealing with European union, were the work of the Ambassador himself. Duncannon marvelled at the slowness of the handwriting, and Lord Lansdowne's comment was: 'I have never seen anyone write so slowly.'

Duff's style of composition remained the same as it had in the 1930s. He would spend a long time in thought and then write, thinking as he formed the letters, rarely crossing out, producing a clear and beautifully written despatch. Like most people with good hand-writing, Duff was extremely fussy about what he used to write with, employing a relief-nibbed dipping-pen; not for him the barbarity of the biro. Between words he would shake his pen, spotting a sheepskin rug kept at the side of his desk for that purpose.

Those who worked under him at the Embassy found him an impressive figure. But he was also a kind one. When one of the junior staff, Barley Alison, found herself being harassed by an unscrupulous landlord and, in distress, turned to her chief, Duff dealt swiftly with the offender and told her to tell him if there was any further trouble. When she left the Service in 1951 he wrote:

I am glad ... to learn that you are leaving the Foreign Office. It is no place for a pretty young woman. You don't know what might have happened to you if you had stayed in it. You might have become exactly like Sir William Strang.*[5]

Duncannon too found that Duff was quite different to the run-of-the-mill Ambassador. Quite apart from the occasional embarrassment caused when a letter not marked 'private' was opened in the office, and then found to be from one of the Ambassador's lady-friends, there were other unconventional moments.

Duff's love of wine has already been noted. He was one who considered that, after breakfast, any meal without a bottle of wine was not complete. His consumption did not, however, leave him noticeably the worse for wear. If he rarely left the dining-table stone-cold sober, it was even rarer that he did so noticeably under the influence; those who tried to match him, however, could find themselves in difficulty. But seasoned drinker though he was, even he could meet a fence too high. His downfall, and Duncannon's, came at the hands of the Russians.[6]

Receptions and dinner-parties at the Russian Embassy were always rather hazardous. Bogomolov, the Russian Ambassador, and his wife were a taciturn couple and, *tête-à-tête*, could have bored at international standard. Receptions, which by their nature lacked this peril, had their own gin-trap. Diana thought that the sole purpose of Soviet diplomacy on these occasions was to drink the other Powers under the table; a cunning and little-known aspect of the Cold War? Duff ought then to have been on guard when invited back to the Russian Embassy along with the American Ambassador, Jefferson Caffery, by Bogomolov in July. The three Ambassadors were accompanied by their private secretaries. At the Embassy they were led upstairs, where two tables had been laid. '*Les trois grands là*', said Bogomolov, gesturing to the larger table, '*et les trois petits grands là*', he told Duncannon and the other secretaries, pointing at the smaller table. Both tables were piled high with caviare and other delicacies; and each place-setting had a carafe of vodka. These last were intended to fuel the toasts. Bogomolov started off with one to his great leader; Duff and Caffery followed suit. On and on they went, down and down the vodka went, until fifteen toasts had been pronounced and two litres of vodka consumed. At this point Bogomolov's private secretary slid under the table vomiting; he was carried out by two burly maids. Duncannon was informed by his host that it was his turn to propose a toast. Being half-French and in Paris, he suggested one to de Gaulle. Bogomolov

* Permanent Under-Secretary at the Foreign Office, 1949–53.

did not agree, but in trying to reach Duncannon to tell him so, he tottered over, pulling him down too. 'Beaming' in a benign fashion at this example of Anglo-Russian collaboration, Duff helped Duncannon up and, leaning the one on the other, they managed to get back to the ambassadorial Rolls. Unfortunately they were both due at a party, but, when the Rolls arrived, Duff 'realized that it would be wiser not to go in, so I sent poor Eric in to collect Diana, Loulou and John Julius. They drove me home and I remember little more.' Eric Duncannon's recollection was that it had been he who had advised Duff to stay put; he was unwise enough to stay at the party and needed to be carried home. Duff felt quite well the next morning, but by the evening he was decidedly unwell; he spent most of the next week in bed recovering. His one consolation was that neither Bogomolov nor Caffery was seen very much in public during the same period. Fortunately for Duff's liver this was one area of conflict in which there was no escalation.

His convalescence was made no easier by the uncertainty which existed about his future by early August. In May the Churchill coalition which Duff had joined five years before finally broke up and a general election was announced for June.

Although a Conservative and a friend of Winston's, Duff's feelings about the possibility of a Churchillian triumph were distinctly mixed. The Prime Minister's antagonism towards de Gaulle was one of the most formidable obstacles in the way of an improvement in Anglo-French relations. Moreover, Duff was well aware of how little confidence his old friend now reposed in him. A change of Government could only improve the prospects of an Anglo-French alliance.

The British election campaign was obscured for Duff by the recrudescence of another obstacle to good relations with the French – the Levant. Churchill's visit to Paris in November 1944 had been accompanied by the announcement that Spears was to leave Beirut; Duff and the Foreign Office were almost as pleased as the French themselves. But his departure was not wholly to the benefit of the French. With him gone, it was easier for the Foreign Office to see the real crux of the problem: that the Syrians and Lebanese wanted independence while the French did not want to give it to them.

As Franco-Syrian relations worsened, Duff did his best to explain the French case to London. It was, he pointed out, only natural for the French to suspect any advice given them by the British – the history of Anglo-French colonial conflict was all the proof needed in

Paris to show that the English coveted French colonies. What was needed, Duff stressed, was tact and diplomacy. Unfortunately, however convinced Eden might have been by a long despatch from Duff along these lines in mid-May, the effect was spoiled by French actions.

At the end of May the French tried to reinforce their garrisons in Syria. The Syrians tried to prevent this and were met with a response in the best traditions of French colonialism – Damascus was bombarded. The Syrians appealed to the British and Americans for help against this aggression. In the face of a threat to the security of the whole Middle East, the British acted decisively, declaring martial law in Syria.

The whole business made Duff despair. It seemed almost a rule of nature that, whenever he tried to improve Anglo–French relations, de Gaulle did something unpardonable. As Ambassador, Duff was charged with the task of conveying the news of the British action to de Gaulle; this proved difficult. 'The General is indisposed', 'he is unavailable', these were all the answer his requests to Palewski elicited. The French press was hostile and there was talk of another 'Fashoda'. Duff, who had first visited Paris at the time of that humiliation for the French, was not anxious to preside over a repeat of the episode.

The 2nd of June 1945 was their twenty-sixth wedding anniversary and Duff had booked seats for himself and Diana at a performance of *A Midsummer Night's Dream*. In view of the diplomatic crisis advice was not lacking that the treat should be postponed. Duff ignored it. In the interval, the theatre manager announced that the British Ambassador and his wife were in the audience; Duff braced himself for the eggs and was correspondingly delighted to receive only applause.

His interview with 'Cheer-up Charlie' (as Diana renamed de Gaulle) on 4 June was less pleasant. Duff came away with the impression that, had he been able to do so, de Gaulle would have liked nothing better than to have declared war on Britain. But the French were not in such a position and diplomacy triumphed. Thanks to Louise, Duff was reassured that neither de Gaulle nor Palewski had any complaint against himself. By the time the crisis was settled in late July both Palewski and de Gaulle had good reason to be nice to the Ambassador – they were afraid he would be removed by the new Labour Government produced by the election.

Popular opinion said that Churchill could not lose, but popular opinion was wrong. Although Duff had given up his seat gladly, he was a 'little melancholy' during the election campaign – the first one for twenty years that he had not contested. The advent of Attlee and his Labour Government gave rise to mixed feelings in Duff's breast. His first reflection was that there was 'no doubt that the removal of Winston, Cherwell and Max will make my task easier'; but then came the rub – 'unless I am removed myself'.

Duff had no reason to fear the Labour Government, but he also had little to hope for from it. Rumours that Ernest Bevin was likely to become Foreign Secretary cheered Duff who had 'always been on good terms' with him. On the debit side of the account were the many rumours that the Labour Party would demand the recall of Ambassadors who were clearly political appointees. Duff was in London on 26 July when the election results were declared and was able to read all the many press reports to this effect. His reaction was, as ever, sanguine: 'I doubt it. Nor should I greatly mind. Curiously enough Diana would mind much more than I should. She loves Paris now although she was not prepared to and did not at first.' He certainly was not prepared to carry on with a cloud of question-marks surrounding his future. He wrote to Bevin on 31 July, congratulating him on his new office, adding an assurance that: 'If you feel you would prefer to be represented in Paris either by a regular member of the Foreign Service or by a politician of your own Party, I shall not resent, though I shall regret your decision.'[7] He asked for, and was granted, an interview with the new Foreign Secretary, at which he unfolded his own hopes and plans for the future of Europe. He told Bevin that: 'A great opportunity awaits the new administration of doing rapidly what both democracies think should have been done already.'

Duff was aware of Diana's agitation at the prospect of leaving *La Bande*; he was soon made aware that there were others who felt the same way. On 31 July Loulou told Duff that Palewski had asked her what steps he and the General could take in London to ensure that there was no change of Ambassador; Duff asked her to tell him to write to the Foreign Office.

Bevin's response to these efforts came on 6 August while Duff was recovering from his bacchanalia with Bogomolov: 'As regards your own position, I will be writing to you in due course; but for the moment, as I am sure you will understand, there is nothing very definite that I can say.'[8] Duff did not 'understand' and was annoyed at what he saw as prevarication. Instead of a clear verdict from Whitehall, there were obscure auguries which could be divined from the gossip-columns and the rumour-mongers.

An invitation to come to London for talks on the future of Anglo–French relations on 8 August seemed to imply that immediate dismissal was not in the offing. When he discovered that there was no intention of removing Halifax from Washington he concluded that he would survive: 'They can hardly keep on the arch-Municheer and sack the man who resigned at Munich.' Conversation with Bevin on 11 August failed to remove the ambiguities: 'He was far from reassuring about by own position. He was evidently not in a position to give me any undertaking, but I felt that he himself was well-disposed.' More satisfactory was the fact that Bevin wanted good Anglo–French relations. Although Duff was never vouchsafed any promise of prolonged tenure, he was, in fact, safe since, as Bruce Lockhart recorded, Bevin was 'in complete agreement on policy' with Duff 'whatever he might think of Diana and the Embassy entourage'.[9] If *La Bande* and the *salon vert* survived to delight Parisian Society it was because the burly ex-carter and the cultivated diplomat were both in favour of a renewal of the *entente cordiale*.

⌒⌒⌒ 23 ⌒⌒⌒

Nunc dimittis

Bevin had made it clear that he wanted to improve Anglo–French relations and had shown sympathy with the idea of an alliance; his 'policy and sentiments towards France could not be better', Duff reflected. This roseate optimism did not last long.

Duff soon discovered that despite the removal of one of the pieces on the diplomatic chess-board, the game was still deadlocked. De Gaulle's intransigence continued to place a formidable obstacle in the way of an Anglo–French alliance; he insisted on linking any treaty to a settlement of the Levantine and Rhineland questions, something Bevin always refused to countenance. Even when de Gaulle quit the scene in January 1946, Bidault insisted on continuing his policy. In French eyes the alliance was a lever for extracting concessions from Britain, a game which the British saw little need to go along with: the French needed Britain more than Britain did France. As the French Government's objective was known to include detaching parts of the Rhineland, the Ruhr and the Saar from Germany, a course of action to which Bevin was opposed, no progress could be made towards an alliance.

But the problems were not all on the French side. Certainly de Gaulle's resentments and his delusions of grandeur did not help matters, and Bidault's belief that the British wanted an alliance enough to pay a high price for it was a clumsy error, but the Foreign Office played its part in the diplomatic stalemate. Although Bevin was 'anxious to move towards a closer association between the Western countries' he 'did not wish to take any active steps towards the conclusion of a Franco–British alliance or the formation of a Western group until he had time to consider possible Russian reactions'.[1] In other words, Bevin's policy differed little from Eden's. Although there continued to be considerable sympathy for Duff's policy inside the

Foreign Office, the paralysis which had gripped Eden's diplomacy soon had Bevin in thrall.

Duff was able to get some idea of Bevin's problems with the Russians when he was summoned to London in September to take part in the Conference of Foreign Ministers which was being held there. This meeting between Bevin, the American Byrnes and the Russian Molotov, was supposed to be a prelude to the final peace conference, but, as Duff discovered, the Russians seemed to place a low premium on co-operation with their allies.

The conference itself bored Duff. Interminable wrangling with a Russian whose mastery of foreign languages seemed to amount to an intimate knowledge of a dozen ways of saying 'no', struck him as a fruitless waste of time. It was true that he and Bevin secured from Molotov a statement that, reports in the Soviet press notwithstanding, he had nothing against a Western bloc, but, as Duff commented: 'It is all very well to say that, but how can one not pay attention to articles in an entirely government-controlled press?'

Apart from being able to visit White's frequently, Duff's stay in London had only one other advantage: he was able to press Bevin more closely about his own future. A pre-conference drinking session on the morning of 23 September provided the opportunity for Duff to ask Bevin how long he could expect to have in Paris:

> He said at once that he would undertake that I should stay in Paris for a year. I might, of course, stay several years, but he could not go further than that. I might stay as long as he did but he did not know how long he would stay himself.

That, thought Duff, was 'good enough'; but he did have some fears about how long Bevin might last:

> I think he finds the work very hard. He complained today that he had been at work since seven. He reads slowly and has very great difficulty on paper. In fact he hardly writes anything. He has injections at intervals. He is very heavy and might easily have a stroke.

Thus it was that Duff continued in place, but on uncertain tenure. He had, however, offers of employment if the worst happened. Churchill wrote to him on 17 September: 'If things go wrong about the Paris Embassy, I will certainly help you in any way I can to get a seat, and of course, once elected you would be welcome to our "shadow" meetings.'

Duff had remained in touch with his former leader and, now that he was out of office, much of their old friendship returned. Duff was able to preside over a friendly meeting between Churchill and de Gaulle in November 1946. Churchill now saw de Gaulle as the one hope against a Communist-dominated France, and so took a kindlier view of him. He wrote to Diana, with reference to the imminent French elections: 'The choice before France seems very serious – whether she will be vertebrate or invertebrate. This is, I believe, a very important division in the animal kingdom.'

Duff shared his old friend's view, but he saw an interesting comparison between the careers of his former bugbears:

> People have sometimes criticized you for identifying yourself with a political party. I believe that not having done so may prove fatal to de Gaulle, for when he falls he will 'fall like Lucifer never to rise again' because he will have no party to fall back upon.

It was an accurate prediction, and, despite de Gaulle's successes in the November elections, Paris was full of rumours about him. Some said he would resign unless given more power; others that he would stage a *coup d'état*, pushed forward by malign forces like Palewski. All these Duff heard, but few did he retail to London, seeing in them emanations of personal malice. He did not much care for Palewski himself, supposing that de Gaulle had chosen him as 'being one of the few men in the world uglier than himself', but that did not make the man a Fascist.

Thus it was that when the Foreign Office asked Duff about rumours of de Gaulle's impending resignation in January 1946, he replied that: 'Paris was full of rumours and gossip which I did not usually report unless I thought it was well-founded.' Unfortunately this was the one rumour which turned out to be true. Duff was suffering from influenza when Bevin's query arrived, and he did not get up from bed until 20 January. That afternoon news came through that the General had given in his resignation; Duff felt like retiring to his sick-bed. He had just been going through one of Louise's increasingly frequent emotional crises, this one caused by his acquisition of another new mistress. The fact that the Foreign Office was bound to think itself better informed than he was, was the last straw.

Still, no lasting damage was done. Indeed, de Gaulle's removal seemed to offer a chance to press forward with the quest for an Anglo-French alliance. Duff settled down to compose another long despatch to continue the series he had opened in May 1944.

Literary composition was seasoned by a fresh love affair with a young Frenchwoman, 'a girl after my own heart, good company, a formidable appetite for pleasure and no nonsense about love'; it was a pleasant contrast to the jealousy of Louise. But other, and less amusing diversions presented themselves.

In early March he received a request for an interview from the Duke of Windsor. Duff had not seen his former sovereign since the abdication and still remembered his cheerful comment that he would find plenty to do; their meeting provided a pathetic commentary on those remarks. The Duke stayed for an hour, talking about politics in England, his desire to serve his country and his resentment at not being allowed to do so, but no matter of substance was raised: 'I expect the truth is that he is so *désœuvré* that Wallis, to get him out of the house said, "Why don't you go round to see Duff one morning and have an interesting talk about politics."' It was, Duff thought,

> Sad to think that he gave up the position of King-Emperor, not to live in an island of the Hesperides with his Queen of Beauty but to share an apartment on the third floor of the Ritz with that harsh-voiced ageing woman who was never even pretty.

Despite all interruptions, Duff finished his despatch on 19 March. It was just over a year since he had last tried to push things along and in this, his first attempt under Bevin, he recapitulated the arguments he had used with Eden, pointing out how time had verified his fears about Russian intentions – fears which had appeared 'fantastic' in 1944. Time had, he argued, removed many of the obstacles in the way of an alliance. It was true that the French remained obstinately wedded to the idea of attaching an alliance to a settlement of their demands in the Rhineland, but this need be no bad thing: 'Some settlement of this all-important question cannot be much longer delayed, and it is my submission that advantage should be taken of it to conclude a firm and close alliance with France.'

It seemed as though Duff's despatch had come at an opportune moment. At the end of March the French *Président du Conseil*, Félix Gouin, pronounced himself in favour of an alliance without any prior conditions. Inside the Foreign Office there was considerable sympathy for Duff's arguments, as well as fear that France might go Communist; an Anglo–French treaty of alliance seemed, to some, a cheap way of supporting Gouin and other French democrats.[2] It was with something approaching indecent haste, at least in Duff's view, that Oliver

Harvey was sent over to Paris on 5 April to sound the French out about an alliance.

Duff was annoyed at not being consulted about Harvey's visit – and rightly so. Instead of bringing an alliance nearer, this *démarche* set it back. Duff had been sounding out Bidault and was aware of the little man's determination to link an alliance to the Rhineland question, as well as of the differences between Bidault and Gouin. As it was, the French, being forced to make a quick choice between the two lines of approach, chose Bidault's and left Bevin feeling snubbed. The latter told Duff that he did not intend to run after the French. This was perilously near the language which had been used by Churchill, but all Duff's attempts to explain away French actions failed to shift Bevin. And there Duff's quest seemed to have fallen.[3]

Another session of the Conference of Foreign Ministers, held in Paris between late April and June, provided Duff with some diversion from the failure of his plans. The fact that the meeting took place in Paris meant that Duff could continue his love affair while helping Bevin; it also gave him a chance of getting to know Bevin.

Duff and 'Ernie' made an ill-assorted pair: the dapper West End clubman, the scholar-diplomat with impeccable upper-class credentials, alongside the untidy, burly ex-carter, the trades unionist with the sort of proletarian credentials that most Labour MPs only dream of having. Most would have failed to guess that it was the great fat man with the huge hands, the bulbous nose and the provincial accent who was the boss.

Duff liked Bevin. He found his uncomplicated patriotism attractive and thought him of far greater calibre than men like Attlee, but he did not find him easy to deal with. Duff's experience of the working class had been limited to canvassing in Oldham, and he found Bevin's boastful delight in his own powers and lack of culture distressing. However great his differences with Eden or Churchill, he had always been able to take for granted a common culture and range of reactions. A private letter had always been a way of circumventing the 'normal channels'. None of these things were true with Bevin. Duff found it hard to fathom his thoughts, and the fact that Bevin had such difficulty in putting pen to paper, meant that all communications between the two went through those 'normal channels'. Duff never felt any affinity with his new chief. At a party at the Embassy in mid 1947 Bevin was in 'remarkably good form and when Diana showed him to his room he made violent advances to her and seriously suggested that she should sleep with him. These people are indeed surprising.' Diana's recollection was of the vast bulk on top of her as she 'like most well-brought-up girls of my generation could only think of crying "No, Ernie, no, Ernie."' He complied with her wishes – but suggested that they meet for 'one sweet night of bliss' at the Dorchester; Diana declined the honour.

Diana may have been reluctant to leave Paris, but she was not *that* reluctant. Suggestions that she deliberately vamped Bevin in order to keep Duff in Paris are wide of the mark; and whatever her intentions, Bevin was unlikely to have kept Duff on merely for the pleasure of her blue eyes.

The Conference of Foreign Ministers gave Duff another chance to ask about his own future in the light of continuing press speculation. From Bevin's entourage Duff learnt that although he was in favour of keeping him in Paris, 'he will probably not be able to resist the pressure much longer'. On 14 June he asked Bevin about the press reports:

> He was embarrassed. He said that matters had not been discussed and then went on to say that when it had been brought up at the Labour Party Executive he had said he was bound to admit that he had always had a soft corner for me because I resigned at Munich. He assured me that he would not be rushed and that he would give me fair warning.

At dinner on 26 June, when someone asked Duff if he intended to return to the Commons, Bevin said:

> 'We're going to send Duff to the 'Ouse of Lords.' When Diana protested he seemed surprised and said, 'Wouldn't you like him to be a Viscount?' She said she didn't want to lose this job, to which he replied, 'Oh, don't worry about that.'

Duff's impression was that 'I shan't go before Christmas and possibly not before next spring. The prospect does not disturb me in the least.'

The knowledge that his mission had, in all probability, not much longer to run made Duff all the more determined to try to push the Foreign Office into concluding an alliance. There seemed, however, little prospect of this. Despite great support within the Foreign Office for the idea of a Western bloc, there were also considerable hesitations. The advent to office in December 1946 of the veteran socialist leader, Léon Blum, at the head of a minority Government, prompted thoughts within Whitehall that a fresh approach should be made to the French; Bevin thought not. He minuted in late December, in one of his rare scribblings, that: 'After giving this considerable thought I am still very doubtful about raising it, until we see what the new Government is like and what their attitude is. I am in favour of waiting a little while longer.'[4]

Duff was unaware of his chief's view, and even had this not been so, it is unlikely that he would have passed up the chance of making another in the series of *démarches* which he had made since 1945. When he saw Blum on Boxing Day he suggested that he might like to conclude an alliance as a memorial to what was bound to be a short-lived administration. This was but one more stone lobbed into the stagnant pond of Anglo–French relations, and Duff had little hope that its ripples would be any greater than on previous occasions. In fact, he had just made the first move which broke the stalemate – if a change of metaphor may be allowed.

Blum wrote to Attlee at the beginning of January 1947 asking for help with French coal shortages; he added that he favoured concluding an alliance without settling the Rhineland question first. Attlee replied a few days later regretting that there was little he could do to help with extra coal supplies, but it was quite otherwise with an alliance; he suggested that Blum might visit London in early January. In Cabinet on 7 January Bevin came out strongly in favour of moving towards an immediate Anglo–French alliance.[5]

The news caused a flurry of excitement at the Embassy. Duff had been contemplating producing a 1947 version of his earlier long despatches and was glad to be relieved of the necessity; but with Harvey's abortive trip to Paris in mind, he warned London that it was no good Blum going to London 'unless they meant business'. A failure at this point would be disastrous.

Duff travelled to London with Blum to take part in the talks, which went well, at least until it came to the drafting of the final communiqué. To Duff's annoyance one of the Foreign Office officials, Mr Hoyar-Millar, kept objecting to the inclusion of a paragraph committing the two countries to the conclusion of an alliance; he was equally delighted when Bevin ruled that the paragraph must go in. He went back to Paris happier than at any time since August 1945.

The Foreign Office had been caught napping by what they assumed to be Blum's initiative – Duff was not going to tell them whose initiative it had been. Duff was determined to ensure that they produced the goods. He telegraphed on 18 January asking them what he should tell the new Minister for Foreign Affairs, Bidault, and suggesting an answer. Duff thought that they ought to move at once towards a 'general alliance' as the first step towards 'a closer understanding'.

Bidault, who returned to the Quai d'Orsay in the Ramadier Government, expressed his willingness to continue along the lines laid out by Blum, much to Duff's delight. News from London was less cheering. Ashley Clarke, who had replaced Holman as Duff's counsellor, reported that the permanent officials were

> being very slow and timid about the French treaty. They are a poor lot
> – all terrified of something – of the Russians, of the Americans, of the
> Chiefs of Staff, of the Board of Trade, of the Treasury – with the result
> that they never want to do anything.

This was a little harsh. The Foreign Office were still hoping to link an Anglo–French treaty with the Anglo–Russian one of 1942, and they were anxious not to offend the Russians. The draft which they produced in early February was, to Duff's eyes, profoundly disappointing. It provided for Anglo–French collaboration 'to prevent a renewal of German aggression' and was, in Duff's view, 'nothing except vague expressions of goodwill'. Writing to Harvey on 7 February, Duff commented that 'the cupboard looks rather bare to me'. He argued that they should 'beware of allowing our respect for Russian susceptibilities to produce a state of paralysis in our foreign policy'. He added that if they pressed on with 'so jejune' a treaty, he hoped that 'there may be found some way of immediately making clear that it is, nevertheless, meant to open a new chapter in our relations with France'. Duff concluded:

> The time has arrived for a most momentous decision in British foreign
> policy. If we now succeed in identifying our interests with those of France,
> we shall with our two vast empires be able to remain not only one, but
> possibly not the least important, of the Big Three.

If Britain failed to grasp the opportunity now presented she would sink 'into being only one of the two smaller Powers very dangerously situated between the two giants of the West and the East'.

Unfortunately the Foreign Office were already acting as though Britain was in such a position, fearing that 'If we give either the Russians or the Americans the idea that we and the French are trying to do too much by bilateral agreement, we may land ourselves in a lot of difficulty.' It was decided, quite deliberately, to avoid 'putting teeth' into the alliance.[6]

Thus it was that Duff's feelings were mixed as the negotiations moved towards a speedy conclusion. It was not thus, with a vague and general treaty of alliance, that he had hoped to lay the foundation of a Western bloc; moreover, in the three years that had passed since he first pressed the issue, Russian power had grown until she did indeed dominate Europe. On the other hand it was a step in the right direction and, however inevitable he believed it to be, there was a measure of personal satisfaction. 'I honestly believe', he recorded in his diary on 28 February, 'that it would not have been done now if I had not said what I did say to Blum.'

On 4 March Duff left for Dunkirk to take part in the signing of the treaty:

> It was cold and damp at Dunkirk. We had nearly an hour to wait for Bevin, and a further rather awkward wait for the treaties which arrived about a quarter of an hour later. However, all went well. Both Bidault and Bevin spoke well, the latter the better of the two. Then they, Massigli and I signed. This was followed by a rather pointless but short excursion to the beaches where we gazed upon the desolate site of a derelict sea-coast under a wintery sky – and shivered.

There, where almost seven years before an alliance had ended, the *entente cordiale* was, Duff hoped, reborn: an 'historic occasion', he wrote in his diary; '*Nunc dimittis* – the alliance was signed today'.

It was the fulfilment of the mission he had set himself in 1944 and he looked forward to pushing on to the next stage – from Anglo-French alliance to Western European union. In the immediate future his main task was to recover from the heavy cold which he had picked up at Dunkirk. Despite two bottles of champagne (shared with Louise) and a 'good deal of port and whiskey' when he got back to Paris, the cold lingered.

The Treaty of Dunkirk brightened up a dull season. He was, as he told his new friend Lady Weymouth,* 'romanceless', his last *grande passion* having departed for Kenya at the end of December 1946. This had made for a dull Christmas, despite his insisting on having a dinner-party for fifty-two guests on Christmas Eve where there were many beautiful women. The fact that he was in love with none of them 'absolutely robs the gingerbread of its gilt for me. Gilt and guilt are spelt differently but are closely connected in my mind. I like to

---

* Daphne Vivian, m. 1926–53 to Viscount Weymouth, later the Marquess of Bath; m. 1953–78 to Major Alexander Fielding. Writer and painter.

have a secret love affair, a hidden life, something to lie about.' He was 'afraid it's my idea of romance. Not a very elevated one perhaps but the habit of a lifetime.'[7]

Excitement was soon to return and the habit of a lifetime remained unbroken. On the evening of 27 March he had 'a very successful dinner-party', and among the guests were a young American diplomat, William Patten, and his wife, Susan Mary; of her Duff recorded: 'I get fonder every time'. With this thought, and plans about how to advance the case for Western European union in his mind, Duff and Diana went off to Monte Carlo for a well-earned rest.

After lunch on 8 April he settled back to read the paper, only to find that he was 'trembling so violently I couldn't reach it'. He then 'had a kind of rigor': he retired to bed with a temperature of a hundred and three degrees. A few days later it was up to a hundred and four degrees; ignoring his protests, Diana called in the doctors; during the next week he was injected with over a million units of penicillin: 'At first I suffered terrible gouty-rheumatic pains in my right foot, but these passed and when, about the fifth day the fever subsided, I was fairly comfortable.' The one bright spot was the arrival of four 'long, charming letters' from Susan Mary Patten: 'She obviously likes writing them, but I flatter myself she must like me rather to write them.'

She, for her part, loved his replies, and expressed mock-indignation when she discovered that a friend of hers had also had 'a lovely letter from Duff Cooper': 'How many wretched women in Paris, London and New York do you write these lovely letters to? A good two dozen, I should think!'[8] Her witty and affectionate letters were just the thing for convalescence: 'They grow more numerous and more affectionate,' he noted, with more than a flash of his old spirit. When he suggested that she had created an image of him and fallen for that, she replied in kind:

> Has it not occurred to you that you might also have created me, out of your illness and boredom? I am not beautiful you know, but have only a sort of surface prettiness that will do as long as it stays fresh, which it won't do for long at this rate!

She did not want, she said, to fall in love with him. She loved her husband and worried about what Diana would think: 'I desperately need all your knowledge of the world and wisdom to help me.'

He was flattered and disturbed. That he could arouse such emotions in a young and pretty woman (he disagreed with her own description of herself) was pleasing, but she was not his usual type. He was no rake. His conquests were usually married women with experience of the world and a complaisant husband; there were rules to the game and he stuck to them. He had no wish to endanger Susan Mary's marriage. There was, as it turned out, no need to do so. Her love was passionate, but discreet. At first she worried that someone was bound to get hurt. She did not think that it would be Diana, and her comments on this point are the most sensible ever made by an observer of that remarkable marriage: 'My instinct tells me that your relationship is a wonderful, undamageable thing, apart from and undisturbed by your relations with other women.' 'You like women,' she wrote, 'you have immense charm, and in your world it is normal', but she worried that his position and her husband's pride might be damaged: 'So subterfuge is the only answer.'[9] So it was that their 'strange, imaginative affair' began.

Susan Mary's love came at a good time for Duff. His illness had been a serious one. His doctor warned him that his 'liver and kidneys are in a bad state' and that he should take it 'as a warning'. A strict diet was prescribed: 'Hardly anything am I allowed to eat except chicken and rabbit.' He was to have 'one or two totally vegetarian days each week and nothing to drink except a little claret'. His reaction was simple: 'I can't do it and don't believe it's necessary.' Duff was a bad patient. Although his foot continued to give him pain, he told no one about it and, within a few months, was eating and drinking at almost his old rate. But there were after-effects. As he wrote to Daphne Bath (as Lady Weymouth had now become) in August 1948 with an air of surprise: 'Do you know that if I drink too much at night I don't feel very well the next day? Can you imagine? It doesn't stop me drinking but I do hate feeling ill.' He did not hate it enough to stop of his own volition. Susan Mary provided a much needed distraction from the state of his health – and from the lack of progress he was making in advancing beyond the achievement of the Treaty of Dunkirk.

Early June 1947 saw him back at the Embassy, just in time to pass on to the French Bevin's enthusiastic reaction to General Marshall's speech offering economic aid to Europe. Anglo–French discussions on 17 June led to 'almost entire agreement on the line that we should take': the important thing was to invite the Russians to participate but to give them 'no opportunity to cause delay and obstruction'.

When, by 3 July, it was obvious that the Soviets were not going to join in a common European plan for economic recovery, Bevin decided to 'go straight ahead with the Duff Cooper plan'. Thus it was that 'the Western bloc which I have always advocated' came about: 'manufactured in Moscow. *Tant mieux.*'

Diplomacy connected with concerting the Anglo–French response to what has become known as 'The Marshall Plan' (although it was the Europeans who drew up the plan) kept Duff in Paris until the summer had almost run its course, and he and Diana planned to take their holiday in September. On 3 September a letter arrived from Bevin; it began: 'Dear Duff, After very careful reflection, I have come to the conclusion that I must make a change at the Embassy in Paris at the end of the year.' That was it; the blow had fallen. None of the flattery that followed these words detracted from their meaning: it was 'the sack'. Late that night he and Diana departed for San Vigilio. He felt a 'greater freedom' than he had for years. Before leaving he penned a gracious reply:

> I will not pretend that the news was welcome, but I can assure you that I received it without the slightest feeling of resentment. I have had, as you say, a good innings, and I shall always consider that the Labour Government has shown great magnanimity in retaining me at this post for two years and a half.[10]

The long expected news gave Duff one bad night on holiday, but otherwise he was unruffled. As he wrote to a friend on 26 September:

> If Bevin were now to change his mind and to ask me to stay on indefinitely, I should feel disappointed. I have thought of so much that I am going to do in the coming year that I should think it all very dull now to have to continue as I have for the last three years.

There were, too, he found, advantages in being a 'lame duck' Ambassador; the greatest of these was a freedom to speak his mind 'in terms that would hardly be proper as coming from a subordinate to his chief'. He was determined to go out preaching the 'gospel'. On 16 October he aimed a 'final broadside' at Bevin, a diplomatic final will and testament.

The letter recapitulated the history of Duff's attempts to sponsor the 'Western bloc' and drove home some lessons which he thought ought to be learnt. One of the fundamental difficulties was that opponents of the scheme never disagreed 'in principle' but always said that now was 'not the suitable moment for taking any action'. This insidious argument had held up an Anglo–French treaty and was even then being used to hold up talks on economic and military collaboration:

> Britain has now become part of the Continent of Europe, and she has to decide whether she will place herself at the head of a confederation of Western democracies or whether she will become a satellite of the United States.

It was natural, he said, for civil servants to oppose radical change, but it was the duty of ministers to construct a policy. In reply to Bevin's answer, Duff once more urged him forward. The pre-war years showed the result of passing up opportunities for co-operation because 'the time was not ripe':

> The attitude of the Government at every turn was always defensible, logical, supported by sound arguments, but it lacked one thing – a guiding policy behind it – and so, in the end, it landed us in a ghastly war without a previously pledged ally or an agreed scheme of defence. We came within an ace of losing that war. For God's sake, and for the sake of humanity, don't let that happen again.

For four years Duff had tried to offer a 'guiding policy' to avoid reproducing the mistakes of the 1930s. He could at least console himself with the thought that he had achieved more this time than he had then. As the end of his mission approached Duff wrote in his diary: 'I feel no melancholy at all at the thought of leaving.'

The news of his departure was not made public until 21 October, after which the letters of condolence poured in. Susan Mary had been told in early September. He had a dinner-date with her the evening of the day Bevin's letter arrived, but said nothing until the following day. It was, as she wrote on 7 September, wonderfully unselfish of him not to spoil their evening together. These were rare enough and precious, and it would have been quite unlike Duff to let anything ruin a lovers' tryst.

A great party was held at the Embassy on the night of 10 December. Susan Mary, who stayed until it ended at five o'clock the following morning, reported that:

> You gave unquestionably the best party that has taken place since 1939 and everyone there said the same thing.... This morning's telephone consensus is that there can never be another party like it because you are leaving the Embassy.

218

But she did not feel inclined to join the mourners because, much as she enjoyed balls, she loved 'very small exclusive parties more, especially parties for two'.[11]

On a freezing morning, 18 December 1947, Duff and Diana left Paris. Friends and staff were there to see them off. The wife of the British military attaché, Guy Salisbury-Jones, commented: 'How too sad, but dear Lady Diana did look so lovely, one must find a bright side somewhere mustn't one?' Nancy Mitford's response to this was: 'I don't see one, they're gone at least for the moment and Paris is going to be dreary without them and my feet are cold and I'm on the verge of tears.' Which was exactly what Susan Mary was thinking.[12] She would, she wrote, have given anything if 'in return I could have the next five minutes sitting on your lap and be held tight, tight against your heart and forget that you were leaving'. She told him that she thought she had heard 'some wonderful tributes to you before you left, but the sadness since is more moving'.[13]

Thus his public career came to an end – on a high and romantic note, just as he would have wished.

~~~ 24 ~~~

A Contented Man

'I have had enough of diplomacy and am looking forward to a different life,' wrote Duff on 31 December 1947. He had arrived back in
England to be met, at Dover, by the Lord Chamberlain, representing
the King, and the Permanent Under-Secretary at the Foreign Office,
Sir Orme Sargent: 'an honour I had not expected'. This helped com-
pensate for one which he had expected. A few days earlier he had
received a letter from Bevin offering him the Grand Cross of the
Order of St Michael and St George. The GCMG, or 'God Calls Me
God', as it was known in the Diplomatic Service, was a coveted order
of knighthood awarded to senior diplomats, but it was not what Duff
wanted: 'This means that I shan't get a peerage to which, as an ex-
Secretary of State, I might consider myself entitled.' He would have
'liked the platform that it affords', but did not 'feel strongly about it'.
Thus it was as Sir Duff Cooper GCMG that he faced retirement.

The Labour Government can be forgiven for not wishing to ennoble
a Conservative, but their reception of a man who had served them
well was lacking in any grace. Bevin did not say thank you and there
was no interview with the Prime Minister; no formal meeting, that is.
Duff was a great admirer of the circus and one of the first things he
did back in London on 19 December was to go to one. In the interval
'I went to relieve nature where I met the Prime Minister. While
buttoning up his flies he congratulated me on the success of my mission and conveyed to me the thanks of His Majesty's Government.'
To which gracious tribute 'I, while unbuttoning mine, expressed my
sense of the honour done to me and my gratitude to Ministers for
their support and confidence.' There cannot be many Ambassadors
who have had their final meeting with the Prime Minister in such
circumstances.

He saw Bevin on 20 December: 'he meant to be very civil and

grateful to me but the Graces were not invited to his christening'. Duff felt 'a little sad as I left the Foreign Office – probably for the last time as a member of the Service'. It was the end of a long association: 'I was very proud when I first went there in October 1913.'

His major regret in leaving the Embassy was that he left the room which was to be a permanent memorial to him. He had been shocked to discover that there was no library in what was, otherwise, a perfect house. The remedy for this he outlined in a letter to Rupert Hart-Davis in March 1946:

> You will be sorry to hear that I am going to leave the greater part of my books in the Embassy when I go from it, which I hope will not be too soon. I hadn't seen any of them since 1940, when under the threat of bombardment I sent them all down to Belvoir. I saw a chance of getting them down here if I could persuade the Office of Works to allow me to install a library, which they did on my promising to leave it fully stocked with books.

He had been delighted to have his books about him once again, and to have a beautiful library to which he could retire. It was a wrench to leave both – even though he had kept the choicer volumes.

One reason for leaving so many books to the Embassy was the feeling that they were becoming an encumbrance. There were, he thought, too many 'for any house we are likely to be able to afford'.

The problem of where to live after his mission was over had been almost as troublesome as the question of what they were to live on. Entertaining at the Embassy was an expensive hobby and they were £4,000 overdrawn at the bank in late 1947; Diana saw penury staring them in the face. Duff, as ever, was more sanguine. He solved the financial problem and she answered the accommodation question.

They had sold the beautiful house at 34 Chapel Street before the war and now had no London address. West House was still theirs, stained by war and neglect. Encroached upon by Bognor and barbed wire, it was no longer a 'terrestrial paradise'. Finding a suitable house in England promised to be difficult – especially with socialist taxation to be paid. It was Diana's insatiable curiosity which made such a search unnecessary.

Some twenty-six miles from Paris lies the great park of Chantilly. Set in it, a mile or so from the great Château de Chantilly, was the exquisite little Château de St Firmin. Dating from the reign of Louis xv, it was the very model of a gentleman's country retreat. The drawing-room windows faced onto a spacious lawn leading down to a lake with ornamental cascades. Diana fell in love with the place the first time she saw it.

She came across it while wandering in the park and set about finding its owner. She discovered that it had been leased to the former American Ambassador, Bill Bullitt, by the *Institut de France*. Bullitt was willing to let the Coopers take over his lease if they could provide linen for the bedrooms, but not all Diana's ingenuity could procure such a thing in wartime Paris. However, they persevered, and were finally able to buy Bullitt out for £2,000 in November 1947. It was here, at the Château de St Firmin, that they proposed to spend Duff's retirement, renting a flat in the Rue de Lille for visits to Paris.

There was only one drawback to this arrangement – but it was a major one, at least for a time. By convention retiring Ambassadors do not visit the scene of their former triumphs for a year or so after quitting the stage. In this instance such an arrangement might have been thought essential. Such had been the prestige enjoyed by the Coopers that their successors, Sir Oliver and Lady Harvey, were bound to be in for a hard time of it. The presence of their predecessors at Chantilly made things even more difficult for them.

Duff was perfectly content to leave the Harveys to get on with their task; it was quite otherwise with Diana. He noted in early January 1948, after they had taken up residence at Chantilly, that she was taking their 'fall from grandeur' far harder than himself; her evident unhappiness touched him. He had enjoyed living at the Embassy, 'but I always felt as though I was living in a hotel'. He supposed she had 'enjoyed the position and enjoyed entertaining, though she often complained of it at the time'. To him: 'The restoration of liberty makes up for everything, but I am sad that she should be sad.'

Her unhappiness took itself out in what was described somewhat melodramatically by the gossips as a 'feud' with the 'Horrible Harveys' (as Diana called them). Raids on the Embassy to 'retrieve' pieces of furniture which had been 'left behind' and the odd disparaging remark about Lady Harvey scarcely amounted to a declaration of hostilities. They did, however, keep the rumour-mongers happy – and provide Nancy Mitford with the raw material for an amusing episode in *Don't tell Alfred*. From Duff's vantage point the real significance of the business was the first manifestation of the melancholia which was to dog Diana for much of the next eighteen months.

Diana's fear that they were going to end up in penury was more easily dealt with. Duff joined the Board of the International Wagons-Lits, which gave him a nice excuse to travel in luxury, and as well as becoming chairman of the Paris subsidiary of Alexander Korda's London Film Productions, he became the Paris adviser for ICI. These posts brought him over £4,000 a year, which was not much less than his salary as Ambassador. Given French tax-rates and no lavish diplomatic parties to spend money on, he and Diana were, if not rich, extremely comfortably off. He could do whatever he wanted.

Although he had enjoyed being an Ambassador, he had a feeling that he would enjoy a change of occupation even more. There had been moments when he had looked forward to release. Sitting in a garden in Deauville in late July 1946 he had mused thus: 'My life is so continually surrounded by people that it is a pleasure to be alone for once and I enjoyed this drive, and this lunch and sitting in the sun.' It occurred to him that 'I was probably an existentialist without knowing it'. It was true that he had 'always denounced it' and that he had 'never quite understood what it stands for. Nor am I clear how it differs from hedonism.' He decided to 'worry less and work less'. He could now do just that.

He once observed to Clarissa Churchill that 'one should be a little interested in everything. It makes life more interesting for oneself and it makes one less boring to others.'[1] Having always followed this admirable precept himself, his retirement was a happy affair. Life remained composed of the same ingredients: politics, literature, pretty women and a hectic social round; all that changed was their relative importance.

Politics, which for so long had been the predominant occupation, now became marginal. Churchill, writing to congratulate him on his time in Paris, offered to take him into the Shadow Cabinet, but Duff was not interested. He was living in France, which would have been a problem. More importantly, politics had lost their charm. The prospect of being in opposition was unappealing. The narrowing effects of that life had seemed bearable when accompanied by the ambition and naïveté of youth; now they were repellent. A look at his old rival Eden gave the awful warning. Mutual friends gave him an uninviting picture of the professional politician in middle age and Opposition:

What a curious man he is – he has no friends and no real interests outside politics. X* says that he never stops trying to make love to her – which

* The name is given in Duff's diary.

she finds tiresome. Caroline says she has broken off with him completely. They both concur that he doesn't like me – but also that he loathes Winston. He thinks of nothing except being leader of the Conservative Party.

That was not the road for Duff. Thanks to his friend Ann Rothermere, the columns of the Continental edition of the *Daily Mail* provided him with a platform for airing his views on the international situation. That was enough for him. Despite invitations, he did no speaking in the 1950 or 1951 general elections. Henceforth he would be one of those who slung the brickbats rather than one of those who received them; it was a refreshing experience.

Literature, that first love of all, now gained the upper hand over politics. In 1946 he had lent his nephew £1,000 to help him start his own publishing firm, Rupert Hart-Davis Limited. In April 1946 he had told Rupert that although he was far too busy to have time to write anything: 'I may get thrown out at any moment and then I shall have to write hard in order to keep that tiresome wolf from the ever-open door.' Thanks to his business connections he was not impelled to write merely to keep that wolf away; he was able to do so for fun. It was only natural that he should choose his nephew as his publisher.

Towards the end of 1948 he conceived the idea of writing a book on Shakespeare's early life. Rupert wrote in February 1949 to enquire how things were going. Duff's reply gives a nice insight into his life at this time. He had, he said, just returned from England:

> I went to lecture to the officers at Aldershot – unpaid. I waste much time doing things like this out of a sense of duty – and things like articles for the *Daily Mail* out of a sense of greed – plus a certain salt of *saeva indignatio*.

He would, he promised, turn to Shakespeare. By the end of June he had completed twenty thousand words and decided that it would be 'a very thin book'. But 'people might buy it at Christmas-time' and it 'may irritate the experts'. It was out in time for the Christmas market, and in a print run of ten thousand. Apart from a few savage mutterings from the dark corners of the Leavisite underworld, *Sergeant Shakespeare* met with a warm reception. Cast in the form of a letter to Diana, it was a delightful essay which toyed with the idea that the Bard had been, in his younger days, a soldier in the Low Countries. J.I.M. Stewart (better known as Michael Innes) welcomed 'this urbane re-entry of the amateur into the dusty arena of professional

Shakespeare scholarship', and among the book's admirers was Ernest Hemingway, who told Duff that it was 'beautifully written, clear, clean and sound – besides giving me great pleasure it moved me very much'. It was an encouraging start.

Duff was already writing his next book, but there was one drawback to the success of *Sergeant Shakespeare*; it reminded his old publisher, Jonathan Cape, that he had an option on Duff's next book after *David* – something he pointed out in a letter in November 1948. Rupert provided the way out of this problem.[2] Drawing on his experience of working for Cape, he suggested that Duff should write to him saying that he was working on a novel and asking for the same advance – £1,000 – that he had received for *David*. This was done. As Rupert had anticipated, Cape's meanness made him jib at the advance. Even better, he suggested that Duff should stick to history. This left the way clear for Duff to abandon Cape. But the problems did not end there.

The book, a novella entitled *Operation Heartbreak*, was based around an historical event. In order to mislead the Germans into thinking that the Allied invasion of Sicily in 1943 was, in fact, intended as an invasion of the Balkans, the British security services had embarked upon an elaborate operation. An aircraft was crashed off the coast of Spain and from it was picked up the corpse of a Major Martin. On his person were top-secret documents. These found their way to the Nazis. What the Germans did not know was that Major Martin had been put into the sea by a British submarine – and that he had been dead for several weeks. The deception worked brilliantly. As head of the Security Executive in 1943, Duff had been privy to *Operation Mincemeat*, and he found in it a peg upon which to hang his own tale. The Cabinet Office were less than amused and wanted the book stopped because, according to them, it breached security. This objection was eventually surmounted and *Operation Heartbreak* was published in November 1950.

It is a beautifully written and very moving book, telling the fictional life-story of the 'man who never was'. Willie Maryngton, the hero, is a decent straightforward soldier whose one desire is to serve his country. Alas, just too young to miss fighting in the Great War, and too old to fight in the Second World War, he dies a sad and frustrated man. Then, having brought the reader close to tears with poor Willie's pathetic end, Duff lifts the spirit with a clever idea: it is Willie's corpse which is used in the deception operation.

It was an exciting story, which Duff told well. He received both good reviews and letters of congratulation from friends. Even better, the book sold well, going into a second impression within a month of publication. It was republished as recently as 1973 in paperback.

Duff's only venture into fiction was not his sole literary production at this time. He had always been a keen versifier and, in retirement, he amused his friends and delighted Diana by his verses. He must be the only President of White's to have composed a sonnet in an hour on the premises to win a prize in a *Spectator* literary competition. The theme of the poem was 'On hearing that Wordsworth had an illegitimate child'. The manuscript of Duff's piece hangs beneath a portrait of him near the bar at White's:

> Byron! thou shouldst be living at this hour,
> We need thy verse, thy venom and thy wit
> To castigate the ancient hypocrite.
> We need thy pith, thy passion and thy power –
> How often did that prim old face turn sour
> Even at the mention of thy honoured name,
> How oft those prudish lips have muttered 'shame'
> In jealous envy of thy golden lyre.
> In words worth reading hadst thou told the tale
> Of what the lakeland bard was really at
> When on those long excursions he set sail;
> For now there echoes through his tedious chat
> Another voice, the third a phantom wail
> Or peevish prattle of a bastard brat.

For a meeting of The Other Club to celebrate Churchill's seventy-ninth birthday in 1953 he produced a poem which took even less than an hour to compose, writing it swiftly in pencil on the back of a bank statement:

> When half the world was deaf and mute
>   You told of doom to come.
> When others fingered on the flute,
>   You thundered on the drum.
>
> When armies marched and cities burned
>   And all you said came true,
> Those who had mocked your warnings turned
>   Almost too late to you.

Then doubt was turned to firm belief
And through five bitter years,
You gave us glory with our grief
And laughter through our tears.

When final honours are bestowed
And last accounts are done
Then shall we know how much was owed
By all the world to one.

In 1949 he brought out a privately printed volume of *Translations and Verses*, which bore testimony to his talents and contained the most beautiful of all his poems to Diana. It was a gift for her on their twenty-ninth wedding anniversary in 1948:

Fear not, sweet love, what time can do
Though silver streaks the gold
Of your soft hair, believe that you
Can change but not grow old.
Though since we married, twenty-nine
Bright years have flown away.
Beauty and wisdom, like good wine,
Grow richer every day.
We will not weep, though spring be past,
And autumn's shadows fall,
These years shall be, although the last,
The loveliest of all.

He loved her as much as ever and found only sadness in her in-creasing melancholia. It was something she had always suffered from, but which became very much worse after the ending of the Paris idyll. Susan Mary Patten, who sympathized with Duff in his attempts to alleviate Diana's gloom, tried to reassure him in August 1948 that: 'With a woman of her character, common sense and humour, this kind of thing is transitory.' She remembered Diana telling her the previous summer that although she was about to 'set off on the perfect holiday with the perfect husband and the perfect son' she was 'so depressed that she could hardly get through the day'. Susan Mary could offer Duff little in the way of constructive advice except that he should 'carry on giving her the love and support that you always have, without which she would be lost'.[3] And that was what he did. Nor were these strains readily apparent, even to friends. As Ann Rothermere wrote to Diana in late 1947: 'You and Duff are by far the happiest married couple I know specially as you have had all the temptations of wit, intelligence and beauty.'

Wit, intelligence and beauty were not temptations which Duff had ever thought needed resisting and, away from the responsibility of office, he devoted himself wholeheartedly to the pursuit of all three. The restraints of office had quite ruined his first visit to Biarritz in Easter 1946, as he told Daphne Bath: 'The weather was very bad and I had to be respectable so that you can imagine it was hell.' He told her to look out for a statue 'of Edward VII or Queen Victoria' next time she was there and to 'think of me and remember that I unveiled them last year – and that was all I did unveil in Biarritz'. Her description of her own stay there made him quite envious: 'A bordel by the sea with raddled blondes, Chateaubriand steaks and whitebait – it's my idea of heaven.'[4] If retirement did not quite take him to this hedonist's heaven, it did provide close approximations.

Diana spent part of every year travelling, finding in it a delight and distraction. Duff, who lacked her pioneering tastes, eschewed North Africa and other exotic locations for the more familiar round of London, the Riviera, San Vigilio and Paris.

His social life was still lived at a hectic pace and could seem arduous to those much younger. Susan Mary warned him that:

> You do too much. I would feel the same if you were twenty years younger. I don't know any pair of our age who do as much as you and Diana do – but it is habit with you both to feel stimulated by people and constant comings and goings.

Visits to England were frequent and filled with activity. He described a typical one to Daphne Bath in March 1948.[5] It began with a weekend in North Wales at Vaynol, the home of Sir Michael Duff. The house-party was a small one: his hostess, 'her pansy boy-friend whose name I never remember because he is always changing it',* his beautiful nieces Liz and Caroline,† and the former's husband, Raimund von Hofmannsthal. It was, he wrote, 'the most heavenly weekend I ever had – perfect weather, excellent food, sufficient drink and – you know, everything. I was very happy.'

Daphne Bath knew Duff well enough to divine the meaning of 'everything'. Susan Mary, in the early days of their affair had, when

---

* Simon Fleet, who changed his name from Harry Cannes for astrological reasons.
† Caroline Paget (1913-76) m. Sir Michael Duff of Vaynol; Elizabeth Paget (1916-80) m. Raimund von Hofmannsthal. Daughters of Diana's sister Marjorie, Marchioness of Anglesey.

his letters mentioned his nieces, told him: 'You seem to think that because they are nieces I won't be jealous. I have seen Lady Elizabeth von H. and thought her the most beautiful thing I had ever seen except her aunt.' She had always, she added, thought that Duff resembled Talleyrand in many ways, and he had enjoyed 'a fairly prolonged walk-out with his niece', so 'this benevolent Uncle Duff role makes me madly nervous'.[6] It also gave her a cold later that year which Duff passed on, having picked it up from Caroline: 'an historic cold of romantic origin', as he called it. For his part, Duff could never decide which of his two nieces was the more beautiful and which of them he loved the most: it was something he was happy to investigate and leave unresolved.

This delightful weekend was followed by a week in London. Monday saw him at 'an amusing bridge-party at Ann Rothermere's'; Tuesday was enlivened by dinner at Lady Cunard's where his neighbour's 'abominable breasts' were 'in my plate most of the time'; Wednesday brought 'an agreeable dinner with Pam Berry'* who had kindly invited Caroline Paget, much to his delight. Each evening saw him at a new night-club, the Orchid Room, 'where I am now regarded as part of the furniture'. On Thursday he dined at The Other Club with 'Winston and a lot of men who are so old that they regard me as a mad little boy'. By the time Friday came he was no doubt ready for the return to Paris.

He also found time to keep up his correspondence with half a dozen pretty women. He was particularly attentive to Lady Bath, not least because he found her replies so delicious. He enjoyed writing letters, and she was the sort of correspondent who brought out the best in him. Described by Susan Mary as 'the most beautiful and fascinating creature',[7] she kept him entertained with tales of her exploits and house-parties in England. He derived great joy from the description of the party at which one of Augustus John's former mistresses opened the proceedings by announcing in 'a rather blasé voice, "I suppose you all want to see my breasts?"' with which she unhooked her bodice and peeled it down – then ran round the room!' But even that was put in the shade by the lady who, in reply to a letter from Duff saying that he had vainly tried to catch her attention from the portals of White's, wrote:

---

* 1914–82, daughter of F.E. Smith, first Earl of Birkenhead. Married to Michael Berry, later Lord Hartwell; political hostess.

My darling sweet Duff – I am most bitterly disappointed that I missed the opportunity of falling into your arms on the steps of White's, and having a spiffing orgasm. It must have been me all right, because I was staying at the Cavendish ... and frequently passing White's generally peering longingly into its tantalizing bow window – thinking of all the good men going to waste behind it.

From Paris, Susan Mary kept up a flow of witty and appreciative letters. Their affair continued, perforce, to be primarily epistolary, but it was a little short-sighted of Bill Patten to say to her in September 1949: 'I don't think Duff likes you as much as I used to think that he did.' She could only reply 'Oh' and feign ignorance of the whole subject.[8] She knew the truth was otherwise from Duff's letters, but sometimes wondered why he did love her:

I think it proof of your extraordinary understanding that you haven't laughed more at me, because, in your wide experience of the world I doubt very much if you ever ran up against the likes of me before. Your friends are the Ann Rothermeres and I have the bourgeois mentality of the Rangoon governor's wife.... Why you should love me ... is an utter mystery.[9]

Part of the answer lay, of course, in her very freshness. She was, moreover, not only a sympathetic and appreciative young woman, she was one possessed of unusual understanding. Early in their love affair she commented about Louise de Vilmorin (whom she thought 'evil') complaining about Duff's neglect of her:

She has, I hope, learned the lesson which I imagine Diana learned long ago and I learned a month ago: i.e. that if you really love someone you don't care what he does so long as he is happy.... I would guess that you're one of those people who like to love three or four different people at the same time for different reasons and in different ways, and that is O.K.[10]

Such perceptiveness, and her delight in the world of literature and history that he opened up to her, explains why he loved her. She was, as she put it in 1948, 'a very steady date honey'.[11]

Thus did life continue to be as pleasant as ever it had been. There was shooting with the President of France at Rambouillet just after Christmas, the spring visit to England followed by a return to France where he would get on with his book and his business interests. Summer would be spent, if possible, at San Vigilio on Lake Garda, his favourite spot in Italy save only for Venice. The autumn would bring the publication of a book, more visits to London and the country houses of friends, and so the round would continue.

Old friends, old books and old haunts, but never a trace of boredom; such was Duff's life as he approached and passed the milestone of his sixtieth birthday. Unlike Diana, he had no fears about getting old. Perhaps he realized that he was unlikely to reach any great age. He had always presumed too much upon a naturally strong constitution, and now he began to pay the price. The severe illness of 1947 was followed by a respite, although when, in July, he allowed himself a whole bottle of red wine with his lunch, he felt very ill. It was, he commented, 'very little compared with what I was accustomed to', but the fact was that he could 'no longer take a normal, or subnormal amount'. But he refused to pay too much attention to the strictures of his doctors or to Diana's pleas. A mild haemorrhage in 1951 should have acted as more of a warning than it did.

25

The Undiscovered Ends

One compensation for advancing age, assuming such a thing was needed, lay in watching the development of John Julius. The war and the Paris Embassy had kept father and son apart for much of the time between 1940 and 1947, interrupting that happy relationship which had grown up in the early 1930s when Diana was so often away from home; now came a chance for them to see more of each other. John Julius was a 'little shy' of his father and suspected that the feeling was reciprocated.[1] Gone were the days when the small boy could wander into the study at West House and ask Papa to cease work and join him in a game of croquet.

During the time his parents were at the Embassy John Julius would visit them in the vacations from Eton. In retrospect it seemed to him that his father showed unwonted patience. 'I was passing through a particularly irritating phase,' he recalled, 'when my main interest was in thumping away for hours on the Embassy piano.' This was in a room next to the library. Duff, who 'hated all noise, but music most because it was deliberate noise', never tried to stop him. For all his father's short temper, John Julius remembers only three occasions when he had to bear the brunt of it. And when John Julius was not playing the piano he was learning how to play the guitar from Louise. He found her charm 'an absolute knockout'; it never struck him at the time that there was anything curious in the fact that this fascinating creature virtually lived at the Embassy: 'At that age one's parents didn't have extra-marital affairs.' It was not until long afterwards that he realized what the relationship had been.

Duff delighted in his son's progress at Eton and then at Oxford. He was not a pushing father and showed no sign of objecting to the fact that John Julius showed little interest in history, art or politics. In so far as he had an ambition for his son, it was that he should go to the

232

Harvard Business School and learn how to make a lot of money. However, blood will out, and by the early 1950s John Julius's interests were following those of his father and he was convinced that if Duff had 'lived for another four or five years we'd have got on like a house on fire'. But it was not to be.

The first major sign of the development of similar interests was John Julius's decision to try for the Foreign Office; so Duff had to put away any hopes of having sired a business genius. He was content to see his son established in diplomacy and raised no objection when, in early 1952, John Julius announced that he wanted to get married to Anne Clifford, the daughter of a former diplomat. As it turned out, his wedding was the last big social event which Duff attended in England.

It is indicative of their relationship that when Duff was at last offered a peerage in 1952 by Churchill, he should have written to New College to ask John Julius's opinion on the matter. He told him that he was inclined to accept but that as doing so would, in effect, preclude his heir from a political career of the first importance, he thought he ought to have his views first. John Julius's reaction was: 'How wonderful about the Viscountcy. And how sweet of you to write and ask me what I think about it.' He urged his father to go ahead and accept it: 'I'm sure you must be longing to. It would be lovely for you, and I can't honestly see that it would make any difference to me.' His only reservation was over the choice of title: 'Must we be known as "the Aldwicks"?'

Duff decided to accept the Viscountcy, but the question of what to call himself proved a tricky one. After racking his brains and consulting Diana, he wrote to John Julius on 22 May:

> You might in your leisure moments – if you have any – give some thought to the name that will be yours. Cooper is condemned. There is one Lord Cooper.... Somebody suggested Duff, but I couldn't be Duff Duff to rhyme with Fluff–Fluff.

Diana hated 'Aldwick' (where West House was situated) as much as John Julius, and suggested 'Erewhon, Lackland or Sansterre, also Love-a-duck and Almighty'. These Duff frowned on: 'One can make a joke but one can't be one, not from choice anyway.' His own preference was to adopt the name of his fictional hero in *Operation Heartbreak*, Maryngton. But he was undecided. Writing to Clarissa Eden (as Clarissa Churchill had now become) on 5 June he expressed his frustration: 'Think, child, think. What will the name be? you ask. I don't know. Have you any suggestions? (not funny ones) We've been thinking for months.'

A week or so later he decided, out of filial piety, that the title should be that of his father's old home, Norwich. Out of courtesy he wrote to the Lord Mayor of Norwich and some local worthies informing them of his choice. It transpired that none of them, except the local Conservative Association, were too keen on the idea; but no objector managed to reach quite the level of pomposity attained by the Lord Mayor who, after waiting a fortnight to reply, said: 'There is unanimous feeling that, in view of the territorial importance of the title of "Norwich" it should only be assumed by a citizen with very intimate and obvious connections with the city.' Duff quoted a letter of approval from the Conservatives to show that the feeling was not 'unanimous'. The Garter Principal King of Arms told Duff that the Lord Mayor's letter had not only displayed, 'not perhaps without plenty of excuse', an ignorance of peerage law and custom, it was, 'to boot, not far short of presumptuous'. Despite a furore of parochial protest in the columns of the *Eastern Daily Press*, Duff went ahead.

Escorted by his old colleagues Rob Hudson and David Margesson, Duff was inducted into the House of Lords on 23 July 1952 as Viscount Norwich of Aldwick in the County of Sussex. His motto was appropriate: *Odi et Amo* – I hate and I love.* According to Chips Channon he looked 'dignified and impressive and immensely pleased as he strutted into their Lordships' chamber'. His own *bon mot* was: 'A little Norwich is a dangerous thing.'[2] He then departed to San Vigilio for the summer.

Writing from there on 1 September to Clarissa Eden, he enclosed an old cheque, payable to Clarissa Churchill and signed 'Duff Cooper': 'I was struck by the thought that although it is less than a year old there are no longer such people as the signee or the drawee.'

Clarissa's marriage to Eden, much approved of by Duff, gave him something of a ringside seat on political life. She did not find modern politics altogether to her taste, seeing them as something of a 'farce'. The observations of Lord Norwich on this were of interest. He told her in a letter on 9 September that they were 'no more farcical

* From his favourite poet, Catullus: '*Odi et amo; quaere id faciam requiris. Nescio, sed fieri; sentio et exerciore*' (I hate and I love; you ask, perhaps, how this can be; I do not know, yet I feel it happening and I am in anguish).

than politics at any other period, and most people become fascinated and absorbed by them'. He acknowledged that he was the last person to say so:

> Because I am one who did grow weary of the routine of politics, though not of politics in themselves. If you read the *Daily Mail* you will see that I still intervene from time to time and I intend to give Their Lordships the benefit of my advice when I think they need it.

Their Lordships, and everything else, could wait until autumn. Summer was spent resting and losing weight at Montecatini. Since the nosebleeds of the year before, Duff had been careful to obey doctor's orders. There was no alcohol, which made him, he feared, a dull companion, and ginger ale was not quite the same thing. Nor could he allow himself much except 'nursery food' to eat. It did not prevent him enjoying the sunshine and the company, but it was a *memento mori*. Some men would have chafed at the restraints, but he took adversity with the same calm good humour as he accepted success.

Back in Paris at the end of September his main thought was:

> And now, thank God, the holidays are over. I have had enough sun for one year and I always enjoy what the French call *la rentrée*, the return to normal life and all the pleasures of autumn, misty mornings, long evenings, oysters and partridges.[3]

From his beautiful small library at Chantilly he could look out over green lawns to lakes and trees. He liked to watch the mist swirl around the early morning grass, obscuring the lake, and making the tall trees drip moisture along with their leaves onto the earth; autumn appealed to the romantic in him. And as he watched, he could order his thoughts for what he would write next. Flicking his pen so that the ink splattered on the carpet, he would carry on writing; slowly, carefully, referring to the letters which he had by him, or to the folders of papers, or perhaps to those diaries which, spasmodically, he had kept. It behoved a man to be careful when writing his own life's story.

He had begun work on his autobiography in 1951. By the summer he had reached the events of 1936 and his plan was to finish by Christmas so that Rupert could publish it in the autumn of 1953. It had been difficult to start with, and where the diaries failed and the letters to Diana gave no help, the going could be tough. Fortunately there was a full diary for 1938. There was, moreover, the incentive of hitting back at the 'filthy Munichois'. He had given something of his side of the story in 1948 in radio talks on Munich, and had said a little more when reviewing the volumes of Churchill's war memoirs as they appeared. The despised minority of a decade before were now respected as voices that had been crying in the wilderness. In retrospect the doubts and the hesitations which had been the daily stuff of life were brushed away by the memory of the heroic days of 1940. Reading the autobiography of Lord Simon in August, Duff wrote that: 'It makes me hate him more.'[4] He had, he knew, something important to contribute to the history of those days. But more than that, he wanted to produce a book which would transcend the normal rank of politicians' memoirs – a genre for which he had little respect. He liked the double- or triple-decker nineteenth-century lives of politicians, but in the modern era only Winston could get away with a multi-volume autobiography. His own work would aim at commendable brevity.

The writing of an autobiography posed peculiar problems for Duff Cooper. In the first place it would have to be, perforce, a partial picture. The Cabinet Office were proving tiresome about what he could and could not publish. No 'Hansardizing' of other Cabinet Ministers, and every time he mentioned the name of a dissentient Cabinet Minister during the Munich crisis, Sir Norman Brook or one of his minions wanted it removed. And then there was the problem that Winston was Prime Minister and Anthony was Foreign Secretary; nothing must be written that would embarrass them. Eden, contacted through Clarissa, proved amenable, but Winston was a little sticky. He did not want Duff to publish his account of the meeting of The Other Club on the night of 28 September; so it was omitted, only to see the light of day twenty-odd years later in Winston's own official biography. These things could be dealt with through his admirable and efficient secretary, Norah Fahie, or else through Rupert. But other problems were for himself alone.

He was writing an autobiography, not a Rousseau-like *Confessions*, and would naturally leave out one vastly important side of his life: of women, save for Diana, nothing could be said. But he was not anxious to present a portrait disfigured by beauty spots put up to hide the warts. The admiration for Charles James Fox was confessed, along with the Fox-like behaviour at the tables. With an elegance that was as characteristic as the bravado, he admitted that:

> Writing in my sixty-fourth year, I can truthfully say that since I reached the age of discretion I have consistently drunk more than most people would say was good for me. Nor do I regret it. Wine has been to me a

236

firm friend and a wise counsellor.... Wine has made me bold but not foolish; has induced me to say silly things but not to do them.[5]

There were some who found such sentiments shocking; but they were those whom Duff had always taken a pleasure in baiting. He was, by nature, a man who was not much given to talking about himself or his past; life was to be lived for the moment. But he had been near to death and there was, about the book, a consciousness of that. The very title, *Old Men Forget*, which caused so many reviewers to comment that Lord Norwich was not that antiquated, demonstrated this. And, most of all, it betrayed itself in the valedictory tone of the last sentence: 'I love the sunlight but I cannot fear the coming of the dark.' But, however conscious he was that his time was limited, he determined to enjoy as much of it as should be vouchsafed him.

Early in the new parliamentary session, Duff gave his maiden speech in the Lords.[6] It was not as cold or as wet as that day twenty-nine years before when he had delivered another maiden speech, one which had launched his career, and inspired Max Beerbohm to draw a picture of Lord Birkenhead telling the young MP that a successful first speech was not everything:[7] not everything, but enough – and useful. Duff's warnings were directed at the Government as he spoke on 6 November. He had never liked or trusted the Germans. He had warned against their intentions in the 1930s after losing so many friends to them between 1914 and 1918; now the British Government was proposing to rearm them. He was surprised that Winston, of all people, did not know better.

Diana, watching from the Peeresses' gallery (despite her dislike of the title 'Lady Norwich', which she never accepted), sent him a note: 'Darling – Everybody thinks it a notable speech. I was so relieved and delighted and proud and adoring.' Susan Mary wrote to him on 12 November: 'I continue to hear nothing but admirers of your speech here, and everyone admires you for having made it. I guess Mr Churchill didn't like it.' Such was the case, but at a meeting of The Other Club a few nights later he and Duff passed off their disagreement quickly enough.

It was a season of notoriety among the mists and mellow fruitfulness. Haig's diaries were published in November 1952. Their editor, the historian Robert Blake, visited Duff at Chantilly in 1950 to ask what he thought of the Francophobe comments in those diaries at last being published. Duff was all in favour.[8] The French press reacted predictably, and there were calls in some quarters for Lord Norwich to resign as Chairman of the Paris branch of the Travellers Club. Susan Mary's comment was apt: 'I can't seem to pick up a paper without seeing that you have won a sonnet contest or been reproved by the Prime Minister or have been the only person to defend the apparently indiscreet Haig.' She thought it was 'about time you settled back into a quiet private life as the Lord of St Firmin', tilling his acres and 'talking gently of peaceful things to come.'

If the acres remained untilled as Duff continued to enjoy life, progress on the book was steady – but very slow. A visit from Daphne Bath (who was about to become Mrs Xan Fielding) enlivened his sixty-third birthday on 22 February 1953, but as he wrote to her three days later:

> How tiresome it is to grow old. Ever since I have had a sort of mild flu. I always have odd forms of illness. I cough a bit, have a little temperature and feel slightly bloody but not bad enough to stay in bed. I shouldn't mind, as I like invalid life, but I want to finish my book next month.

His illness certainly impeded progress. By the beginning of February he had reached the end of the chapter on the Ministry of Information: 'It was a period I did not much enjoy and I fear it is on that account a dull chapter.' He did not see, he told Rupert, how he could get the book finished by the end of the month.

Most of the problems with the Cabinet Office were now solved, but in their place came a new one, reviving echoes of an old antagonism. It had been thought only right to let Louis Spears see the chapters on the Levant in 1944. He replied on 29 April with a long argument designed to show that he had been right and Duff wrong, but no obstacle was raised to publication. He hoped, he wrote, 'to tell this story myself one day. Meanwhile *M. le Vicomte, tirez le premier.*' It was thus with some surprise that Duff and Rupert found him threatening legal action after *Old Men Forget* was published.

That the book had reached such an advanced stage was largely the result of a visit by Rupert to Chantilly. By early May there was only a chapter to complete. On the morning of Sunday 2 May Duff was in the happy position of having finished the book. He was just rereading the last two chapters when his nose began to bleed; he tried to carry on, but when he started vomiting blood it was too much. He was rushed to hospital in Paris where, thanks to the skill of the doctors and massive blood-transfusions, his life was saved.

Diana was, not unnaturally, terrified that he was going to die, but he made a remarkably speedy return to something like his old self. Diana reported that he was 'so cheerful and uncomplaining', and when he telephoned Susan Mary on the evening of 4 May she thought 'your voice sounded like your own'. The worst part of the illness was the pain from the nosebleed and the thirst: patients who have had a bad haemorrhage are not allowed to drink. By 10 May he was well enough to write (in pencil) to Rupert, asking him to be his literary executor: 'It was a great satisfaction to me when I felt I might be dying to know that I had finished the book.' The following day he was well enough to be allowed back to Chantilly, from where he reported: 'I'm getting better slowly. I don't mind an invalid's life but I hate an invalid's fare.'

The one major inconvenience of an invalid's life was that he was unable to attend the Coronation of Elizabeth II, and had to be content watching it on television with Daphne Fielding and her husband Xan. This was a disappointment, for, as he had written after receiving his GCMG in 1948: 'When I get to Buckingham Palace I hunt the royalties with the same avidity with which at the age of 18 I hunted the tarts at the Empire *promenoir*.' On this occasion 'the sporting spirit' had produced a 'bag' of:

> A few words with Queen Mary, a glass of wine with the King (concealing behind my back an empty glass which I had just finished when he invited me), a couple of Travellers Club jokes with the Duke of Edinburgh, and a real killing with the Queen.

The Queen (now the Queen Mother) was something of a fan of Duff's books and, after the publication of *Operation Heartbreak*, wrote to tell him that it had brought tears to her eyes. He would have enjoyed being at the Abbey among the Viscounts.

As he contemplated the coming of autumn and the publication of *Old Men Forget*, he had a new and, as it turned out, final round of an old argument to distract him.

Reference has been made many times to Duff's 'veiners', those fits of temper when the vein in the middle of his forehead would bulge and his face would purple. To his friends they were an essential part of his reputation, and some of them, like Randolph Churchill, who were also of an irascible nature, would delight in provoking him and in the ding-dong argument that would follow. There were occasions on which, by a quick flash of wit, the veiners might be circumvented. When a dining companion remarked: 'Well, anyway Duff, there's one thing no one can take away from you and that is the reputation of being the worst Secretary of State for War this country ever had', the result seemed inevitable. Randolph Churchill described what happened next: ' "How *dare* you say that," he replied, his voice a livid tremolo of rage, and then, a flash of genius coming to the rescue of his angered brain, he added, "... in the presence of Jack Seely." ' Seely, who had been Asquith's War Minister, joined in the laughter.[9]

But there were other occasions when an outbreak of the veiners could give mortal offence – and not always to those of a pacific nature. When he was invited to stay with Randolph Churchill in early July 1953, he learnt that Evelyn Waugh, who had also been invited, had cried off because he found his presence intolerable.[10] The reasons behind this action cast Waugh in an oddly unfamiliar light. After all, he was known for his bullying and his caustic wit, but could not, it seems, take the medicine when it was dished out to him.

Christopher Sykes, Waugh's biographer, has written that his subject's behaviour to Duff was 'foolish' and attributed his otherwise 'inexplicable' jealousy of him to sexual envy.[11] While never doubting Waugh's assertion to Duff that 'it is possible for a gentleman to have a deep love for a married woman without adulterous intentions',[12] there may be something in Mr Sykes's speculation. When told that he had laughed at rumours that she was *une grande amoureuse*, Diana's response was: 'How the hell can he tell if I am or not? Just because I never responded to his dribbling, dwarfish little amorous *singeries*, he need not be so sure!'[13]

Whatever part was played in the process by sexual jealousy, Waugh's dislike of Duff was shown in many ways, the most obvious of which was the spreading of fantastical rumours about him. After dinner one June evening at Chantilly in 1949, Waugh even tried his 'needling' to Duff's face, taunting him with having been responsible while Minister of Information for praising the Russians. Like most bullies, Waugh was normally careful to pick on those who could not or would not fight back, but it was after dinner and he was, perhaps, a little careless. Duff's response was a full-scale veiner: 'He took to random abuse of the wildest, coarsest kind. "It's rotten little rats like you", he yelled, "who have brought about the downfall of the country." ' Vein pulsing, he accused Waugh of cynicism, hatred of decency, homosexualism, cowardice, pacifism 'and other enormities'. Having got that out of his system, he asked Christopher Sykes to take some port and pass the decanter round.[14]

It seems to have been the recollection of this which prompted Waugh to refuse to share Randolph Churchill's hospitality with Duff.[15] Recalling the many times he had given house room to the novelist, Duff wrote to tick him off for his lack of manners. Waugh responded with a suitable letter of apology on 8 September, saying that the use of the word 'intolerable' was 'in itself intolerable because it was false' and also 'unsuitable applied to a slightly older and very much more distinguished man'. There was, he continued, 'no excuse for my using it' and he was, he said, 'deeply grateful to you for allowing me to come so often to your and Diana's various delightful homes'. He disagreed that there was any dishonour in accepting joint hospitality while abusing the host, but admitted that it was 'dishonourable to express the feeling – especially with the violence I used'. If not quite unconditional surrender, honours lay with Lord Norwich in this final set-to.[16]

Duff's temper may have been short, but so was his memory of offences committed against himself, and those who knew him best rarely took his veiners with the seriousness that Evelyn Waugh did.

Epistolary warfare provided one way of passing the time before the publication of *Old Men Forget*, another was to think about his next book – a history of Venice. He made a few notes for this and gathered his materials, but it could wait until the spring. The doctors had advised him to winter in a warm climate and he and Diana had gladly accepted the invitation of an old friend, Lord Brownlow, to stay with him in Jamaica.

Before that, however, there was the launching of the book on 3 November. It was the most enormous success, fulfilling all Duff's hopes, and was welcomed as a contribution to history and to literature. The reviewers were kinder than they had been since *Talleyrand* and it was gratifying to be told that it was a classic of autobiography.

He and Diana planned to spend Christmas at Vaynol with Caroline and her husband, Sir Michael Duff. It was a pleasant occasion, if somewhat marred by a heavy cold which Duff picked up. Before going away, he dropped in to see Rupert Hart-Davis at Soho Square. It was an occasion which stuck in the mind:

> It was very cold and he was wearing a heavy black overcoat. As he came into the room he said: 'I've brought you a Christmas present. I hope you haven't got it,' and from each overcoat pocket he pulled out two little volumes. They were first editions of *Northanger Abbey* and *Persuasion*, and

in the front of the first volume Duff had written: 'Old men forget, but they are grateful when they remember.'

Rupert 'never saw him again'.[17]

From White's, on 30 December, he wrote to Clarissa Eden to say how sorry he was not to have seen her before setting sail: 'I shall look forward to seeing you in the spring.' It was the last letter he wrote and must have made odd reading after the headlines in *The Times* on 2 January 1954.

Diana was worried by his coughing as they went on the boat-train to Southampton. He did not feel much like seeing the various people who had gathered there to see him off. He felt unwell as he boarded the liner.

Epilogue

It was not given him to 'cease upon the midnight with no pain', but he was, nevertheless, happy in the timing of his death. A brief twilight, during which his vital faculties were unclouded, was followed by a swift sunset. He lived to see his memoirs hailed as a classic and they provided a full stop to a busy life.

Diana accompanied his body back from Vigo to England. On 6 January 1954 they laid him to rest in the family mausoleum at Belvoir Castle. It was a bitterly cold day, the snow emphasizing the black of the mourners and making a thin white pall on the coffin. Diana was too grief-stricken to attend. She was at the memorial service at St Margaret's, Westminster, the following day, along with dozens of his friends.

He would be missed and mourned by many. Diana was inconsolable. No doubt life would go on somehow. Friends were kind, and John Julius and Rupert Hart-Davis did all that love and tact could contrive; but the centre of her life had gone. She would always miss him. Susan Mary, who had lent lustre to his later years, would miss him too: his wise and witty letters, his voice on the telephone, dinner *à deux* and the pleasure of his company. Others too would treasure his memory.

Few men can have enjoyed life more than Duff. It was, he thought, rare 'to appreciate properly one's own period', nor was there 'much to be said in favour of this one', but as he told Clarissa Churchill in April 1947, 'I have had a pretty happy life on the whole.' This thought had comforted him when he thought he was dying; it may be that it returned to do so that final night.

More than most men, he was the architect of his own fate. He believed that variety was the soul of pleasure and, though many passions drove him, none of them possessed him. He loved politics, literature, wine, women and the gaming-tables; but he had them on his own terms. If *The Times* imagined that this made him a failure it forgot what Duff never did, the comment of Bacon that: 'It is a strange desire to seek power and to lose liberty.' He came near enough to power to know that its fruits are those of the Dead Sea which turn to ashes in the mouth; 'laughter and the love of friends' provided a better reward.

He loved life fiercely. To him politics was an adventure, yet he was not an adventurer, for in addition to wanting to *be* someone he wanted to *do* something. If 'rightly to be great/ is not to stir without great argument/ but greatly to find quarrels in a straw/ when honour's at the stake', then there was in him an element of greatness. His patriotism saved his career from the charge of careerism – even if it ruined his prospects of advancement.

The inscription upon his tombstone, written by Diana herself, speaks of this:

> This perishable stone marks the grave of
> DUFF COOPER
> whose name is imperishable in the memory of
> England and of those who loved him.
> Attached to this world but free of its trammels
> he loved the light and did not fear
> the coming of the dark.

As lapidary inscriptions go it is an accurate one, although one might raise an eyebrow at 'free of its trammels'.

Each year leaves fewer of those who knew him. Most of those who remain recall the statesmanlike Ambassador, and there are few now whose memories reach back to those gilded Edwardian summers to conjure up the young diplomat who hated work and loved play. But when Diana talks of him the years seem to fall away; whatever might be true of old men, old ladies do not forget.

Notes

The main source for the book has been the Duff Cooper papers. These were divided into two portions: the diaries and material from the Paris Embassy, which are in the possession of Sir Rupert Hart-Davis; and other political and private papers, which I discovered in the cellar at Lady Diana Cooper's London home. This material is not archived and therefore I saw no point in footnoting my use of it. It is clear when I am quoting from Duff's papers and the precise location is apparent from the date of the quotation. I have not footnoted references to Duff's and Diana's letters, even when an extract is from the published edition of the letters.

Chapter 1

My main source for this chapter is Sir Rupert Hart-Davis, *The Arms of Time* (London, 1979). I am very grateful to Rupert for his help on this chapter.

Chapters 2–5

These are based so heavily on Duff's papers and Duff and Diana's correspondence that I have felt it otiose to add footnotes.

Chapter 6

1 Lord Vansittart, *The Mist Procession* (London, 1958), p. 277
2 Interview with the author, 25 January 1983
3 Liverpool Record Office, Papers of the 17th Earl of Derby, 920 DER/17, 31/3, Hall to Derby, 28 April, 31 May 1923
4 Bodleian Library, Oxford, Grigg papers, MS. Film 1001 for Duff's letters

Chapter 7

1 Beaverbrook papers, BBK C/257

Chapter 8

1 Beaverbrook papers, BBK C/259
2 Letter to the author, 16 February 1985

Chapter 9

1 *Evening Standard*, 11 June 1929. My thanks are due to my colleague Geoffrey Searle for pointing out this reference to me.
2 Bodleian Library, Worthington-Evans papers, MS. Eng. Hist. C.897
3 T. Jones, *A Diary with Letters* (London, 1954), p. 2
4 A. J. P. Taylor, *Beaverbrook* (London, 1972), p. 304
5 G. Peele, 'St George's and the Empire Crusade', in C. Cook and J. Ramsden (eds), *By-elections in British Politics* (London, 1969), p. 95

Chapter 10

1 Diana Cooper, *The Light of Common Day* (London, 1959), p. 103
2 *Ibid.*, p. 87
3 Information from Sir Rupert Hart-Davis
4 King's College, London, Liddell Hart papers, Section 11/1935 contains his criticisms of Haig
5 Information from Lord Blake
6 Diana Cooper, *op. cit.*, p. 147
7 Duff to Kakoo Rutland, 11 September 1933. I am most grateful to Her Grace the Dowager Duchess of Rutland for letting me quote from this and other letters in her possession and for talking to me about Duff.
8 M. Gilbert, *Winston S. Churchill*, Vol. v (London, 1976), p. 489
9 Beaverbrook papers, BBK C/257
10 Letter to Kakoo Rutland, Easter 1934
11 Diana Cooper, *op. cit.*, p. 155
12 R. R. James, *Chips* (London, 1967), p. 34
13 T. Jones, *A Diary with Letters*, p. 267

Chapter 11

1 J. Campbell, *F. E. Smith* (London, 1983), p. 689
2 British Library, Lord Robert Cecil papers, Add. MSS. 51082, Cecil to Lord Irwin, 7 June 1927
3 Campbell, *op. cit.*, p. 646
4 Duff to Kakoo Rutland, June 1936
5 For the background to, and details of, the debate, see: N. Gibbs, *Grand Strategy*, Vol. 1 (London, 1976), Parts II and III; Brian Bond, *British*

Military Policy between the Two World Wars (London, 1980), Chapter 8; R. Shay, *British Rearmament in the 1930s* (Princeton, 1977), Chapter 2

6 Duff Cooper, *Old Men Forget*, p. 205

7 Gibbs, *op. cit.*, pp. 440–50; Bond, *op. cit.*, pp. 198–230

8 Bond, *ibid.*, p. 223

9 *Alfred Duff Cooper* (privately printed, 1954), p. 78

10 *Old Men Forget*, pp. 197–9

11 Liddell Hart papers, section 11/1936/56, LH's note, 7 May 1936

12 *Hansard*, House of Commons, 5th series, Vol. 314, cols 39, 115ff.

13 R. R. James, *Chips*, p. 73

14 *Ibid.*, p. 78

15 *Ibid.*, pp. 80–81

16 House of Lords Record Office, Lloyd George papers, G/2/6/33

Chapter 12

1 R. R. James, *Chips*, p. 78

2 *Alfred Duff Cooper*, p. 53

3 *Ibid.*, p. 83

4 *Ibid.*, p. 79

5 *Ibid.*, p. 105

6 James, *op. cit.*, p. 72

7 Duff Cooper, *Horace* (privately printed, 1937), p. 11

8 This account of the abdication crisis is taken from the relevant portions of Duff's diary which he had typed up while 'the facts are still fresh in my memory'.

9 Beaverbrook papers, BBK C/257, Duff to B, 16 December

10 PRO. Cabinet Memoranda, Cab. 24/266 C.P.326(36), 3 December

11 *Ibid.*, C.P.334(36), 11 December

12 *Ibid.*, C.P.337(36), 14 December

13 N. Gibbs, *Grand Strategy*, pp. 448–9

14 *Ibid.*, pp. 455–9

15 *Ibid.*, p. 459

16 N. Thompson, *The Anti-Appeasers* (London, 1971), p. 138

17 Liddell Hart papers, 1/247/22, Duff to LH, 4 May 1937

18 Gibbs, *op. cit.*, p. 459

19 *Ibid.*

20 Liddell Hart papers, 11/1937/49, LH MS. note 3 June

21 Diana Cooper, *The Light of Common Day*, p. 193

22 Cambridge University Library, Baldwin papers, Vol. 152, fol. 113^{r}ff.

23 R. Shay, *British Rearmament in the 1930s*, p. 158

24 R. R. James, *Churchill: A Study in Failure* (London, 1973 edn), p. 358ff. for this view, which is supported by Duff's own impressions recorded in Chapter 10 of this book

Chapter 13

1 Diana Cooper, *The Light of Common Day*, pp. 194-5
2 *Ibid.*, pp. 199-202
3 N. Gibbs, *Grand Strategy*, pp. 279-81
4 P. M. Kennedy, *The Realities behind Diplomacy* (London, 1981), pp. 223-57
5 Liddell Hart papers 11/1938/98, note 20, September 1938
6 *Alfred Duff Cooper*, p. 44
7 Birmingham University Library, Neville Chamberlain papers, NC 18/1/1032
8 *Loc. cit.*, NC 7/11/30/29, NC to DC, 17 December
9 *Loc. cit.*, NC 7/11/30/40, DC to NC, 19 December
10 PRO. Admiralty Files, ADM 167/102
11 PRO. Cabinet Registered Files, Cab. 21/531
12 PRO. Cabinet Memoranda, Cab. 24/274 C.P. 29(38)
13 *Old Men Forget*, p. 216
14 PRO. Prime Minister's papers, Prem. 1/346
15 Templewood papers xviii/1, 15 March
16 *Old Men Forget*, p. 218
17 Phipps papers, PHPS 3/2, 20 April
18 PRO. CID minutes, Cab. 2/7, 319th meeting, 11 April; Gibbs, *op. cit.*, p. 635
19 Cabinet Registered Files, Cab.21/531, C.P.104(38), not circulated
20 Cabinet Registered Files, Prem. 1/346, NC MS. note
21 Templewood papers, x/3
22 *Old Men Forget*, p. 222

Chapter 14

1 Diana Cooper, *The Light of Common Day*, pp. 227-8
2 PRO. Halifax papers, FO 800/309 H/1/1, Duff's letter, 8 August
3 *Ibid.*, H/vii/95, Duff's letter, 12 August
4 K. Feiling, *Neville Chamberlain* (London, 1946), p. 364
5 A. J. P. Taylor, *The Origins of the Second World War* (London, 1972 edn), p. 157
6 PRO. Cabinet Minutes, Cab. 23/94, Cab. Cons. 36(38). The rest of the Cabinet meetings are in Cab. 23/95. I have not cited each Cabinet but I have made reference in the text to the date. I have quoted extensively from Duff's diary.
7 I am, once again, indebted to Her Grace for letting me see Duff's letters to her and for allowing me to quote from them.
8 R. F. V. Heuston, *Lives of the Lord Chancellors* (London, 1964), p. 593

9 D. Dilks (ed.). *The Diaries of Sir Alexander Cadogan* (London, 1971), p. 102
10 *Ibid.*, pp. 105–6

Chapter 15

1 N. Nicolson (ed.), *Harold Nicolson: Diaries and Letters* (London, 1966), pp. 368–71
2 D. Dilks (ed.), *The Diaries of Sir Alexander Cadogan*, pp. 108–9
3 The description of the dinner is based on Duff's diary, in C. Coote, *A Companion of Honour* (London, 1965), pp. 173–4, and Lord Boothby, *Recollections of a Rebel* (London, 1978), p. 129, supplemented by an interview with Lord Boothby in the House of Lords on 24 February 1983.
4 A. J. P. Taylor, *Beaverbrook*, pp. 385–6, which account is accepted by M. Cowling, *The Impact of Hitler* (Cambridge, 1975), p. 329
5 See my letter in the *Spectator*, 1 June 1983, and Mr Taylor to John Julius Norwich, 28 June 1983
6 There is a draft of this at PRO. Admiralty Files, ADM 1/9456
7 Duff Cooper, *The Second World War* (London, 1939), pp. 16–31
8 Bodleian Library, Crookshank diary, 1–8 October 1938

Chapter 16

1 N. Thompson, *The Anti-Appeasers*, pp. 192–3
2 *Ibid.*, pp. 193–4
3 N. Nicolson (ed.), *Harold Nicolson: Diaries and Letters*, pp. 377–8
4 *Hansard*, House of Commons, 5th series, Vol. 341, col. 1177
5 Thompson, *op. cit.*, p. 199; M. Gilbert, *Winston S. Churchill*, Vol. v, p. 1023
6 Neville Chamberlain papers, NC 7/11/31/76, DC to NC, 23 December 1938
7 *Loc. cit.*, NC 18/1/1071–1091, NC to Ida, 12 March 1939
8 Churchill College, Phipps papers, PHPS 3/2
9 Halifax papers, FO 800/315 H/xv/138, DC to EH, 22 March 1939
10 Duff Cooper and Coudenhove-Kalergi, *L'Europe de demain* (Paris, 1939)
11 Chamberlain papers, NC 7/9/59, WSC to NC, 29 September 1939
12 *Ibid.*, NC 7/9/60 for NC's reply
13 *Old Men Forget*, p. 268
14 Ross D. Rogers to Duff, 5 February 1940
15 Halifax papers, FO 800/321 H/xxiv/2, minute by Mr Perowne, 16 January 1940
16 Cranborne to DC, 9 February 1940; Bracken to DC, 10 November 1939
17 I am grateful to Mrs Daphne Wakefield for sending me a tape of this speech
18 Thompson, *op. cit.*, pp. 227–8

Chapter 17

1 John Julius Norwich to the author, 23 March 1984
2 Kenneth Clark, *The Other Half* (London, 1977), p. 18
3 PRO. Prime Minister's papers, Prem.4/83/1A fols 139 and 142
4 *Ibid.*, fols 140-1, DC to WSC, 12 June 1940
5 BBC Written Archives, Caversham, file on the MOI; I. McLaine, *Ministry of Morale* (London, 1979), pp. 81-4
6 McLaine, *ibid.*, pp. 84-5
7 Templewood papers, xiii/7, B to Hoare, 14 July
8 *Ibid.*, RAB to Hoare, 20 July 1940
9 British Library of Political and Economic Science, Hugh Dalton diary, Vol. 23, p. 28, 31 July 1940
10 Balliol College, Oxford, Nicolson diary, 3 August 1940
11 Bodleian Library, Oxford, MS. Eng. Hist. C.498, Wallace diary, 1 August 1940
12 *Ibid.*, 4 August 1940
13 Beaverbrook papers, BBK C/257
14 Templewood papers, xiii/7, B to Hoare, 14 August 1940
15 Dalton diary, March and April *passim* for Dalton's thoughts and plans
16 Churchill College, Cambridge, Inskip diary, INKP 1/2, 19 September 1939
17 Dalton diary, 23 April 1941
18 Nicolson diary, 27 March 1941
19 Lord Birkenhead, *Walter Monckton* (London, 1969), p. 185
20 PRO. Ministry of Information files, INF 1/857
21 *Ibid.*
22 *Ibid.*, written in pencil
23 Halifax papers, Prem.3/365/7, fols 46-7
24 Dalton diary, 12 June 1941
25 PRO. War Cabinet Memoranda, Cab. 66/17, W.P.(41)139
26 PRO. War Cabinet Minutes, Cab. 65/18, W.M.(41)64
27 Dalton diary, 1 July 1941
28 Francis Williams, *Nothing So Strange* (London, 1970), pp. 164-5
29 Bodleian Library, Selborne papers, MS. Eng. Hist. C.1075, Bracken to Lord Wolmer, 23 July 1941
30 I. Sproat, *Wodehouse at War* (London, 1981), and F. Donaldson, *P. G. Wodehouse* (London, 1982), give the fullest accounts of this episode
31 Williams, *op. cit.*, pp. 165-6; Donaldson, *ibid.*, p. 239
32 BBC Written Archives, Cassandra file, Mr Ryan to the Chairman of the BBC, 14 July 1941
33 Donaldson, *op. cit.*, pp. 241-2 for the texts of this correspondence
34 BBC, Cassandra file, memo. by R. G. Barnes, 12 July 1941
35 Nicolson diary, 4 July 1941

36 BBC Cassandra file for press-cuttings on the broadcast
37 Donaldson, *op. cit.*, p. 248
38 Copies of letters from Wodehouse dated 21 November 1942 and 4 September 1944 are in Duff's papers. They are the only material relating to the Wodehouse affair to be found there.
39 Williams, *op. cit.*, p. 166
40 Selborne papers, MS. Eng. Hist. C.1075, DC to Wolmer, 22 July 1941

Chapter 18

1 K. Young (ed.), *The Diaries of Sir Robert Bruce Lockhart 1939–65* (London, 1980), p. 110
2 PRO. Prem.3/155, fols 158–69
3 *Ibid.*, fol. 161, Attlee to WSC, 11 July
4 Beaverbrook papers, BBK/C259
5 Borthwick Institute, York, Hickleton papers, Papers of the First Earl of Halifax, Washington diary, 14 August 1941. I am grateful to Miss Lesley Neal for this reference.
6 Duff's letter, 22 September. I am very grateful to Lady Lindsay for allowing me to copy and quote from Duff's letters to her.
7 Leo Amery diary, 24 July 1941. I am grateful to the Rt Hon. Julian Amery, MP, for allowing me to consult his father's diary.
8 W.P.(41)286, 29 October 1941, copy in Duff's papers
9 Prem.3/155, fol. 94
10 *Ibid.*, WSC note, 29 November
11 Duff to Loelia Westminster, 4 December 1941
12 Prem.3/155, fol. 90, DC to WSC, 8 December 1941
13 *Ibid.*, fol. 91, Bracken to WSC, 8 December 1941
14 W.S. Churchill, *The Grand Alliance* (London, 1950), p. 544
15 Oliver Lyttelton, *The Memoirs of Lord Chandos* (London, 1962), p. 228
16 Brian Montgomery, *Shenton of Singapore* (London, 1984), p. 77. My thanks are due to Mr Leo Cooper for drawing my attention to this book before I wrote this chapter.
17 *Ibid.*
18 Martin Russell's notes on *Shenton of Singapore*. My debt to Martin Russell for discussing this period of Duff's career with me is enormous.
19 Montgomery, *op. cit.*, p. 114; Martin Russell's notes. Lady Diana has confirmed Martin Russell's denial of this story.
20 Duff's diary of the Singapore mission, 11 December 1941
21 Montgomery, *op. cit.*, p. 87, dates this 10 December
22 Duff's diary, 11 December
23 Montgomery, *op. cit.*, p. 97
24 Martin Russell's notes

25 Montgomery, *op. cit.*, p. 94
26 *Ibid.*, pp. 95-100; Duff's diary for the quotation
27 Montgomery, *op. cit.*, p. 115

Chapter 19

1 Leo Amery diary, 25 February 1942
2 J. Harvey (ed.), *The War Diaries of Oliver Harvey* (London, 1978), pp. 96-7
3 See below, Chapter 24
4 R. R. James, *Chips*, pp. 327, 339
5 Amery diary, 17 October 1943
6 James, *op. cit.*, p. 360
7 PRO. Avon papers, FO 954/25A, fol. 112, DC to AE, 22 April 1942
8 James, *op. cit.*, p. 349
9 M. Amory (ed.), *The Letters of Evelyn Waugh* (London, 1980), p. 167
10 British Library, Add. MSS. 56391, Oliver Harvey diary, 23 September 1943
11 *Ibid.*, 5 October 1943
12 *Ibid.*, 28 September, 5 October
13 *Ibid.*, 30 September
14 Prem.3/273/1 for the texts of WSC's letters to AE and Duff, and for Duff's replies
15 Memorandum in Duff's papers on his appointment. Other quotations on this subject should be assumed to come from the same source unless otherwise attributed.
16 Harvey diary, 5 October 1943
17 PRO. Foreign Office General Correspondence, FO 371 series (henceforth FO 371) file 36351/Z11729, P. Viénot to Eden, 12 November 1943

Chapter 20

1 *Old Men Forget*, pp. 320-1
2 Prem.3/177/6, M.33/4 WSC to Eden, 26 January 1944
3 Prem.3/177/3, fols 270-1, 266-7, tels. 377 from Duff, 306 from WSC, 28 March
4 Prem.3/182/8, fol. 141, T.577/4, WSC to Duff, 16 March
5 *Ibid.*, fol. 140, tel. 360, Duff to WSC, 21 March
6 *Ibid.*, fol. 137, tel. 294, WSC to Duff, 22 March
7 Sir Rupert Hart-Davis to the author, 17 May 1980
8 PRO. Avon papers, FO 954/15, pt.2/me/44ff. for FO views of Spears
9 Prem.3/423/15, M.251/4 WSC to Eden, 10 March
10 St Antony's College, Spears papers, Box 11/7, ELS to WSC, 14 March

11 Prem.3/423/15, M.349/4 WSC to Eden, 2 April
12 *Ibid.*, P.M./44/397 AE to WSC, 1 June
13 PRO. Papers of the British Representative to the FCNL, FO 660/194/v/ 121, n.d. minute by Duff
14 *Old Men Forget*, p. 326
15 PRO. Foreign Office General Correspondence, FO 371/42000/Z4379/ 3636/17
16 Sir Rupert Hart-Davis to the author, 16 February 1985
17 Prem.3/177/4, fol. 488
18 *Old Men Forget*, p. 332
19 Pierson Dixon diary, 8 June 1944. I am grateful to Mr Piers Dixon for allowing me to consult his father's papers.
20 Prem.3/423/15, M.717/4 WSC to Eden, 11 June
21 FO 954/15, pt.3/me/46/102, Duff to Eden, 26 July
22 *Old Men Forget*, pp. 335–6

Chapter 21

1 M. Amory (ed.), *The Letters of Evelyn Waugh*, p. 185
2 *Ibid.*, p. 186
3 Duff's despatch and Eden's response were printed for the War Cabinet as W.P.(44)409
4 FO 660/199, Duff's marginalia
5 N. Nicolson (ed.), *Harold Nicolson: Diaries and Letters 1939-45* (London, 1967), p. 403
6 FO 371/42024/Z6470, tel. 149
7 FO 660/221 describes the reactions at the Embassy
8 FO 371/42025/Z7118, DC to WSC, 24 October
9 Prem.4/30/8, for WSC's and AE's minutes in late December 1944
10 FO 954/9, M.58/5 WSC to AE, 11 January 1945
11 Prem.3/182/8 for the texts
12 FO 371/49067/Z4378, tel. 177 SAVING
13 *Ibid.*, M.298/5 WSC to AE and following papers
14 *Loc. cit.*, Z4920, T.542/5 WSC to DC, 20 April
15 *Ibid.*, Z5274, tel. 640, 22 April

Chapter 22

1 Harold Macmillan, *War Diaries* (London, 1984), p. 589
2 This and other unattributed quotations in this and the following chapter come from Duff's diary
3 R. R. James, *Chips*, p. 393
4 This paragraph and the following ones are based upon interviews with

Miss Barley Alison, Lord Bessborough, Sir John Coulson, Sir Robin Hooper, Lord Lansdowne and Sir Brooks Richards. I am very grateful to them all for giving me such a vivid picture of Duff as Ambassador, and to Lord Rothschild for his stories of life in Paris at this time.

5 Duff to Barley Alison 24.VIII.15(51?). My thanks are due to Miss Alison for talking to me about Duff and for allowing me to see Duff's letters to her.

6 Lord Bessborough, *Return to the Forest* (London, 1962), pp. 123–5; Duff's diary; supplemented by an interview with Lord Bessborough on 30 May 1983 – all provide the material for the next paragraph.

7 PRO. Bevin papers, FO 800/464, Fr/45/1, DC to Bevin, 31 July 1945

8 *Ibid.*, Fr/45/2, Bevin to DC, 4 August 1945

9 K. Young (ed.), *The Diaries of Sir Robert Bruce Lockhart 1939–65*, p. 493

Chapter 23

1 FO 371/49069/Z9535, FO minute, 21 August 1945

2 FO 371/59952/Z2780 for FO reactions to Duff's despatch

3 Details of this can be found in my article on 'Duff Cooper and Western European Union', *Review of International Studies* (1985), 11, pp. 58–9

4 FO 371/67670/Z25, undated minute by Bevin

5 Alan Bullock, *Ernest Bevin: Foreign Secretary* (London, 1985), pp. 357–8

6 For detailed reference see Charmley, *op. cit.*, p. 59ff.

7 Duff to Daphne Weymouth, 28 December 1946. I am very grateful to Mrs Fielding for allowing me to use Duff's letters to her and for talking to me about him.

8 Susan Mary Patten to Duff, 23 April 1947. I am very grateful to Mrs Alsop for allowing me to quote from her letters to Duff.

9 SMP to Duff, 21 May 1947

10 FO 800/465, Fr/47/20, Duff to Bevin, 3 September 1947

11 SMP to Duff, 11 December 1947

12 *Ibid.*, 18 December 1947

13 *Ibid.*, 21 December 1947

Chapter 24

1 Duff to Clarissa Churchill, 'The Ides of March 1947'. I am very grateful to Clarissa, Countess of Avon, for allowing me to see Duff's letter to her.

2 Rupert Hart-Davis to the author, 16 February 1985

3 SMP to Duff, 24 August 1948

4 Duff to Daphne Bath, 13 March 1947

5 *Ibid.*, 19 March 1948

6 SMP to Duff, 24 May 1947

7 *Ibid.*, 14 June 1948
8 *Ibid.*, 7 September 1949
9 *Ibid.*, 9 March 1949
10 *Ibid.*, 30 June 1947
11 *Ibid.*, 30 September 1948

Chapter 25

1 These paragraphs are based on conversations with John Julius Norwich. Quotations are from interviews on 25 January 1983 and 3 and 10 February 1983.
2 R. R. James, *Chips*, p. 469
3 Duff to Clarissa Eden, 24 September 1952
4 *Ibid.*, 21 August 1952
5 *Old Men Forget*, p. 94
6 *Hansard*, House of Lords, Vol. 179
7 Max Beerbohm, *Observations* (London, 1925). I owe this reference to Sir Rupert Hart-Davis.
8 Information from Lord Blake
9 *Alfred Duff Cooper*, p. 78
10 M. Amory (ed.), *The Letters of Evelyn Waugh*, p. 406
11 C. Sykes, *Evelyn Waugh* (London, 1978 edn), p. 180
12 Evelyn Waugh to Duff, 8 September 1953 (Duff Cooper papers)
13 Philip Ziegler, *Diana Cooper* (London, 1981), p. 160
14 Sykes, *op. cit.*, pp. 422-3
15 Amory, *op. cit.*, pp. 406-7
16 Evelyn Waugh to Duff, 8 September 1953
17 Sir Rupert Hart-Davis to the author, 16 February 1985

COPYRIGHT: ACKNOWLEDGEMENTS

I am grateful to the following for permission to publish copyright material: the Keeper of the Public Records for documents which are Crown Copyright; the Rt Hon. Julian Amery for his father's papers; the Rt Hon. Paul Channon for his father's papers; Mr Auberon Waugh for his father's papers. If I have inadvertently infringed anyone's copyright I hope that they will accept my apologies and contact me so that this can be put right in any subsequent editions of the book.

Bibliography

The main source for this book was the Duff and Diana Cooper papers. Other manuscript sources fall into three groups:

A. Public Record Office, Kew
    Cabinet Minutes, Cab. 23
    Cabinet Memoranda, Cab. 24
    Cabinet Registered Files, Cab. 21
    War Office Files
    Admiralty Files
    Prime Minister's papers (Chamberlain) Prem. 1
    Ministry of Information files, INF. 1
    Prime Minister's papers (Churchill) Prem. 3, Prem. 4
    Prime Minister's papers (Attlee) Prem. 8
    War Cabinet Minutes, Cab. 65
    War Cabinet Memoranda, Cab. 66
    Foreign Office General Correspondence, FO 371 (for 1944–7)
    Papers of the British Representative to the FCNL, FO 660
    Minutes of the Committee of Imperial Defence, Cab. 2

    Private Collections
    Avon papers, FO 954
    Halifax papers, FO 800
    Bevin papers, FO 800
    Ronald MacNeill papers, FO 800

B. Other archives
    BBC Written Archives Centre, Caversham – files on Lord Norwich, the MOI, and Cassandra

    Balliol College, Oxford
    Harold Nicolson diary

Birmingham University Library
Austen and Neville Chamberlain papers

Bodleian Library, Oxford
Viscount Crookshank diaries
Sir Edward Grigg (Lord Altrincham) papers (on microfilm)
Sir Laming Worthington-Evans papers
Papers of the 3rd Earl of Selborne
Euan Wallace diary

British Library
Viscount Cecil of Chelwood papers
Oliver Harvey diary and papers

British Library of Political and Economic Science
Hugh Dalton diary and papers

Cambridge University Library
Baldwin papers
Templewood papers

Churchill College, Cambridge
Bevin papers
Cadogan papers
Lord Lloyd papers (by permission of David Lloyd)
Inskip diary
Phipps papers
Spears papers

House of Lords Record Office
Beaverbrook papers
Lloyd George papers

Liverpool Record Office
Papers of the 17th Earl of Derby

King's College, London
Alanbrooke diaries
Liddell Hart papers
Ismay papers
Brooke-Popham papers

Quai d'Orsay, Paris
René Massigli papers (by permission of M. Massigli)

St Anthony's College, Oxford
Spears papers relating to the Middle East

C. Private collections
    Leo Amery diaries (by courtesy of the Rt Hon. Julian Amery MP)
    Pierson Dixon diaries (by courtesy of Mr Piers Dixon)
    Duff's letters to:
    Barley Alison (courtesy of Miss Barley Alison)
    Clarissa Avon (courtesy of the Countess of Avon)
    Daphne Bath (courtesy of Mrs Daphne Fielding)
    Susan Pary Patten (courtesy of Mrs Susan Mary Alsop)
    Kakoo Rutland (courtesy of the Dowager Duchess of Rutland)
    Daphne Wakefield (courtesy of Mrs Daphne Wakefield)
    Loelia Westminster (courtesy of Lady Lindsay).

D. *Hansard*

Index

259